MARILLION MISADVENTURES & MARATHONS
The Life & Times Of Mad Jack

MARK KELLY

MARILLION
MISADVENTURES
& MARATHONS
The Life & Times Of Mad Jack

KINGMAKER PUBLISHING
First published in Great Britain by Kingmaker Publishing Limited in 2022
© 2022 Kingmaker Publishing Limited
www.kingmakerpublishing.com

Copyright © Mark Kelly

Mark Kelly has asserted his moral right under the
Copyright, Designs and Patents Act, 1988, to be identified
as the author of this work.

ISBN 978-1-8384918-1-9

Printed in Great Britain by
Biddles Books Limited, King's Lynn, Norfolk

CONTENTS

PROLOGUE

Y ou know the old adage: there's no such thing as a free lunch. Especially when you're being charged £15 for your rocket salad. Not that I was paying.

Imagine the scene, a fabulous Soho eatery, it's 2015, the late summer light coming through the tall windows, the waiter hovering just at the periphery of my sight line. Somewhere a car revved an engine probably too powerful for these slender London streets.

I was staring at my sprig of rocket and thinking, 15 quid? My hand resting around the stem of my glass of sauvignon blanc, I hadn't dared look at the wine list for fear of clocking the prices and choking on a mouthful of rocket. Though the price of a bottle of wine wasn't going to be that day's only revelation.

"Would Marillion be interested in getting back together with Fish for a tour?"

Not the waiter, sadly. It's always nice meeting an unexpected fan, especially one who's doling out the wine.

It was Stuart Galbraith, from across the table. For the uninitiated, Stuart is a music promoter and the founder of Kilimanjaro Live Group. He, I like to imagine, thinks 15 quid for a rocket salad is a pretty good deal, for the restaurant at least. He's been doing deals all his life and here was one more.

I knew when he invited me to lunch that it wasn't just because he liked my company, but I wasn't expecting this. I didn't have to think very long before answering, but I listened patiently to what he had to say.

Over lunch, he tried to persuade me that it was a great idea. I know there's a lot of fans out there that would love to see Marillion back together with Fish one last time. Christ, Fish had left the band 27 years previously when we were at the height of our fame. Admittedly, the cracks were beginning to show back then, but only to our inner circle. Stuart said we could play arena shows all over Europe and walk away with a decent six figure sum each at the end of it. At this stage in our career, things were going well for Marillion, but not so well that we could retire. Also, I had recently split up with my long-term partner, Angie, so I wasn't exactly in the chips. Reuniting with Fish would be a few months of our lives in exchange for a nice retirement pot.

I wasn't sure how I would sell it to the rest of the band either. Stuart hadn't really considered how many of our current fans would react to such a seismic move. Steve Hogarth (aka 'h') had been our singer since 1989, making 13 studio albums with the band (compared to Fish's four). For many people, h is Marillion's singer and they wouldn't want it any other way. I didn't waste too much time thinking about Stuart's suggestion because I knew that it wasn't going to work.

Not least because Fish couldn't sing the old songs anymore. His voice had sadly deteriorated over the years. Either through age, smoking, drink, drugs, genetics or a combination of all of the above, he wasn't the singer he once was. When he performed the old Marillion songs like, say, *Sugar Mice*, he dropped the key a whole fifth so he could manage some semblance of hitting the high notes. It meant that Steve Rothery's guitar part, which underpins the song, can't be played the way he originally wrote it. So, the idea of going out and playing those old Marillion songs to an audience that would be expecting so much and knowing that we wouldn't be able to deliver, whilst trousering big piles of cash, didn't seem right.

So, I said no. I didn't even discuss it with the rest of the band. It was a non-starter.

But as we sat together having lunch, I knew there was something else that I could ask Stuart about. According to the Beatles, it would take 4,000 holes to fill the Albert Hall. I'm no mathematics whizz (as you'll see when we get to my school years), so I can't vouch for the Fab Four's thinking, but, like those infamous holes, we too wanted to fill the Albert Hall.

The Royal Albert Hall is a beautiful building, steeped in history, with as striking an exterior as its interior. The lively acoustics have been tamed by a forest of inverted, giant mushrooms planted in the ceiling, looking down on a circle of boxes and neat rows of swivelling chairs.

When I was growing up it was always Hammersmith Odeon and Wembley Arena that meant success to me. h described the RAH as his 'show to end all shows'. It was on his bucket list. So, I asked Stuart if he could get us a night at the Royal Albert Hall.

He was candid in his response: it was difficult as the RAH was booked up years in advance with annual long running events like The Proms and Cirque du Soleil. If we were patient, he would secure a date for us eventually.

From time to time, our manager, Lucy Jordache, would get an email from Kilimanjaro suggesting a Tuesday or a Wednesday, maybe even a Thursday. But we knew it was going to be a tall order for us to fill the place. We hadn't played anywhere that big in London for many years, so we held out for a Friday or Saturday to maximise our chances of not embarrassing ourselves.

Then, eventually, we were offered Friday 13th October 2017. Very Marillion, but as we aren't superstitious, we booked it. Besides, 2017, that was years away…

Until, of course, it wasn't. On the day itself I was nervous from the second I woke from a fitful sleep. I wasn't the only one. From the moment we arrived at the venue, we felt and acted like a bunch of kids about to play our first big gig. It was like those 1,800 gigs and 35 years of touring had melted away to reveal these five young men, excited, nervous, agitated, pacing around as we waited for the show to start.

Entering the stage door of the Royal Albert Hall is like stepping back in time. It reminded me of the BBC's Maida Vale studios in the old days. There are staff everywhere. Somebody on the door, caterers busy putting small bowls of nibbles and flowers in the dressing rooms. People, some uniformed, some not, quietly going about their work. Your eye occasionally met with a glance and a silent nod and then they were gone, back among the shadows preparing for the night ahead.

History is writ large on those walls, covered as they are with images of the events which the RAH has played host to over the years: Everything from the Ford Motor show, championship tennis and even servants' balls in the 1930s. The gentle curve of the circular building, a series of corridors of wood and velvet trim, crimson curtains and gold brocade. Brass balustrades, the impossibly high ceiling, the grandeur of the boxes as rows of empty oblongs filled with plush, red seating. Tradition hung heavily in the air. It's an overused phrase, but this really was history in the making. The sense of responsibility was overwhelming; that we'd soon be standing on the spot where so many great performers have stood in the last 150 years.

The soundcheck is always the moment when the venue reveals itself to me. Just how different it is from the same place a few hours later when you walk on to (what you hope is) the roar of the crowd. The clubs where we started out were almost always painted black up to and including the ceiling. Under the fluorescent workday lights everything looked scuffed and dirty. The air smelt of stale beer and disinfectant. Then, later, almost magically, when the place was filled with people, those rooms are transformed into something overwhelming and alive. Not the Albert Hall. Even devoid of people and with the lights on, it's still utterly thrilling.

They ran out of money when they were building the Royal Albert Hall, so to raise the funds needed to finish it, they sold 999 year leases on about 1,200 seats. I guess it was a forerunner to the internet crowdfunding I'd suggest to the band in 2000 that set us on the path out of falling sales and on to something like a secure future, but more of that later.

Today, the total capacity of the Royal Albert Hall is around 5,200. Before the introduction of more sensible fire limits, the place would regularly pack in 8,000 and on occasion had as many as 12,000 punters in there.

That night we had sold every ticket available to us. The other 1,200 leased seats were also filled; we were officially a hot ticket. The people who own the seats, or debentures, will sell them if they aren't interested in attending themselves unless the show that night isn't in demand, in which case the debenture seats are often left empty, leaving no option for the artist or promoter other than to give them away to 'guests' or to 'paper the room'. This means that even with a sold out show, unless you have a particularly high ticket price, it's difficult to make a profit at the Royal Albert Hall. Plus, fancy filming it? That'll be an extra £20,000.

But let's leave the machinations of business aside momentarily. It's quite rare for Marillion to leave the stage and all say what a fantastic night it was, because, well, have you met us? Plus, a lot of things need to come together in just the right way for Marillion to have a great gig or even a good gig.

We set ourselves high standards, but on that night, a once in a decade event, we exceeded even those standards. It wasn't just how we played or how we felt about it, because quite often we'll play a gig that seems like a stinker to us and the audience love it. We often joke about the fact that we can never tell whether our gigs are good or bad. But on that night, we walked off dazed and elated, knowing that we'd nailed it and the audience had been with us through every beat, every colourful musical nuance and vibration.

As well as playing the RAH, it was also another first for Marillion that night as we had some extra classical musicians with us on stage. They added to what I like to think of as the majesty of the occasion.

The Space might not be my favourite Marillion song, but the place erupted when I played the opening bars. I'll never forget it. Such a feeling of power, like I was driving a finely tuned racer, or team of stampeding horses, and I was completely in the moment, totally in control. *The Space* was ideally suited to the RAH and to the four string players (in praise of folly), horn player and flautist that were part of Marillion that night.

If I'm honest, I don't usually get overly excited about gigs. I went from being terrified about performing when I was younger to struggling to tune into the frenetic energy of a live audience. I don't know if it's something to do with what I do, but I can't often get lost in the music. Maybe it's because there's too much technical stuff to worry about that isn't musical? Making sure samples or loops begin or end where they should. Making sure computers are not falling over and software is running smoothly. It's not a musician's job that I do up there a lot of the time, it's a technician's role. Occasionally, I unwittingly relinquish that, and something goes into overdrive and my feet leave the floor and I soar with the rest of the band. Which is what happened that night. I performed rather than simply operating the machinery.

The audience were startling, not least in the moment in the song *Go* when they all took out their finger lights and surprised everybody in the band with their LED synchronicity, lighting up the RAH with what looked like the most incredible display of indoor fireworks known to man. It wasn't just any audience either, there were some people in attendance very dear to me.

It's funny that my three youngest children, Tallulah, Delilah and Jude, never expressed much interest in my career as a musician. On the one hand, they think it's quite cool that I'm in a band, but, on the other, I think they're a little bit embarrassed because quite often their friends will say that their parents are fans or the teachers at school say they're fans and, like I was at their age, they don't relish being singled out. So, understandably, they haven't seen me play many times.

Consequently, I was so happy that for this of all nights they and my eldest son, Kai, were all there. They were all on my side of the stage too, so that I could turn my head and pick out their faces in the shadows, lit up in the bursts of colour emanating from the stage.

So, there they were, my children, all except Freya. My mum. My dad had died a year earlier. Four of my brothers; the other two were in Ireland and New Zealand respectively. My future wife, Karina, and her two children, Arthur and Pedro.

I was sad that my dad didn't live to see that show. I always wondered what he really thought about my chosen career. I remember at one of our early Marquee shows, he took me to one side and, apart from urging me not to marry my pregnant girlfriend of three months (probably good advice generally in case you were wondering), he asked if I thought I'd ever make any money from playing in a band. I didn't know and I didn't care, and I told him as much.

A few years later we were selling out Hammersmith Odeon and he said to me: "Do you remember when I asked if you thought you'd ever make any money doing this?" I said I did. He said, and I remember this as if it were yesterday, "I feel a bit silly now". I didn't have the heart to tell him that I really wasn't making any money then either.

I think it was Clive James who said, and I'm paraphrasing, that a rock star makes two kinds of money: not as much as you think or more than you can possibly imagine. Clive knew what he was talking about. It's a fallacy that any band makes money in their first few years, even if they appear to be doing well. Everyone wants to believe that rock stars make loads of money. But, sadly, that's not true.

People think it's like winning the lottery. My younger brother, Barry, told me that, as soon as we became even a tiny bit famous, kids at school would say to him, "you've got it made now", as if one record in the charts and a few appearances on *Top Of The Pops* was enough to elevate an entire family into the upper echelons of the super wealthy.

And speaking of families, it's probably time you met mine…

CHAPTER 1

In Dublin's Fair City

Picture this: the rooftops of Romford under a slate grey sky. It's going to rain before midday, inevitably. Drop down to the warren of streets below and into the newsagents on the corner. That's where you'd find me, one eye on the shopkeeper, one hand rifling pineapple chunks and packets of Opal Fruits into the lining of my jacket. I'd realised quite early on that the overhead security cameras – a modified half globe studded with cameras hanging from the ceiling that looked like a Dalek had crash landed headfirst through the shop's roof – were a ruse. There were no cameras blinking into life, monitoring the shoppers below. It was a decoy designed to prevent little urchins like me pilfering the stock. Fat chance.

Did I mention my 'nicking coat'? A design, I say design, it was more like I'd assaulted my own clothing with a Stanley knife. I'd slashed the lining down both sides to make two enormous pockets that meant that in one swift, well-practised move an item could disappear from the shelf into the coat unnoticed by the shop assistant. I'd swagger out of there into the half-light of a low Essex sky, my coat rattling with my sugary swag, making a sound like an old pill bottle being shook.

But I'm getting ahead of myself. How, you're thinking, did we get here?

It was former US President Jimmy Carter who said of the immigrants who had washed up on America's shores over the years: "We have become not a melting pot but a beautiful mosaic. Different people, different beliefs, different yearnings, different hopes, different dreams." It seems unlikely he was singling out my almost entirely Irish family who emigrated to the United States in the late '60s and early '70s, but I'd like to think they added something to the landscape. Even if that something came in the shape of a bar popular with the type of men and women who liked to get fall down drunk and possibly fit in a fight before they did so.

But let me digress: my maternal grandfather, Douglas Crumel, was born in Toronto, Canada. The family story goes that his grandmother was from the Canadian Blackfoot tribe. So that makes me one sixteenth Blackfoot. In truth, I'm probably more closely related to the Queen than I am to the Blackfoot tribe. But it's part of our family story, possibly because it made us sound more interesting and exotic. I liked the story enough to include the name Blackfoot in my three youngest children's middle names along with nine other names each. (I'm sure they're delighted by this.) Much further down the exotic register comes my middle name, Colbert, which has a much more troubling origin. More on that shortly.

My maternal grandmother was a Londoner from Islington. Hetty Wilkinson was her name and during the Second World War Douglas, her husband, was posted to Burma. Both my mum and my mum's sister were born during the war years, and after the war ended the family spent the next decade living in Chelsea, west London. The family were now blessed with three more sons before the government's move to shift people out of the grey of the capital and into the leafy suburbs of Essex. Aveley to be precise, settling down on the quiet streets of a new estate, London now a train ride away.

My paternal grandfather was called Michael Colbert Kelly. My father was called Michael Colbert Kelly. My oldest brother is called Michael too. Are you seeing a pattern yet? Though his middle name was Douglas after our maternal grandfather, so the name Colbert went to me. I hated that name as a kid, and if asked what my middle initial stood for, I'd say Colin or Chris. Anything but Colbert, which always made other kids snort with laughter.

I found out much later that my paternal grandfather, born in June 1916, was christened Colbert in honour of the Irish rebel Cornelius "Con" Colbert who participated in the 1916 Easter Rising and was executed by firing squad in May 1916. My grandfather's nickname throughout his life was Con. My dad was also known as Con by everyone. I was happy with Mark. My grandfather was a member of the Irish Republican Brotherhood back in the 1930s, when the IRA was an army rather than a terrorist organisation. He was as tough as flint (imagine a breeze block with a frown and fists raised and you're close).

As I mentioned earlier, the whole clan emigrated (by dawn's early light perhaps) to the US in the late '60s. My grandmother, Maggie, was a staunch Catholic who went to church every Sunday. I don't think my grandfather was such a strong Catholic. He was a thin, wiry man with hands like boulders. A former Dublin lightweight boxing champion, who was not above getting into a punch up or two, even into his seventies.

My dad's brother, Wally, ran a bar in Elizabeth, a part of New Jersey that was about as genial as a hand grenade. It was called Kelly's Bar. It looked more like a shop with a big white sign above the door, with the customary green lettering, shamrocks and Celtic patterns. It was the sort of place where drunks stopped by for a vodka and grapefruit to steady their hands on their way to work in the morning. Populated by life's wreckage and the occasional character from New Jersey's underworld, the interior of the pub looked like something Charles Dickens might have conjured up in a fever dream. All of this overseen from behind the bar by my grandad while occasionally working a cloth around the rim of a pint pot. I think Wally just let him work there to keep an eye on him because he was always getting into trouble.

One day a woman walked in wearing red shoes and my grandad threw her out because he thought she was a prostitute, as nothing screams 'working girl' like a pair of red pumps. Another time, a young man came in wearing a Union Jack T-shirt. My grandad told him he could get a drink, but he'd have to leave his shirt outside. Unsurprisingly, the kid and his Union Jack T-shirt took exception to that and, with an emphatic 'no', poked my grandad in the neck. Wally leapt between them to stop a fight breaking out, which he almost succeeded in doing, the kid stepping back unaware that Wally was protecting him. Too late alas, Con's fist flying past Wally's head to knock the kid into a set of barstools, going over like so many skittles being hit with a bowling ball. He came round later in the back alleyway and one can only assume found somewhere else to get a drink.

Con was scared of no one. Well, maybe one person: my grandmother's brother, Dick Timmins, who was nicknamed 'the Gunman', and with good reason. Dick was part of the republican brotherhood and served time in prison for his part in a botched attempt to blow up King George VI by planting a bomb under Hammersmith Bridge. As history bears out, King George came to no harm, probably because he came nowhere near Hammersmith Bridge either. Timmins escaped from prison twice, once from Wakefield Prison and again from Leyhill Prison in 1947, from which he managed to get across the water and back to Dublin. In 1952 the government decided that it wasn't in the public interest to force his return to the UK to serve the rest of his sentence. It wasn't reported what King George might have made of this, but I like to think he sighed with relief at the news.

The other notable member of my dad's family in Ireland was my great aunt, Maura (Kelly) Laverty, who wrote a number of banned novels – I hear good things about *The Cottage In The Bog* and *Lift Up Your Gates* if you like that sort of thing – and was the creator of the first Irish TV soap in 1964. It was called *Tolka Row* and was the Dublin equivalent of *Coronation Street*. She was also famous for her cookery books which are still in print today.

The first time I saw my grandparents in their home in the USA was in the summer of 1983. It was my first time in the States. Marillion were there on tour, a selection of club shows of up to 800 people on a good night, and a handful of gigs opening for Todd Rundgren. I went to visit my grandparents in Elizabeth. My grandfather gave me a crucifix that was probably once part of a set of rosary beads. The figure of Christ was made of brass mounted on a wooden crucifix. The face of Christ worn smooth by the constant rubbing of whoever held it whilst praying. I have a feeling it wasn't him.

He also gave me a bullet, a live bullet. I know it's the thought that counts, but I'm not quite sure what he was thinking as he placed it in the palm of my hand.

When my grandmother saw what he'd given me, she called him an old fool and asked him if he was trying to get me arrested at the border. I gave the bullet back, but I took Jesus with me. My lack of faith is still unresolved, but I still have the crucifix.

My dad was born in 1940 in Crumlin, Dublin. He was, and let me put this delicately, a bit of a lad. We had quite the gene pool, I'm sure you'll agree. When my dad was young, he was getting into a lot of trouble and most of the kids he hung around with ended up in prison. Growing up in Crumlin in the 1950s was tough. There was a movie made about Christy Brown (played by Daniel Day-Lewis) based on his autobiography of the same name called *My Left Foot*, which was about his life in Crumlin. My dad said the family lived in the next street to his and they were the worst of the neighbours and that was in the face of some pretty stiff competition. Brown was one of 23 children, nine of whom died in infancy. My dad was taken away from a potential life of crime by his father, who spirited him away to Liverpool to become an apprentice fitter. Almost inevitably, he never finished his apprenticeship, but called himself a diesel fitter anyway.

As a boy, I was always curious about what he actually did. When asked he would say, "I'm a diesel fitter. I measure women's knickers. I hold them up and say, 'These'll fit her'". My dad was the oldest boy in the family, and he had two younger brothers and four sisters. Mark Twain wrote that history doesn't repeat itself, but it often rhymes. My dad went on to have seven children too. Like the Waltons, but less idyllic.

In May 1958 my mum had just left school aged 16 and was due to start work in a shipping office in London the following week. There was a village fair on, and my mum persuaded her older sister, Sylvia, to go with her to the fair, and that was where she met my dad. They got talking and after that spent every night together. Soon the inevitable happened and she got pregnant, so they got married the following July in 1959. They lived with my mum's parents until my oldest brother, Michael, was born in January 1960.

My dad's father persuaded him to go back to Ireland with him. My brother, Michael, was only six months old at that time and my mum was up for going. It was, she said, an adventure. She was in love and wanted to see what Ireland was like.

They moved in with my paternal grandparents in Crumlin. Sleeping in my grandparents' front room didn't stop my mum becoming pregnant again. When my mum went into labour, she had to take the bus to hospital as they didn't have a car. She only made it with minutes to spare. I was born on 9th April 1961 in Dublin. That summer my parents took us to England to visit my maternal grandparents. Once there, my mum didn't want to go back to Ireland, perhaps understandably, having experienced Crumlin first hand. So, they put their names down for a council house and lived with my mother's parents while they waited for one to become available.

But – and you might see a pattern forming here – my dad and my grandmother had what might be described as words. He told her to shut the fuck up and they were forced to leave. My dad always had a bit of a short fuse even when he was older. I can't imagine he was any better at 22 with two kids and living at the in-laws. My parents went to stay with my dad's sister, Rose, and her husband, Jerry, and their two kids in Reading. Rose and Jerry split up soon after and she moved out with the kids, leaving us to live in their house with Jerry. My parents were happy there for a few years and my brother, Greg, was born there in January 1963.

Jerry decided to sell the house in Reading, making us homeless once more, and so there was nothing else for my parents to do except make the journey back to Dublin.

We moved back in with my Irish grandparents for another two years, in which time my mum gave birth to another two boys, Barry and Garrett.

Again my parents applied for a council house and eventually we landed a brand new house in Raheny, a northern suburb of Dublin, grey brick and not without its share of problems. But it was a step up from Crumlin and it was home. The members of U2 met at Mount Temple Comprehensive School, a few miles down the road from Raheny. Had we stayed in Dublin I'm not sure I could have persuaded them to include a keyboard player.

It wasn't a very big house; I remember box rooms set atop the other. The back garden was how the builders left it when they finished the house. Mud everywhere with some huge holes that resembled fishponds when it rained. It was more Somme than garden. We also had a swing that our dad made from scaffolding poles and big heavy chains he purloined from work. It was huge and, on reflection, quite deadly.

All five of us kids were sharing a double bed, three at one end and two at the other. Not unlike the grandparents in *Willy Wonka*, but without the promise of the Golden Ticket and a lifetime's supply of free chocolate.

There were no carpets on the floor. I distinctly remember that because one Saturday morning, while my parents were probably trying to have a lie in, I was busy pouring water into a knot hole in the bedroom floor, wondering where the water was going to, quite enjoying the experience, not realising that, of course, it was soaking the ceiling below. My dad worked shifts at CIÉ (Córas Iompair Éireann, or the Irish Transport System to me and you) and would often leap out of bed to shout at us all to be quiet if he was trying to sleep. Totally naked with one hand in the air, waving and shouting, and the other hand holding on to his tackle. He was scary and funny at the same time. You never knew when he was going to blow up, but he could also be amusing at times.

I don't remember seeing much of our dad when we were growing up, what with the shift work and the time down the pub. As he was heading out the door I'd ask, "Dad, where are you going?" He'd reply: "I'm going to see a man about a dog." The first few times I would get excited thinking he was planning to get a puppy. The dog he was talking about was the sort you bet on, but what he really meant was "I'm going down the pub". And with a wave he'd be gone for the next few hours at least.

One evening I had just gone to bed and I was scared out of my wits by a leg crashing through the plasterboard ceiling right above my bed. Years later I learned that my dad had come home from the pub a bit worse for wear and, as we had no firewood or coal, he had gone up into the loft of our new house to 'harvest' some firewood from the rafters. There were plenty of 4x2 planks up there. Sawing off a few probably wouldn't weaken the roof too much, would it? It's hard not to admire his endeavour, his logic less so.

We didn't really holiday anywhere. There were five of us, plus we didn't have a car, not unless you count the static motor that was permanently parked outside the house, which didn't work. We used to use it as a playground. I can remember sitting inside it, pretending to drive, and persuading the girl next door to sit on the windscreen with her knickers down while we were inside. We made our own fun.

———

I attended St. Malachy's Boys' School, which was a short walk down the road. I didn't like school very much.

I don't remember my first day at school, although I do remember the first day that I skipped school. On the way to morning registration, I decided I didn't want to go, so I just climbed into a ditch at the side of the road and waited for everybody else to disappear inside the school gates. And then realised that I was kind of stuck, because if I came out of the ditch and somebody saw me, they would know I was playing hooky and I would get into trouble. I spent the rest of the day in the ditch, watching the light go out of the sky, waiting for the school to come out so I could walk home and pretend I'd been there too. It was, without doubt, the most singularly boring day of my entire life.

Though that didn't stop me skipping school one other time when I was in my teens. I was selected to read something in assembly to the whole school. It was like the worst nightmare for me. And rather than read this passage, I bunked off school pretending I was ill. I had a stammer when I was young which got much worse when I was nervous. I would get stuck on words starting with vowels. I got pretty good at substituting consonant words for vowel words to hide my stammer. It probably helped to broaden my vocabulary, but for the most part I think it made me seem stupid because the words I substituted were rarely as apposite as the original.

Saying my birthday was a particular trap I couldn't escape. I distinctly remember everyone in class being told to stand up in turn and tell the whole class theirs. I had plenty of time to get really nervous, so when my turn came, I stammered "A-A-A-A-A–April 9th" while turning a nice shade of crimson as everyone laughed, including the teacher.

———

Sometime around 1968 my parents decided to emigrate and follow the Irish tradition, joining the great diaspora to the United States. Eyeing New Jersey, Boston or Philadelphia, where some of my Irish family had already settled, my parents applied for immigration status, but they didn't hear anything for a while. Then one day a stranger came knocking at the door. He asked my dad if he was interested in joining the Communist Party.

He replied, "Well, I would, but I don't have the time."

He didn't have the time by that point as he had six children to look after, but he later realised that it was probably somebody checking him out on behalf of the American Embassy. Needless to say, our application to emigrate to the United States was refused on the grounds that he was a communist.

That said, I think there's probably more to that story than meets the eye, because many years later in 1999 when my grandad was dying from cancer my dad went to visit him one last time and he was arrested when he got off the plane, held in a room for 12 hours without even a drink of water and then escorted in handcuffs on to the next plane home. They removed the handcuffs in full sight of all the other passengers, which made for an uncomfortable eight hours for him and everyone else on board. I never understood why he was treated that way, and he never chose to enlighten me.

As America was no longer an option and the strain of raising so many children was wearing my mother down, she finally gave my dad the ultimatum that she was going back to England and he could come too if he wanted. Ultimately, it was decided that my dad would go to England to look for work and when he had a job and somewhere for us to live, we would join him.

My dad asked Dick "the Gunman" to keep an eye on things while he was gone. My mum said Dick was always a polite, softly spoken man when she saw him, but there was one incident that happened around that time that's always stayed with me.

For reasons that still elude me to this day, a local hard man sent a thug around to see Dick and rough him up. It didn't quite go the way as planned and Dick beat him black and blue. Then, after extracting the information as to who had sent him, Dick bundled him into the boot of his car, and drove round to the hard man's house. On seeing a spry looking Dick on his doorstep, the hard man immediately denied all knowledge of the thug, claiming he'd never met the guy. He left Dick alone after that.

Back over in England, my dad quickly found a job, paying twice what he was earning in Ireland, and in May 1969 he arrived in a van to collect us all. We loaded up our worldly possessions and the seven boys, all wearing red jumpers my mother had knitted especially for the trip, plus some white goods that were bought on the never-never but hadn't been paid for yet. My family didn't leave a forwarding address.

When we got off the ferry at the other end the customs man counted all seven of us out of the van and said to my mum: "You must be Snow White then."

We rented a two bedroom flat in Hornchurch, Essex, above a shop on the High Street and went to the local Catholic school, St. Mary's.

For no reason I can fathom, my dad believed that Catholic schools gave a better quality of education than non-Catholic schools. I wasn't so sure about that. Being taught by nuns was pretty grim. His own short education at the hands of the Christian Brothers was brutal even by the standards of the day.

On my first day at St. Mary's a kid jumped on my back, put his arm around my neck and demanded to know which team I supported. Thankfully, he offered two options: West Ham or Tottenham. Not knowing what he was on about (I didn't even know they were football teams), I took a guess and said West Ham. His response was positive, and by that I mean he didn't try to strangle me. So, from that point on, I was a West Ham supporter. I only ever saw them play once, on a rare outing with Mike, Greg and our dad to Upton Park.

I'm not sure at which point I decided I didn't believe in God, but it was fairly early on. The three eldest boys used to go through the weekly charade of being sent by our dad to the church next to St Mary's School. Instead of going to church, we'd go to the park next door and play for a while. Our parents gave us some coins to put on the collection plate, which we happily spent on sweets or transfers, which gave us something to do while we were in the park.

Each week we took it in turns to sneak into the vestibule of the church while the service was going on and grab a newsletter to bring home and place nonchalantly on the kitchen table as unspoken indication that we'd actually been to church.

I remember one Sunday morning dad said, "Get ready for church."

It struck me that he never went to church, so I asked, "Why don't you go to church?" He replied, "Because I don't believe in God."

I said, "If you don't believe in God, why are you sending us to church?"

He said, "I'm not sending you. I'm just telling you to get ready for church." And I said, "Well, I don't want to go to church." He said, "Don't then" and that was it. We didn't go to church any more after that.

That's sort of how things went generally. My dad seemed to be following a script that was handed down to him by his mother and his Catholic upbringing. When challenged, he was quite happy to acquiesce.

My parents were fairly relaxed. I suppose they had to be with seven boys. We didn't have many rules in the house, and I'm surprised that none of us ended up in real trouble or locked up considering how closely we sailed to the wind.

I used to have a friend whose mum worked in the local laundrette. She would empty the washers and dryers of their coins once a week and keep the money at home before it was collected. Every Saturday he would steal a few pounds in 10p pieces, and we would head into Romford town centre to The Golden Egg café and order a full English breakfast, feeling like the ten year old kings we imagined we might be.

Emboldened by fried eggs, bread and sugary tea, we'd then go 'shopping'. Which is where the aforementioned 'nicking coat' came into play. Luckily, I was never caught, and my life of crime was over when I moved to secondary school and made new friends.

Though not before my habit of snaffling sweets had escalated to targeting all the things my parents couldn't afford to give us. I was interested in science so, naturally, I stole a microscope and another time a chemistry set. I was getting bolder and simply put my coat over the boxes and walked out of the shop with them. The only problem was I couldn't take them home without having to answer lots of awkward questions, so I took the chemistry set to the local park and spent the afternoon experimenting. Simply put, that mostly involved setting fire to things.

Like a lot of pre-pubescent boys, I was fascinated with fire, but before I got to the stage of setting fire to a public building, I managed to scare myself straight when a small fire I started in the corner of a field quickly got out of control. The grass was like tinder and it spread like, well, wildfire. I didn't hang around long enough to see what happened. Though at the point I was overtaken by a team of fleeing horses I realised it was getting serious and determined, with the smell of smoke in my nostrils and the thunder of hooves in my ears, to leave the Swan Vestas, and my one-man crime wave, behind me.

CHAPTER 2

The Best Days Of Our Lives

"I have never let my schooling interfere with my education." Mark Twain said that, but at one point in my errant youth I was starting to think along similar lines. Not that I'm about to draw parallels with the celebrated wit and American literary icon; for one thing he could read *and* write, something that was missing in the Mark Kelly skill set, but we'll come to that in a moment. Let's just say that none of Twain's brilliance was shining any sort of light upon my world. When it came to bookish endeavours I was still sitting in the dark.

Look at me there, idling at the back of the class, barely tuning into the teacher's words. I was both callow and a youth. You were unlikely to see me with my hand poised to shoot in the air before the question was even out of the teacher's mouth. My learning pace was more sedate: a mess-around-with-my-mates, homework-on-the-bus sort of student.

My mum was far too busy trying to put food on the table and clean clothes on our backs to think much about our education. For a while my dad took an interest in Mike, the brightest one in the family, but it wasn't the sort of interest I envied. Dad would get angry and bang the table if Mike couldn't complete his homework to our dad's satisfaction. I felt lucky to be under dad's radar.

My relaxed attitude to learning at school began in Ireland where I managed to avoid learning to read entirely. Quite a feat when you think about it and that may have been the school's fault as much as it was mine. On my first day at St Mary's, apart from my initiation as a Happy Hammer, I was asked to stand up in class and read out loud from *Green Book One*. For the uninitiated among you, it's from the *Wide Range Reader* series. An epithet I wasn't about to give myself.

As I recall, the cover was mostly green, an airborne witch on her broomstick flying through the night sky. And that was all I could have told you about that book because I couldn't read a word of it. That moment yawned interminably as the words on the page refused to disentangle themselves and surrender to my untrained eye. But God bless St. Mary's (which I'm guessing he must have done at some point in religious folklore) and the school she had graced with her name, as they managed to turn me from illiteracy and into something of an avid reader, I was hooked.

The local libraries in Hornchurch and Romford were something of a godsend to the young Kelly clan. Library books were free to borrow which suited our empty pockets perfectly. To say we were careless about returning books on time is to downplay it somewhat. Each late returned book came with a small fine, so to circumvent the cost, we chose not to return them at all. Over time we amassed an entire bookcase full of books, almost a library's worth you might say.

Dad, after countless attempts to persuade, cajole and threaten us into taking them back, packed the whole lot into boxes and left them on the steps of the library like an unmarried mum abandoning her baby in the hope of a better life for the unwanted child. I can see him now, placing the box on the steps, casting furtive glances left and right as the day bleached the darkness from the streets around him, his breath coming in exasperated clouds before he climbed back into his car and drove away.

When we weren't poring over late library books, you could find us happily splashing about in the local swimming pool. Every Saturday was spent in a happy idyll of six or seven hours in the chlorinated water until we'd drag ourselves home, exhausted and starving with our fingers and toes like white prunes.

During the long summer holidays, if we weren't poolside, we'd buy a Red Rover travel ticket, one single fare that let you run wild through London's bus and underground train network. We'd come racing into the light from the tube at South Kensington and make for the museums. I especially loved the Natural History and Science Museums. The impressively lofty ceilings, the slats of oblong daylight lighting up the high arches, the sedate yet giant dinosaurs below. If we had time, there was also the V&A. Strange to think that, while we haunted those corridors, the Royal Albert Hall was sitting just around the corner, out of sight and mind.

In 1971 we moved from Hornchurch to Harold Hill. With less than a year to go at junior school and an Eleven Plus pass already under his belt, brother Mike spent the remainder of his final year at St Mary's. He was destined to attend Campion Grammar School for Boys and go on from there to university and a successful career in science.

The rest of us moved to a school closer to home, St. Ursula's. Academically speaking, it was a big step down from St. Mary's. That, together with my devil-may-care attitude to learning, meant I sleepwalked into failing the Eleven Plus exam.

The Eleven Plus was introduced post World War II as a way of determining, at the tender age of 11, which children were destined for grammar school, university and a nice white collar job and which were heading for a comprehensive school, and probably leaving there at 16 with very few qualifications. Those in the latter category wouldn't need many qualifications as they would be building houses and roads and making the cars to run on them.

The Eleven Plus was essentially an IQ test, a test whose significance wasn't really impressed upon our young minds at the time. Nobody explained that it would pretty much set the course of my life from that point onwards, and if they did then I clearly wasn't listening.

Because I failed the Eleven Plus my choices were limited to one of the comprehensive schools in the area. I chose Bishop Ward Boys' School in Dagenham for no other reason than that's where my friends were going. It was a Roman Catholic school too, which got my dad's approval.

It was a blow to my confidence that I failed the Eleven Plus and didn't follow Mike to Campion. When I started in secondary school, I was in the top stream for Maths and English and diligently worked my way downwards from there.

I failed my Maths O Level and barely scraped a grade C in English. My reputation was so bad that one of my teachers refused to enter me for the Chemistry O Level because he was sure I would fail, and it would be a waste of money. I offered to pay for the exam myself, as I was earning money from my Saturday job, and was vindicated when I passed with a grade C.

At best you could say our school buildings looked unscrubbed. Like most schools, the teachers were a mixed bunch: some kind and inspiring, with the occasional weirdo and sadist added to the mix for good measure.

Dagenham was in a rough part of east London and the school had its share of bullies, although I was never bullied. That might have been because I got into a couple of fights in the first few years and once the bullies know you are prepared to fight, even if you didn't win, they tend to leave you alone. I spent a couple of evenings a week for a year or two training at the Five Star Boxing Club in Harold Hill.

I really enjoyed the training and still occasionally enjoy skipping with a rope today. Because of the training I felt more confident than I should have when a fight was brewing. Instead of sensibly backing down I put my fists up. The first time I easily beat the kid who was picking on me. The second time not so much, as my opponent seemed unfamiliar with the Queensberry Rules. After some fancy footwork and a few well-placed jabs from me, his face was a bloody mess. But then he got really mad and surprised me by grabbing my long hair and set to work kicking me in the face like he was kicking a football in a string bag. I caught hold of his leg, upended him and he went down with a clump of my hair still in his hand and the fight came to an awkward end.

There was a bully in our year, Andrew Connolly. He called himself Bozo (presumably the irony of naming yourself after a clown had eluded him, not that I nor anyone else was going to point that out to him). He was very tall and well-built for an 11 year old. He was also pretty smart and funny, but something in his past had brought out the tormentor in him.

A few weeks into our first year Connolly was looking for a kid called Brian Biggins. Apparently, I looked like Biggins. I know this because Bozo cornered me in the playground, sure that I was him. I quickly put him straight. He took some convincing but eventually relented and I hurried off to class. Whenever I saw Connolly around the school after that, he would greet me with a friendly, 'Alright, Biggins'. The name caught on and everybody started calling me Biggins, even some of the teachers, and that was the name I was known by throughout my seven years in secondary school.

Aged 12, I discovered something I was good at and enjoyed doing: drawing. My rudimentary years were spent sketching out the escapades of comic book characters like Spiderman caught between New York's skyscrapers, thin ropes of webbing emanating from his wrists. Within a few years I was imagining myself as an illustrator or a draughtsman of some sort or even a graphic artist designing record sleeves.

I was good with my hands generally. I loved taking things apart and I was interested in electronics from an early age, which started when we were in Ireland. We had an old radiogram player, which was essentially a big wooden sideboard with a single speaker mounted inside, a valve radio and a Bakelite turntable topped with a brown felt pad where the record being played rested.

I'm not suggesting my parents were trying to cull a few of us, but, for some weird reason, it didn't have a plug attached. If you wanted to play a record, you had to stuff the bare wires into the wall socket and cross your fingers. I can remember getting a couple of nasty shocks until I mastered the technique of inserting a pointed object into the top hole to raise the 'child proof' spring loaded shutters and jamming the bare wires in, releasing the shutters onto the wires, all without touching the exposed copper wire. Like Tom Cruise in *Mission Impossible*, but on a budget. I'd like to report that it gave me a healthy respect for electricity but throughout my teens I received more electric shocks than a tight-lipped Russian dissident in a Moscow prison.

My interest in music was ignited when my brother Greg and I were given a joint Christmas present in 1972 of a cassette recorder. It was an expensive item for my parents to buy and so we shared it. Apart from creating our own radio plays like a pair of budding Orson Welles, we used to record songs off the radio. We both liked glam rock bands like Sweet, Slade, T. Rex, Cockney Rebel and Mott The Hoople. This led us down the rabbit hole to more sophisticated artists like Roxy Music and Elton John. It wouldn't be long before I was moving towards progressive music, something I would totally fall for a few years later.

My parents' taste in music was a big influence too: Cream, Stevie Wonder, Rory Gallagher, Bread, The Hollies, The Moody Blues, ELO and The Beatles too, naturally. They even went on a rare night out together to see Free playing at the Royal Albert Hall in 1972. With some pestering from us older boys they also bought some Pink Floyd, Queen and Led Zeppelin.

We probably only had about 30 albums in total, so whenever we obtained a new record it was played until the vinyl threatened to wear thin as I absorbed every musical and lyrical detail.

Apart from our limited record collection, we also listened to the radio, especially the Saturday afternoon rock show on the BBC, presented by Alan 'Fluff' Freeman. And as well as Fluff and his eclectic mix of tunes, there was the infamous pirate station floating somewhere off in the North Sea, Radio Caroline.

Every evening they played a wide range of music from the progressive rock bands we were used to hearing from Fluff Freeman, but then threw in some musical curveballs from artists like Dutch band Kayak, as well as some songs you were never going to hear on the BBC: *She Moved The Dishes First* by Liverpool band Supercharge. A song about a guy who brings a girl home to his parents' house late at night and so as not to wake them she pees in the kitchen sink. Marriage material, clearly.

Radio Caroline was the brainchild of an Irish hippy businessman, Ronan O'Rahilly. He used the station to promote a cod, pseudo eastern philosophy he called Loving Awareness. He put together a band under the same name and they recorded an album which was heavily promoted on the station. My brother Mike and I went to see them play at the Marquee Club in 1976. It was my first proper gig. They were much better than their album might have suggested, with some very good players who went on to become The Blockheads, Ian Dury's backing band.

It was Rick Wakeman who truly turned my head though. His *Journey To The Centre Of The Earth* album changed my life. I first heard it playing in my uncle Alan's car. I was probably 13 years old and it hit me like a thunderbolt. I don't think I'd ever heard an album that told a story before – an actual concept album. There was the narration, the orchestration and, most of all, the keyboard solos. The sound of the Minimoog was wonderful, although you could have put a gun to my head at that point and I wouldn't have been able to tell you what a Minimoog actually was.

My best friend at the time was Anthony Burke. We didn't share much in the way of musical taste except for a love of Queen, but his mother worked as a shop assistant in the Co-op in Romford. Through his mother, Tony got a part-time job there, stacking shelves. I couldn't help noticing how much money he had and I wanted a piece of that action. I was 15 when I started working at the Co-op. The hours were all day Saturday and four hours every Monday, Tuesday and Wednesday evenings after school. It didn't help elevate my academic performance at all, but the £11.60 it paid blinded me to that.

At the end of my first day at work with my pay packet burning a hole in my pocket, I headed straight for Downtown Records in Romford and bought *Journey To The Centre Of The Earth*. I played it continuously, as I'm sure any of my family will bear out. I was so hooked on the music that I would listen to it before leaving for school because I couldn't bear the thought that I wouldn't hear it again until I got home.

Eventually, for everyone's sake, I bought a pair of headphones to sate my Wakeman obsession and not drive my parents half crazy. I quickly completed my Wakeman collection as soon as I could afford it: *The Six Wives Of Henry VIII*, *The Myths And Legends Of King Arthur And The Knights Of The Round Table*, *No Earthly Connection* and even the soundtrack to the movie *Lisztomania*. Yes, I even found space in my heart for *Lisztomania*.

Unlike children, I didn't love all his albums equally. But Wakeman's incredible playing always managed to spirit me away, in particular on *Six Wives* where he was at his best and members of Yes and Strawbs played on several tracks.

Around the same time, brother Mike asked for *Yessongs* by Yes for Christmas after seeing them perform *Roundabout* on the TV. I didn't like the sound of Yes and told Mike so. Which was when he pointed out to me that the keyboard player was one Rick Wakeman. Reluctantly, I gave them another chance and quickly succumbed to their musical charms.

I firmly believe that a major contribution to my taking up drawing and my later dedication to the keyboards was TV, or more precisely, the lack of it.

When we lived in Ireland, we had a black and white TV. The next-door neighbours bought a colour TV, which was a big deal on our street. We finally got our own colour set after we moved to the UK. Like a lot of people, we rented it from Radio Rentals or Rumbelows, two high street names familiar to people of a certain age. One day my dad brought home a brand new TV (probably best not to dwell on where it came from), so the rental went back to the shop. Which was great until the new TV broke down. Unable to afford to get it repaired, we lived without a TV for the best part of a year.

The TV wasn't the only thing my dad brought home. On one occasion there was a few hundred tins of corned beef. My mum became pretty inventive with corned beef recipes. We had corned beef with everything and, while I liked it, I wasn't sad when the little key rolled open the seal on that last tin. I haven't eaten corned beef since. Another time he brought home a nice stool which I grabbed as it was perfect for playing the organ. Years later, when I was old enough to frequent pubs, I noticed it matched the stools in our local.

Mike took up playing the guitar, but I had my sights set on the keyboards. Somehow, in 1976 I persuaded our mum to buy me an organ. I was drooling over these huge organs (bear with me), but, as they were all so expensive, I had to settle for a small single keyboard. It was a Hammond Everett. It had the famous Hammond name but that was where the similarity to the mighty C3 or B3 that Wakeman, Keith Emerson and Jon Lord rocked out on ended. Sporting a small three octave keyboard with a bunch of chord buttons to the side, it resembled an accordion as much as an organ.

I realised early on that the chord buttons were not much use unless you were planning to take up the accordion (and I wasn't). I wanted to learn to play properly, but with only a three octave keyboard two handed playing is somewhat restricted. As a result, my left hand playing is underwhelming and my hand independence is nowhere near where it should be. For those of you currently staring at the page the way a dog looks at a biscuit, hand independence is the ability to play using both hands in such a way that each seems to be working independently of the other. Mine, shall we say, are less independently minded.

The organ cost £185, roughly equivalent to £1,500 in today's money. Which, when you consider our family's fortunes, was way too much for my mum to cough up in one go. She arranged to pay for it in instalments and I would pay her back £5 per week from my Saturday job. To begin with I paid her every week, but over time, to my shame, I started skipping payments and eventually stopped paying her altogether before my debt was completely discharged.

I don't know if she really believed I was serious about wanting to learn to play or if she figured it didn't matter as I had committed to repaying her, so the folly was all mine if I gave up after the first week. Whatever, I am forever grateful that she took the gamble.

It's not unusual for teenagers to take up a hobby with great enthusiasm only to find after a few months that initial fervour wanes. We've all been there, but the passion I felt for playing the keyboards was different. I didn't lose interest. I became obsessive about learning to play. I would spend every waking hour that I wasn't at school or stacking supermarket shelves sat at that keyboard.

Children today have so many distractions – smartphones, iPads, computers and game consoles – that they have no time to be bored. Boredom is a great motivator. If you're never bored, then at what point will you find a new hobby, or will it find you? Learning to play a musical instrument takes a lot of effort with little initial reward. In these days of instant gratification, picking up the guitar or sitting down at the piano might seem like too much effort. It makes me wonder where the next generation of musicians might come from.

I was passionate about wanting to play the keyboards, and over time I gradually improved: Learning to play by ear and teaching myself the rudiments of music theory. Within the first year of starting to play I discovered a friend, Jerome Sopher, played drums in his garage with another boy from our school, David O'Neil. It would be a stretch to call them a band because they didn't have a name and never ventured out of Joe's garage (unlike the musicians featured in the Frank Zappa song of the same name). I persuaded them to let me join even though I was terrible, but as they were equally terrible it didn't matter.

I can't recommend joining a band enough, even if you are just starting out and all you can manage is a cacophonous racket. Having the discipline of regular band practice and songs to learn is a great way to improve your playing.

A major hurdle every budding young musician faces when they join a band is transport or lack thereof. My solution was simple: invite my bandmates round to set up in my bedroom. This idea was met with some resistance from my mum, but she was a bit of a pushover, so I got my way, and it became a regular Sunday afternoon fixture in our house for a while. That was until the next-door neighbour came banging on the door, having been disturbed sleeping off a lunch time drinking session. In his strong Mancunian accent, he bellowed, "You've 'ad yer 'ammer, now curb it!" And our Sunday band practice came to an end.

No sooner was the Hammond Everett set up in my bedroom than I had the back off it to see how it worked while I attempted to connect a wah-wah pedal to the thing to broaden my sound palette. I was surprised how empty it was inside. The Everett was the first transistor-based organ Hammond produced. It didn't sound anywhere near as rich and earthy as the fabulous tonewheel organs they made from the 1930s until the 1970s. Hammond went out of business in the 1980s when sales fell in response to their switch to inferior transistor-based organs.

The tonewheel organs were originally intended as a cheaper alternative to the air-powered pipe organs usually installed in churches. The Hammond quickly caught on in jazz music and by the 1960s was a major feature in rock music. Cranking up their valve amps to 11 produced a warm distortion that suited guitar bands perfectly. Jon Lord took the concept even further by putting his Hammond through a guitar amp.

It was common to ditch the pedals altogether and cut the organ in half so it could be transported more easily for touring. The fact that I was some way off playing live, let alone in a touring band, did nothing to dissuade me and I cut the bottom three quarters off mine with a saw. The few circuit boards inside were easily repositioned safely behind the keyboard. This turned my upright piano sized organ into a keyboard I could carry on my own. A few years later I cut it down further, removing the useless chord buttons, making it small enough to fit under one arm.

I'm not sure what my poor mother must have thought about my keyboard butchery as I hammered and sawed away as she stumped up cash to pay for it each week.

I drifted between bands over the next few years playing the odd gig. Odd as in strange, as well as infrequent. It was a hobby, I loved it, but didn't think for a minute that I had the chops to consider it as a career choice. It was a fantastical idea, something to dream about.

When Yes released *Going For The One* in 1977 Mike and I went to see them play at Wembley Arena. I saw Pink Floyd there too a few months earlier. Music was becoming an all-consuming part of my life.

In this happy idyll of 13/8 time signatures and cape-wearing keyboard players, I wasn't aware that the natural order of things was about to be washed away by a cultural tsunami. I had grown to think that good musicianship and well-crafted songs were, it was universally agreed, something worth striving for, the songwriting higher ground.

And then, like someone throwing a house brick through your window, along came punk.

CHAPTER 3

A Chip Off The Old Communist Bloc

S wearing is neither big nor clever, but it's akin to a booster rocket if you crave the wide skies of overnight notoriety and the front pages of tabloid newspapers nationwide.

It was the balmy, long days of the summer of '77, the sun set high over our Essex home. A few months previously, The Sex Pistols had ushered in the age of punk rock with a cacophony of swearing and general bad behaviour, bringing anarchy to early evening TV and upending middle England on its ear. *Never Mind The Bollocks* was about to drop on an unsuspecting world. The Pistols had already been dropped by a nervy EMI and then scooped up by Richard Branson's Virgin label.

Talking of unsuspecting, my parents had somehow been persuaded to let my brother Mike throw a party. They agreed to go out for a few hours so that we could party unsupervised, like adults. Playing to our strengths, I prepared a nice selection of classy pop, prog and rock on my reel-to-reel tape recorder and Mike had two 40 pint polypins of beer delivered. He did a pretty good job of publicising the party too. I know this because most of the 200 students from his sixth form turned up, whether they were invited or not.

Some of the students arrived wearing black bin liners held together with safety pins. They brought their own music too. A handful of singles they played endlessly while bouncing up and down headbutting the lampshade and pulverising the rug. This was my first sight of punk fashion and pogoing as it was known. It was nothing compared to the dreadful din that assaulted my ears.

The Pistols' *God Save The Queen*, *New Rose* by The Damned, The Clash's *White Riot*, The Jam's *In The City* and *Gary Gilmore's Eyes* by The Adverts blared out on a discordant loop, a hideous soundtrack matched only by the ugly events playing out before my eyes.

To paraphrase Ron Burgundy, things escalated quickly. Luckily my parents arrived home in time to break it up before the police arrived. My dad was most upset about the two women he found sitting on the stairs, who were quickly escorted from the premises. "Who let those prostitutes in!?" he shouted at my inebriated brother. My only thought was how does he know they're prostitutes? They weren't even wearing red shoes.

It subsequently transpired that, at some point prior to their expedited departure, the two women had rifled through the house and found the money that Mike had previously collected from his class towards the polypins of ale which our dad had fronted. To spare Mike further trouble, I lent him the stolen money from my keyboard saving stash.

Overnight everything I held dear musically was considered naff and past its sell-by date. Any fool could start a band and write songs. To my ears, punk held almost nothing of interest for me. However, there was one band that I could listen to: The Stranglers. At least they had a keyboard player who sounded like he knew what he was doing.

Over time my hostile attitude to punk and the new wave that followed softened and I started to see some merit in it. Also, I found it hard to argue with the notion that bands like Emerson Lake & Palmer had outstayed their welcome and should quietly retire after releasing the bloated *Works Volumes I & II* and the risible *Love Beach*.

Inspiration comes in many guises and I wouldn't have guessed that a teacher with slight paralysis of the face would be such an influence on my life.

John Germain was my art teacher and, still built like the rugby player he once was, almost as wide as he was tall. His face placid on one side and deaf in one ear, both caused by nerve damage when an operation following a rugby accident went awry.

He was a cool guy. He treated the kids as human beings, equals almost. He wore sweatshirts, jeans and Kickers boots when his colleagues were all wearing cheap, dandruff covered suits and brown Hush Puppies.

He loved music and was happy to spread that love around, even going so far as to lend me records from his own collection. I particularly remember him handing me *Foxtrot* by Genesis, and the world it opened up to me.

And it wasn't just music that Mr. Germain was turning me on to. He encouraged me in my art and gave me the confidence to apply to Bath Academy of Art in Corsham to study. He convinced me that I should become a fine artist and that Corsham was the place to be.

He didn't sugar coat the future either and made no secret of the fact that art wouldn't pay the bills and I'd need to do something else like teaching to earn money. That wasn't what I saw myself doing, but by then I'd been offered a place and it was settled. I was going to Corsham.

Anyway, I was looking forward to starting a band in art college. Keith Richards, Jimmy Page and members of Queen and Pink Floyd all went to art school, so my hopes were high. Art schools were clearly a fertile breeding ground for the budding rock star, though, as it turned out, not my art school. Bath Academy of Art was a musical wasteland. I didn't meet a single musician the entire time I was there.

I took my Grundig reel-to-reel tape recorder and my first monophonic synth, a Kawai 100F, (both bought with saved money as my credit line had been withdrawn) with me to Corsham and made my first tentative attempts at composing and recording. Nothing survives from my early forays into composition, which is probably for the best.

As with rock 'n' roll, I was a late starter when it came to sex and drugs too.

It was Remembrance Sunday, and I woke up with a thumping head, the morning sunshine casting a watery light on the far wall. I was sharing a single bed in a room I didn't recognise with a young woman whose name I couldn't remember. I was part way through my first term at Bath Academy of Art and I was no longer a virgin. Hallelujah!

The previous night gradually floated to the surface like so much flotsam and jetsam. Like most Saturday evenings, I spent it at the Pack Horse pub drinking Guinness and killing aliens on the newly installed Space Invaders machine. I was by far the best player in Corsham and proud of it. Though not so proud of how much of my student grant had disappeared into the slot to get me there. The young lady lying beside me worked behind the bar and at closing time had invited me back to her digs for a coffee.

I remembered she was a second year student, but her name was a complete blank. How embarrassing. We had chatted and listened to some music and before I knew it, we were in bed together. Now it was morning, and I was sober. My usual shyness around talking to women had returned. Time to leave but how to say goodbye when I didn't know her name? Then it came to me. I remembered seeing a name badge on her bedroom door (she shared a big house with several other students). I went to the bathroom, taking care to clock her name on the way back in. "See you around, Alison", I said with a breezy confidence as I stepped out into the bright and cold November day, content in the knowledge that I had finally lost my virginity.

My dedication to playing the keyboards over the previous four years meant I had little time for nights out with friends or meeting girls, not that I would know what to say to them had I met any. Growing up in a house of all boys and attending an all boys' school meant that girls were an alien species to me. They weren't just from Venus: they were from another galaxy completely.

Alison and I spent a few more nights together after that first encounter but there was never any question of us becoming an item. I think it suited both of us to meet up now and again for a night in her single bed. And not only did she open me up to a whole new world of sex; she introduced me to Kraftwerk too. Thank you, Alison.

When studying art, it was customary to complete a one year foundation course, followed by a three year degree course. To continue in Corsham for the degree course I had to go through an interview process. I was interviewed by a man and a woman, both strangers to me. "Pleased to meet you", I smiled and shook the lady's hand. She arched an eyebrow. "Strange that we haven't met", she said. "I was your History of Art teacher for the last two terms."

Had I made the effort to attend at least one History of Art lecture the course of my life might have been different. As it was, at the end of term I said goodbye to Corsham for good and a life in art with it.

I moved back in with my parents and determined to have a fresh start at something completely different. I applied for a job as an apprentice fireman. The idea of scaling a burning building and carrying a terrified damsel down a ladder before an admiring crowd appealed, but it wasn't to be. They rejected my application: myopic firemen are frowned upon apparently.

1980 became a shifting tableau of cash in hand jobs working for employers with as much regard for worker wellbeing as they did the taxman. I tried my hand at tiling roofs. It was backbreaking and dangerous work. Climbing a ladder with ten concrete tiles on your shoulder requires strength, balance and a reckless disregard for health and safety. I liked being outdoors though, and the heights didn't bother me one bit, but I knew it wasn't what I wanted to be doing for the rest of my life.

For a few days while tiling a roof in north London I heard a band rehearsing in a house across the street. As I stood on that rooftop, the green of the London suburbs laid out before me, I clearly remember thinking how lucky they were to be able to spend their days making music. A dream was forming in my head, a dream fuelled by a recently published biography of Genesis by Armando Gallo. In it he described how Genesis spent six months living and writing music in Richard Macphail's parents' holiday cottage. That was my idea of heaven.

Back in the real world, I got a job lining boilers. This involved climbing inside these gigantic furnaces and replacing the fire bricks that lined their inners. It was like stepping into a miniature version of hell. The dust was horrendous. It blocked the nose and turned hair into dried straw. I'd come out of there like a goldfish upended from its bowl and gasping for air. Unsurprisingly, I lasted little more than a few weeks.

My next job was working in a factory making double-glazed windows. This was a job I was familiar with, having spent the previous summer holidays working in similar factory, although the working conditions here were much worse. The breaks were shorter and there were no washing facilities to speak of. The workers, mostly young men like me, constantly complained about the conditions, so after a few weeks I suggested we get organised. I explained that if we joined a trade union, we could demand better conditions.

The following day I was called into the boss's office, handed my P45 and told to leave via the side door. I ignored him and marched through the factory shouting that I was being fired and if my now former colleagues really wanted conditions to improve, they should follow me out the door and strike. To a man, they looked at their feet. Fuck 'em, I thought and didn't look back.

When I got home, I was worried what my dad would say about getting fired after only six weeks in the job. To my surprise, he couldn't have been prouder. He explained how I should have joined a union before opening my mouth. In that instance, they wouldn't have been able to fire me so easily with a union behind me. I was a chip off the old communist bloc.

To fuel my dreams of making music, I'd been saving my cash, and as soon as I had enough money, I replaced the Kawai synth with a Yamaha CS15. Nothing like the famous CS80, the CS15 was a dual oscillator, monophonic synth. Not a Minimoog but better than the Kawai. My organ also needed retiring. A friend told me that he knew somebody who had an old Farfisa organ they were getting rid of as it was not working. I went round to take a look and I instantly recognised that it was a Compact Duo. The same model that Rick Wright played in the early days of Pink Floyd.

The lights came on when powered up, but it made no sound. I figured that there couldn't be too much awry but concealed my optimism that it could be easily fixed and offered the owner £40 to take it off his hands. I have to admit that with my limited knowledge of electronics I got lucky in identifying a faulty transistor in the audio output stage. The replacement cost me 30p.

Apart from working to earn some money, I was keen to reconnect with some of the people I'd been playing with in bands before going to college. One of them, Jack Grigor, a lovely chap and solid bass player with a Pink Floyd obsession, introduced me to guitarist Dave Weston and drummer Phil Stubbs. Dave had a plan to form a band in the vein of Hawkwind, Gong, Steve Hillage and Here & Now.

He wanted it to be a 'jam band', a style of creating music made popular in the US by the Grateful Dead, but it was a concept that had yet to reach the UK. Dave wanted to call the band Chemical Alice. The name was plucked from the pages of a Michael Moorcock fantasy novel. Moorcock had a long association with Hawkwind, contributing to their *Warrior On The Edge Of Time* album. I liked science fiction and fantasy so it was a good fit, although I found Dave's preoccupation with gnomes and flying teapots a little wearing. We even wrote a song which Dave called *The Gnome Song*, a loosely arranged jam that varied in length depending on how stoned we were.

I had ambitions to write more structured songs, but for the time being I was just happy to be in a band. We played a strange mix of covers including Pink Floyd's *Echoes*, *Like A Hurricane* by Neil Young and Hawkwind's *Master Of The Universe*. More excitingly, for me at least, we also started writing our own songs. Dave treated the vocal parts almost as an afterthought and was quite happy to share the lead vocals with me. We were the sum of our parts: two not especially good singers. A lot of the material we played had long instrumental workouts, so the vocals were less important, but if we wanted to grow as a band, then we needed a real singer.

It takes a certain kind of person to want to be a lead singer. Many singers start off as instrumentalists and move into the role when they discover they are the best voice the band has. Dave Gilmour, Don Henley and our own Steve Hogarth spring to mind. Steve started off as the keyboard player in his first serious band, The Europeans, and gradually moved into the role of lead vocalist. By the time he joined Marillion he was a lead singer who also happened to play keys.

I can't remember how I met Tim Kelly (no relation), but he was the first decent singer I worked with. He had a pleasant voice and personality to match. I persuaded Dave and Jack to give him a try. Tim was a big Genesis fan too and with Jack's help we moved Chemical Alice into more progressive rock territory with structured songs rather than jams.

Fed up with 'Kosmik Rock', Tim departed the band in May 1981 after only a few gigs, but by then we had written a few songs that were more to my taste and built up a small following in the Romford area. Tim's replacement was Andy Grant. He couldn't sing like Tim, but he was more of a front man. He had more confidence than his limited singing ability warranted but with little ego, and he proved to be a better lyricist than either Dave or me, which wasn't saying much. Andy brought drummer Richard 'Cretin' Crighton with him following Phil Stubbs' departure. Cretin was much easier going and more fun than his nickname might suggest.

Around the same time Dave found us a dream rehearsal facility. The railway line at Romford Station is high above the road and the bridge that supports it built on high brick arches. Each of those arches was enclosed with a wooden front and rented out as lockups. They were inexpensive and had a power supply and there was no problem with making as much noise as you liked day or night. It was hardly the Palace of Versailles, but we adored it.

So much so that we practically moved in. It had two floors. We used one to rehearse and the other for partying. We had a few lights, a mirror ball and some cushions. Plenty of speakers and amplifiers. And drugs. Hash and magic mushrooms mainly and, just to take the edge off, the occasional tab of acid. Which was handy, as a lot of Chemical Alice's music made more sense when our states were altered.

Dave and I lived on opposite sides of a golf course. We had heard that at the right time of year it was possible to find *Psilocybe Semilanceata* or 'Liberty Cap' mushrooms there. Some of you will already be ahead of me here, that's if the words have stopped moving about on the page before your eyes, but they are one of the most potent hallucinogenic fungi found in the UK. They feed off decaying grass roots and the short grass of a golf course was the perfect place to find them.

Of course, this was before the internet and so we had no idea what they looked like. Undeterred, we spent a pleasant afternoon wandering around the fairways picking any fungus we could find. Later that night we went to see Hawkwind play in London and ate the assortment of mushrooms we had found earlier that day. All I can remember of that gig was the trouble I had standing up straight, in part because of mushrooms but also because of the raked floor. Luckily, we didn't come to any harm from our reckless experiment, and I determined to visit Romford Library to research the fungi of the UK before we went hunting for mushrooms again.

Once we knew what to look for, they were easy to spot and in plentiful supply. We would quite often just eat them one by one as we picked them and stop looking as soon as we started tripping. Imagine foragers with enlarged pupils and a perpetual and sudden sense of wonder and you're halfway there.

Dave suggested that we should go to the Stonehenge Free Festival for the summer solstice. The festival was a loosely organised (I'm using the word 'organised' in its freest sense) event spanning a few weeks culminating with the solstice. It started in 1974 and grew by word of mouth until more than 30,000 people turned up just ten years later. A victim of its own success, the authorities clamped down on subsequent attempts to hold the festival.

In 1981, even during the solstice weekend, I'd say there were less than 10,000 in attendance. We weren't invited to play, but that didn't prevent us turning up with a van full of equipment, a borrowed generator and a willingness to play. We set up on the periphery of the site and played a number of sets over a few days to passing festival goers that grew into a crowd as the set progressed.

The rest of the time we were stoned, tripping or both. Drugs were openly on sale everywhere. The police didn't enter the site but anybody who left it was a target for stop and search. We wandered the site watching bands like the remarkably monikered Tibetan Ukrainian Mountain Troupe, which I'd still like on a T-shirt. Staying up all night and sleeping most of the day. I can't say that we made many new fans, but we had fun. If you consider dropping a few IQ points fun.

It was late summer before we got our first break at a real gig. The Electric Stadium in Chadwell Heath. Less glamorous than the name suggests, it was actually a pub called The Greyhound, but it had a stage and held about 300 people if you ignored the fire limit, which we did.

We also booked ourselves a day at Spaceward Studios in Cambridge to record four songs to be pressed up onto a vinyl EP which we titled *Curiouser And Curiouser*. For those that never thought to spend their hard-earned cash on our debut on its release, I'll walk you through its many and varied highlights.

Henry The King - Cretin's drumming giving Chemical Alice a punk energy that goes against the prog/hippy vibe the rest of us were trying to project, although the second half slows down to a Floyd influenced extended guitar and keyboard workout.

The Judge - This song opens with a keyboard and guitar melody that owes more than a little to *Lady Of The Lake* by Starcastle. Let's just say I was happy their lawyer never got to hear it. It's not a bad song, but the structure is repetitive and could have benefited from judicious editing.

Goodnight Vienna - This is probably the most sophisticated arrangement of the four. It has my trademark widdly-widdly (as I like to call it) lead synth that I would use to good effect a few years later in Marillion.

Lands Of Home - The other three songs were mostly written by me with lyrics from Andy. *Lands Of Home* was Dave's idea of what Chemical Alice should be doing. It has a heavy Hawkwind influence. Lots of heavy chugging guitar riffs and sweeping synths with fantasy themed lyrics, some of which I wrote. My only lyrical contribution to make it onto record, thankfully.

We only had one day to record and mix four songs, so unsurprisingly it was a bit rough around the edges. That said, at the time I remember we were very pleased with the results and the 1,000 copies we had pressed up sold well at gigs.

The gigs at the Electric Stadium became a regular spot and we were soon selling it out and playing there once or twice a month to enthusiastic crowds.

Despite Chemical Alice growing in popularity locally, we were a long way from breaking into the London gig circuit. We hadn't even made it out of Essex at that point. I figured that I needed a Plan B, and as electronics was my other interest (a career in music seemed like a pipe dream) I applied to study electronics at Havering Tech and was accepted. I started in September, already a full two years older than everyone else in my class.

Around that time, I was approached by two songwriters/guitarists to join them for a rehearsal with a view to me possibly joining their fledgling band, Split Grass. Mike Caswell and his friend, whose name is lost to me now, were only 17 but both were better musicians than anyone in Chemical Alice, including me. Their songwriting was more mature too, if a little poppy. I was excited about the prospect of working with them but decided to keep it to myself until I'd made my mind up whether to leave Chemical Alice or not.

A few weeks later a local music fanzine asked to interview me. I was both delighted and flattered. I might even have puffed out my chest a little bit, and, as we know, pride inevitably comes before a fall. The interview was to take place in a pub and the rest of Chemical Alice sat on the next table within earshot.

I remember the first question like it was yesterday: "How do the rest of Chemical Alice feel about your decision to leave them and join Split Grass?" I'd been ambushed, it was a set-up. I was stunned (though possibly not as stunned as my bandmates nursing pints of lager on the next table) and stammered that I had no plans to leave Chemical Alice. I was annoyed with Mike too. Was this their way to force my hand into committing to Split Grass? I wasn't sure, but it had the opposite effect.

I don't know what happened to the rest of Split Grass, but Mike Caswell went on to be a successful session guitarist, touring with Brian May, Steve Hackett and others. He tragically drowned while on holiday in Spain in 2016.

For a lot of young men, the allure of a rock 'n' roll lifestyle is mixed in with the promise of fame, fortune and female fans. Not me, I was in it for the music. I didn't relish the thought of being in the spotlight. It terrified me. Don't get me wrong, I wasn't about to be canonised, I liked girls a lot, but I was too shy to talk to them.

That's why it hit me like a casually tossed tin of beans when Debbie Smith, suddenly sitting closer to me than I'd first realised, blurted out that she'd like it very much if I took her on a white horse and rode away with her. Two things: there was no white horse and we were both starry eyed from the magic mushrooms we'd taken. Which would probably explain her florid language and my sense of being physically struck. Though that could also have had something to do with the fact that her recently jilted boyfriend was sitting almost within earshot and that ex just happened to be Andy, our singer.

It's difficult for me to express how unexpected this was. A girl, and a pretty one at that, was interested in me. She admitted that I had been in her sights since Andy joined Chemical Alice. I naturally wondered if it had something to do with their relationship ending. I didn't dig too deeply, but he certainly didn't seem especially happy about it.

Rather than do the sensible thing and politely decline Debbie's advances I started seeing her in secret. The excitement of being in a relationship was only enhanced by the covert nature of our romance. I had recently turned 20 but I was like a lovestruck teenager, completely infatuated with my first girlfriend. But even I could see there might be trouble ahead when Andy inevitably found us out, but I was caught happily in the moment.

On Wednesday 11th November 1981 we set up our equipment for one of our regular sold out gigs at the Electric Stadium. I asked Dave if he knew who the support act was that night. "I think you'll like them", he said. "They're called Marillion."

CHAPTER 4

Fifteen Stone First Footer

You never know when lightning might strike. Standing there in the shadows of the Electric Stadium watching our support act that night, little did I know that I was about to be speared by a bolt from the blue. Marillion hit me like the sky falling in. Dave Weston was right; I did like them.

It was hard to look away, not least from the towering frontman. As if his height wasn't imposing enough, he was dressed in a long black robe, though it hardly had the dramatic impact of, say, Christopher Lee appearing out of the mist, a glint in his black eyes, blood at his lip. It looked more like Fish might have slept in it. The band were similarly strangely attired, as if they had come to gig directly from sleeping under a bridge.

Guitarist Steve Rothery and bassist Diz Minnitt were both wearing brown, roughly hewn undergarments and a bright red cloak affair that might have come from a Roman centurion they had robbed. Keyboardist Brian Jelleyman was also wearing a sackcloth outfit in a sage green with a large eye embroidered on the chest. Which not only gave them a look that suggested they had just returned from a festival, but had also fallen in with a cult while they'd been camping.

In the gloom, I realised that all three of them had eyes stitched on to their clothes: Diz and Steve's were on their backs. The overall effect was striking, but not perhaps in the way the band might have imagined. Though you couldn't knock their ambition. This was a support slot in a pub gig in Essex and they were taking it very seriously indeed. Not content with a cloak that looked like it had been left outside in a storm, Fish had foregone shoes, his giant, pale feet an occasional flash of dull white from the stage. His face was a smear of garish greasepaint, a tribal mask of reds and greens peering out of the darkness.

As the support band, they probably only played for 45 minutes, but what a 45 minutes: *He Knows You Know*, *Garden Party*, *Forgotten Sons*, *The Web* and possibly *Grendel* too. I was mesmerised; it's hard to overstate the impact their brief set had on me. They were passionate and energised, Steve's playing cut through the room, as did Fish's vocals. It was prog rock, but with a newly found fervour. It didn't feel like a musical relic, it sounded vital and fresh. I remember being especially struck by the 'The flytrap needs the insect...' section of *The Web*; that was ringing around my head for days afterwards. And the seismic moment in *Forgotten Sons* where Fish spits out the words: 'From the dole queue to the regiment...'

Perhaps tellingly, I remember next to nothing of our set that night. I'm guessing it was mostly original material with a few covers thrown in. In those days I was in the habit of rocking the organ violently backwards and forwards during parts of the set where the keyboard playing was less challenging. Like Keith Emerson without the knives. With one hand on the CS15, and the other gripping chords on the Farfisa, I'd thrust my groin against the front of the organ to tilt it backwards, then, with precious moments to spare, pull it back before it flattened some unsuspecting fan in the front row. I liked it and so, apparently, did Fish and Mick Pointer, their drummer.

Brian Jelleyman, who I was about to usurp, was not a bad player at all and was also responsible for coming up with a few of the iconic Marillion keyboard parts that I got credited with when *Script For A Jester's Tear* was released more than a year after his departure. The *Garden Party* riff, the synth lines in *Forgotten Sons* and *The Web* widdly-widdly, they were all Brian's. But whereas the rest of the band looked like they might have hitchhiked to the gig, Brian looked like he'd just strolled in from the office. No amount of sackcloth could disguise that.

He actually did work in the Unemployment Benefit Office in Aylesbury. He was only a few years away from a management role. He had a steady girlfriend he was soon destined to marry, and he drove a white Ford Capri, which would make an appearance in the lyric for *Chelsea Monday*, affording Brian some sort of immortality in Marillion folklore.

He was the antitheses of everything Fish wanted for Marillion's keys player. Fish worked in the UBO for a few months too, but he approached the job in a way that would furrow any middle manager's brow with consternation. Fish dropped acid in that beige and white office space once and, perhaps unsurprisingly, suffered a terrible trip, but managed to snatch the lyrics for *He Knows You Know* from its psychedelic jaws. Simply put, Fish was gunning for Brian. I don't know what put him in Fish's sights, but he was a marked man and Fish the assassin. This, I later realised, was a pattern that was set to repeat itself over the coming years.

Ironically, after I joined Marillion I don't think I ever rocked the keys in the same way. I was probably too scared in case I broke something or flattened a fan. Mellotrons are unreliable enough without tossing them around the stage like a Heathrow baggage handler.

When Chemical Alice finished our set, I noticed Marillion were still there. Considering they had a three hour drive home this was unusual. Most support bands disappear as soon as their set is over, and the gear's packed away. What were they hanging around for?

Fish and Mick were standing at the bar, so I went over to tell them how much I enjoyed their set. Fish, never backwards in coming forwards, didn't waste any time: "We'd like you to join our band." I motioned across the room towards the unwitting Brian: "What about your current keyboard player?" Fish, with what would become a familiar flourish, drew a dramatic finger across his throat: "He's history", he said. And then almost airily, "Of course, you'll have to move to Aylesbury".

It was as ruthless as they were focused. I was wary, but I was also fascinated. Also, where the fuck was Aylesbury? It might as well have been Middle Earth for all I knew. I didn't drive and I'd never really been outside Essex apart from to London to watch gigs. I'd have to think about it. This was a big step. My thoughts were racing.

To buy some time I suggested that I could come and see them play a gig on their own turf. We finally settled on Chesham as I could reach it on the tube. Admittedly, that was using the tube to traverse pretty much the whole of London, but I was keen.

One of the things that pushed me firmly towards saying yes was reading a Marillion gig review by Xavier Russell in *Sounds* that week. 'A return to kaftans and loon pants', it said. I was very impressed! *Sounds*! They had made it as far as I was concerned.

Ten days later I made the trip to the Elgiva Hall in Chesham with Debbie, my clandestine girlfriend. It was agreed that we would travel back to Aylesbury after the show with Fish, his girlfriend, Kay Atkinson, and Guy Hewison, who passed for Marillion's road crew in those days. We'd make the journey in their 1960s Commer Walk-Thru van, which was affectionately known as Margaret.

It wasn't a particularly well-attended gig, but I was still impressed with what I heard. They had their own mixing desk and a sound engineer, Christopher 'Privet' Hedge, and he was good, very good considering the equipment he had to work with. This was all very slick compared to what I'd been used to.

I found out early on that Fish rarely drove Margaret home after gigs. He usually managed to avoid helping with the load out at the end of the night too. His excuse was that he needed to schmooze the local promoter and anybody else at the gig who might be in a position to further our careers. Inevitably, this involved some drinking, making him ineligible to drive. I had the perfect excuse – I couldn't drive. In reality, I genuinely enjoyed breaking the gear down and loading it into the van.

When Marillion were playing arenas in the mid-80s I tried to join in helping with the load out. I was feeling nostalgic for the old days. Andy Field, the crew boss, politely explained that should my finger get crushed by a 300lb flight case I wouldn't be able to play the next night, the tour would end, and the crew would be out of their jobs, so would I kindly go to the dressing room and get pissed with the rest of the band and stay out of trouble?

The rest of Marillion drove themselves home after the Chesham show, but not before Brian noticed me and Debbie hanging around. He recognised me and wondered what I was doing so far from home. Brian wouldn't have long to wait for an answer.

Fish and Guy shared a small cottage at 64 Weston Road, Aston Clinton. Kay was friendly and she and Debbie spent the next few hours getting to know each other while Fish, Guy and I talked. Fish's enthusiasm and knowledge of music impressed me. He was intense and articulate with a wicked sense of humour, though I occasionally had difficulty following his accent. He came from Dalkeith, a posh suburb of Edinburgh, but his accent was broader than such an upbringing might suggest. I suspected he would like to be thought of as working class rather than the son of a relatively well-heeled garage owner with a holiday home in North Berwick. He had also created his own idiom, which I later discovered the rest of the band had christened 'Fisherisms'.

We discussed common musical ground and he played me albums that I'd never heard of, two of which I still occasionally listen to today: *Still Life* by Van Der Graaf Generator and *The Friends Of Mr Cairo* by Jon and Vangelis. The girls fell asleep on the sofa while we talked all night. I was running on pure adrenaline. For his part, Fish had dropped a tab of acid earlier that evening. I think it says a lot about Fish's constitution that after dropping acid he was able to play a gig and talk all night without me suspecting a thing.

Most people would have trouble holding a coherent conversation while tripping through inner space and time. Fish was perfectly articulate and seemed unaffected if you ignored his gargantuan pupils. My heart sank a bit when he told me, not because I was feeling judgmental, but because I was hoping to leave the drugs behind with Chemical Alice, as it felt like they were getting in the way of the music at times.

By the end of the night, I was pretty sure I wanted to be part of this weird but committed band of brothers. I had only really met Fish properly, but I knew he and I shared more in common musically than anyone in Chemical Alice (with the possible exception of Jack) and that's without even touching on his lyrics. Fish was a force of nature with a fire burning inside of him. It was obvious that if anybody was going to make it, it would be him. I wanted in on this journey. The trick was not to get burnt along the way.

As the slowly creeping daylight moved across the carpet, I decided to throw in my lot with Marillion. Right away, Fish summoned the rest of the band and off they went to unceremoniously fire Brian.

They sent me home with a demo tape containing three songs to learn: *Garden Party*, *He Knows You Know* and *Charting The Single*. This was the tape the band recorded in July of '81 at Roxon Studios, with Les Payne.

Firstly, I had to break the news to my parents that I was planning to leave college and home to throw my lot in with a band of minstrels. I was lucky that they were so easy going. If not exactly throwing me a party, they were supportive enough, especially when I told them that my tutor at college had agreed to take me back after a year if things didn't work out with Marillion. I neglected to mention that he also told me he thought I'd lost my mind.

Debbie was behind my decision too. We both saw leaving Chemical Alice as a timely way of dealing with the problem of Andy, the ex-boyfriend who was starting to suspect something was going on between us. We wouldn't see much of each other, Debbie being in Romford and me in Aylesbury, but love would find a way, or so we thought.

I didn't consider taking Garrett, my 16 year old brother, with me. He had been my keyboard roadie the whole time I was in Chemical Alice and naturally assumed that he was coming with me to Aylesbury. How Marillion would have reacted to the idea I have no idea because I didn't ask them. Years later Garrett told me that he was crushed by my decision not to take him with me.

In retrospect, he might have been better off if I had. After I moved out, some of my younger brothers continued with harvesting mushrooms at the local golf course. They also experimented with other drugs, sometimes to excess. The fact that I didn't exactly hide my activities from Garrett, combined with my parents' relaxed attitude, meant that any number of young minds were often in thrall to uncontrolled experimentation with all manner of drugs. The first time that Greg, Barry and Garrett came to see Marillion play, Fish nicknamed them The Mark's Brothers collectively and Stono, Pisso and Trippo individually. I'm pleased to say that they suffered no long-term effects from their misspent youth.

Follow the camera down, coming low through the Essex streets, it's Friday 27th November 1981, and there I am, laden down with my worldly possessions: my Farfisa organ, Yamaha CS15 synth and a Crumar electric piano. Oh, and a few clothes. Steve and Guy pull up to the curb to take me away and with a slam of Margaret's big green door I disappear into my future.

We had three days booked at Leyland Farm rehearsal studio for me to learn the set before my first gig at the Great Northern pub in Cambridge on 1st December.

The tape was a big help for learning 20 minutes of the set, but with no recordings of the rest of the songs it was a challenge. *Grendel* alone was nearly 20 minutes of music that wasn't written down and none of them had much of an idea of what Brian played. Steve, the most musically talented member of the band, was a big help because he knew the chord structures and could remember some of the keyboard lines which he played to me on the guitar.

Luckily, none of it was overly complicated and I was given free rein to conjure up my own parts for those moments where Brian's handiwork escaped them. I wrote notes too. Not musical notation, I was self-taught, so my notes were more like prompt sheets with just the chords written out for each section. No timing or melodies.

This was fine as long as I wasn't the one kicking the song off. While I knew the titles, I couldn't recall the music in my head prior to hearing the song's intro. As Steve played the opening to *Grendel*, it gave me enough time to prepare myself for when I was due to come in.

It was utterly nerve-racking being so underprepared. Plus, we were a bit short of songs for a full set, so we opened and closed the night with *Garden Party*. I'm sure I made loads of mistakes, but I was still their keyboard player at the end of the night and things only got better from there.

As an added bonus, I inherited Brian's mellotron. The band had paid for it, so when Brian departed, it stayed. I had never played a mellotron before and was thrilled until I found out how unreliable they were. This one had a lot of miles on the clock. It kept blowing fuses, so some bright spark stuck a bolt in the fuse holder to fix it. Hey presto, no more blown fuses, but now we had a mellotron that could burn a building down. A small price to pay.

On the downside, I also inherited Brian's stage outfit. The green one with the eye emblazoned across the front. Brian was smaller in the chest than me, so I struggled to fit into it. The stage clothes weren't always washed after every gig and they often smelt of stale sweat. At least there was a wash day between Brian's exit and my entry.

Moving in with Guy and Fish wasn't exactly as I imagined it might be. I still harboured fantasies about the early days of Genesis, with everyone living an idyllic cottage life and making music all day. In terms of a rehearsal space Chemical Alice had a better set-up than Marillion, but in every other respect Marillion were streets ahead.

Guy had his own room and I shared with Fish. Guy had a job working at a printers in Aylesbury. Fish, having recently quit his job at the UBO, was, like me, unemployed. Steve had also quit his job as a driver for Shaws Pet Products down the road in Aston Clinton. Mick was still working as a kitchen fitter but planned to 'turn professional' like the rest of us soon. Diz had a job too but wasn't opposed to quitting it when the time was right. 'Turning professional' was our euphemism for signing on the dole. As welcoming as the bright lights of Aylesbury were, the gig circuit in and around the town wasn't yet capable of generating the big money to fuel our dreams.

In every other respect, Marillion were complete professionals. Everything we did was in pursuit of furthering our careers. If we weren't rehearsing or writing new songs, then we were poring over music papers and magazines, looking for possible gigs. Fish would spend most of the day on the phone trying to convince poor pub landlords near and far to book Marillion. Introducing himself as Fish was very useful in reducing the time spent explaining who we were. After the second or third call it was enough to say, "Hello, it's Fish", and they would reply "Oh yeah, the guy with the funny name looking for a gig".

People often asked where Fish got his name. He usually told them it was because he stayed in the bath too long when he worked for the Forestry Commission in Scotland. This story was familiar to me because Chris Squire had said the exact same thing when he was in Yes. In a candid moment, Fish admitted to me that he copied the story and just started calling himself Fish when he moved down from Scotland. It was a smart move whatever its genesis. Better than Derek Willie Dick, which has a certain something, but you'd be hard pushed to get an arena crowd chanting that.

Fish didn't take no for an answer. Sometimes I wish he had. The sky was the colour of a bruise and we were all crowded around Margaret, sleet and wind playing through our hair. The bonnet was open, and the engine block was covered in the silvery sheen of ice. Needless to say, it wouldn't start. Guy had somehow managed to mix up the spark plug leads from the distributor cap, ensuring that it would never go, no matter how many cans of Easy-Start (or Start Ya Bastard as the Australians like to call it) he used. The AA arrived, sorted out Guy's mix up and we were off to the gig in no time.

Sometimes I wonder if that storm and icy engine were some sort of warning. We drove for three hours to the Green Man pub in Leytonstone to play to four people. Literally four. We outnumbered our audience. Instead of overpowering them and taking their wallets, we took requests as they seemed familiar with our songs. They were probably from Aylesbury too.

We spent December playing more gigs, including a few at my old haunt, the Electric Stadium. It was especially weird for me because I agreed to play the rest of the Chemical Alice shows we'd already committed to, which included a few at the Electric Stadium. So, for the rest of December, I played there a number of times with both bands. Thankfully, they found a new keyboard player and I was released from my Chemical Alice commitments by Christmas.

I went home for a few weeks over Christmas 1981 to spend time with Debbie and see my family. By the time I returned to Aston Clinton we were in the middle of the worst winter for 20 years. The cottage had no central heating, and we were broke, so food was in short supply too. We had a paraffin heater in the small living room. We joked that it was central heating because it sat in the middle of the carpet. Every other room in the house was freezing cold with ice on the inside of the windows like frost in a freezer compartment (or Margaret's engine block). The bathroom at the back of the house was particularly cold. One morning I took a pee and was surprised to see the water in the bowl was frozen. Undeterred, I flushed it expecting the weight of the water to break the ice. It didn't and my bare feet were suddenly standing in two inches of diluted pee.

Don't get me wrong. I'm not complaining about any of it. I was having the time of my life. Steve and Privet lived in a part of Aylesbury called Bedgrove in a similarly slipshod house to ours, except it was, if anything, even worse. I remember visiting once or twice and, apart from being wary about sitting anywhere, I couldn't help but notice the walls were covered in some garish, childlike murals. Privet's motorbike was in pieces in the kitchen, a semi-permanent state of affairs, according to Steve. Mick and Diz both lived in relative luxury as they had girlfriends.

Both Mick and his girlfriend, Stef Jeffries, were still holding on to their jobs. Which made it even more impressive that Stef showed up at almost every gig, helping us out in any way she could. She was like a mother hen to Marillion. When the band decided to launch a newsletter shortly after I joined, we settled on calling it *The Web*, naturally. Founder Tim Hollings, with help from Stef, wrote it for few issues and then, when Tim stepped down, Stef continued to produce it for a number of years, even after Mick's departure from the band.

As we lived in the same house, Fish and I hung out together a lot. He showed me around Aylesbury, which meant we had to hitch a ride from Aston Clinton into town. It was a surprisingly efficient way to get about and it was free. I can't imagine who would want to stop for two scruffy herberts like us, especially with Fish towering over everyone with his 6' 5" frame, but they did, and, even more surprisingly, we usually didn't have to wait long for a lift.

On one trip we went to visit David Stopps, as Fish was keen that we meet. David was the promoter of the famous Friars Club, which was a favourite touring stop for many legendary artists, including Genesis, Mott The Hoople and David Bowie, who often started his tours there because he liked the venue so much. Stopps was personal friends with the members of Genesis, which was hugely impressive to me. That aside, he was charming, polite, down to earth, and also passionate about music.

He was also vital to the Marillion story because he gave the band so many breaks at the start of their career. He also managed us for all of five weeks, but I'll get to that later.

Fish kept an A4 size, hard cover book containing all his lyrics. He was a prolific writer in those days and was always ready with a complete lyric when the need arose. In fact, by the time I joined the band he had already written some of the lyrics that would appear on *Fugazi*, including *She Chameleon* and *Jigsaw*. Fish's lyrics were not just good, they were better than any lyrics by any songwriters I knew, with the possible exception of Roger Waters. Disclaimer: I was yet to discover Joni Mitchell and Peter Hammill, two writers that Fish was heavily influenced by.

Lyrically speaking (and Pink Floyd aside), Marillion were head and shoulders above the great prog rock bands of the 1970s. Genesis, King Crimson, Camel, Caravan and ELP could all lay claim to moments spent on the literary higher ground, but there was a lot of chaff in amongst that wheat too. It just went to prove that Marillion were much more than a rehash of what came before them all those years before. Symphonic music with a modern edge, juxtaposed with hard-hitting and well-crafted lyrics delivered by a charismatic singer. No wonder I was excited to be part of it.

I first had a chance to write some music with Marillion a few weeks after joining them. We set up in the living room at Aston Clinton and Steve and Diz came round to join us. Fish had already written the lyrics to *Three Boats Down From The Candy* some eight months before. Steve brought along the three different musical sections that make up the first two thirds of the song. I came up with the last third.

Listening now, I can hear just how much I was enjoying the mellotron; I used it almost exclusively to accompany Steve's guitar in the first part of the song. In the piece I wrote you can hear Steve and I playing complementary lead parts for the first time. On reflection, that was something we could have done more of over the years. I also feel that the music could have done some of the heavy lifting with a little more development from around one minute 30, where Fish clearly had a lot to say but the music less so. Apart from one crescendo it stays on one short motif for over a minute.

All in all, not a bad effort for our first attempt at writing together, but it wasn't good enough for the debut album, so it was relegated to one of the B-sides of *Market Square Heroes*, *Grendel* being the other. It was the right decision.

As I became more settled, I started to become aware of some tensions within the band. I was being gently ribbed for being Fish's new favourite. I'm not sure who I replaced in that role, but there was a growing animosity between Fish and Mick. Mick was the founder of Marillion and, quite understandably, saw it as his band. In the early days, certainly before my time, Mick also contributed to the songwriting. It was Mick that came up with the 'Let the blood flow' section in *Grendel* that Marillion have been given so much stick for over the years due to its similarity to *Apocalypse In 9/8* from *Supper's Ready* by Genesis.

The *Grendel* section originated from an exercise that Mick used for practising octaves on his flute. Up-down-down-up-down-up-up-down and so on. It's in 4/4 time (8 notes before the pattern repeats, you were bound to ask) not 9/8 time (9 notes before the pattern repeats), but as it's played on bass it gives the impression of an unusual time signature because of where the accents fall. So, it sounds not dissimilar to that part in *Supper's Ready*. Too close for comfort? Probably.

The focus of the band had also shifted from mostly instrumental music with Mick at the heart of the band. Fish was now very much the centre of attention. I'm not sure Mick liked the power shift. This thought usually struck me when Mick referred to Fish as the "big jock twat". Sensibly he did this behind Fish's back. Over time we would become ever more polarised; a band pushed into an 'us and them' scenario, but that was still some years off. For me, Fish was my friend, and I enjoyed his company and working with him was both exciting and rewarding.

I started to get to know the rest of the band as we travelled around the Home Counties and in and out of London. Steve was always calm, polite and thoughtful. Difficult to read but I always got a good vibe from him. Diz was dry with a sharp sense of humour. He had a good rapport with everyone in the band and seemed popular. How could I bring up what seemed obvious to me: his playing just wasn't up to scratch? Besides, was I spending too much time with Fish? Was I starting to think like him? Diz would have to go, surely? Was it even my place to say that? And if I did, then how long before it was my turn in the firing line?

CHAPTER 5

All Change

The dictionary definition of 'seismic' is something that is of enormous proportions or effect. Not that any of us were thinking that 1982 was shaping up to be anything like seismic, especially when we were looking down the barrel of those 12 months from the front seat of a beat-up, old van, and that was when we weren't sleeping on floors or firing band members. By the end of the year, we would have signed a record deal worth half a million quid with EMI Records. But that was something which felt impossibly far off.

Not that the start of 1982 didn't show some promise, as we kicked off the new year with my first ever gig at the infamous Marquee Club in Wardour Street in London. The boys had already played there the previous October opening for glam rockers Girl. What their coiffured audience made of a rangy and lairy Scotsman and a band dressed like escapees from the Heaven's Gate cult is lost to the sands of time, sadly. But I like to think that the odd, carefully tweezered eyebrow was raised in bafflement.

Marillion got that first coveted Marquee support slot thanks to music PR Keith Goodwin. Keith was one of the first music publicists in London and he worked for a lot of successful '70s artists including Cat Stevens, Black Sabbath, Argent and Yes. Fish persuaded him to take Marillion on at a stage in their careers where Goodwin would normally have given them short shrift. It was a smart move, and Fish and Keith became firm friends until Keith's death in 2004.

This time around we were opening for tea-drinking scousers Spider. A nice bunch of lads who had more bad luck than any band deserves, even if they were everything the music press said they were: Status Quo without the hits.

Spider were managed by Maggi Farren, whose partner Tony Wilson was the producer of the BBC's *Friday Rock Show*, presented by Tommy Vance. Taking over from Alan Freeman's Saturday afternoon show, it was the most important radio show for any rock band in the early 1980s. Tommy would prove to be a big supporter of Marillion throughout the '80s and early '90s, up to when the show was finally taken off air.

Wilson, probably in a show of solidarity to Maggi Farren, was in the audience that night. He watched our set and a few weeks later we were invited to record a session at the BBC studios in Maida Vale.

We chose to record versions of *The Web*, *Forgotten Sons* and *Three Boats Down From The Candy*. The first two because they were the rockiest songs we had (it was the *Friday Rock Show* after all) and *Three Boats* because it was shiny and new.

It's hard to overstate just how important a break this was for Marillion. The session, when broadcast in late February, was well-received and helped carry our name nationwide. Through our *The Web* newsletter we encouraged our fans to write to the BBC to ask for the session to be repeated. They obliged in sufficient numbers for this to happen in May. An early sign that we already understood how harnessing fan power could help us.

Talking of fans, we had organised a coach to ferry some of them from Aylesbury to London to ensure we were playing to friendly and receptive faces when opening for Spider. This had the desired effect because Nigel Hutchings, the Marquee manager, was impressed enough to book us to return as headliners on the 25th January. We would go on to play another 13 sold out gigs that year at the Marquee. There was a buzz building about Marillion.

Away from the lights of Soho and back in the real world, it was a frigid morning in February when Guy let us know that we were being evicted from the cottage in Aston Clinton for non-payment of rent. This was confusing as Fish and I had been paying our share to Guy, which was when he confessed that we were six months in arrears. The buck really had been stopping with Guy. In case you were wondering, we were claiming rent from the UBO. Benefits were pretty generous in those days, which is just as well as the gig earnings barely covered the petrol for the van.

Guy had ambitions to steer the band's career but lacked any of the qualities you would look for in a manager: he wasn't good with money, as the rent fiasco showed. Neither did he have the people management skills required. Navigating band politics while keeping everyone onside requires a delicate balance of leadership, empathy and patience. Guy was a nice bloke but not up to the job and we would part company with him a few months later. Finding a manager with a business head and honesty was going to be difficult, but we felt that David Stopps from Friars was a strong contender.

As we were all homeless, Diz and his girlfriend, Helen, kindly offered to let us stay with them in Victoria Road, Aylesbury. Guy had a room upstairs and Fish and I set up camp in the front room.

On 6th February we played at Westhill College, Birmingham. Diz drove there with Helen. The journeys to and from gigs were getting longer as we cast further afield for gigs having exhausted the Aylesbury scene months ago, but Birmingham was comparatively local. The idea of staying in a hotel was out of the question as we were always short of money. After the gig, on the way home, everyone in the band started bitching about Diz and I couldn't help but chip in: "He's not very good. You know that, don't you?"

I wasn't exactly thinking we should fire him, but rather just stating the obvious. Diz was a basic, if you'll forgive the pun, player. There was no flair in what he did, he was simply adequate, and it showed. Little did I know, but I had planted the seed that would gradually take root in the coming weeks.

In an effort to get more gigs and capitalise on the exposure from the *Friday Rock Show* session we decided to take on an agency, Terry King Associates. They offered us three gigs in Wales.

A Welsh tour in February. The glamour.

The Bangor University gig was a success and, because the brakes on the van needed to be fixed, we played a second night in the students' union bar. The other two gigs were in Tonypandy and Newbridge in the south of Wales. Mining country. We were offered somewhere to stay by the university after the Bangor gigs but driving home from Tonypandy (a small village clinging to the side of the Rhondda Valley) was out of the question, especially as Newbridge was only 20 miles down the road. Fish confidently assured us that we would be fine as all he had to do was announce from the Naval Club stage that we needed somewhere to stay, and the Welsh fans would come to our aid. The Welsh even had a song about keeping a welcome in the hillside.

Unfortunately, Fish asking if anyone had somewhere for us to crash in his broad Scottish accent was met with blank stares. Lost in translation? As a last resort we asked the venue if we could spend the night there. It wasn't allowed they said, but we could leave our equipment inside overnight so at least there was room on the floor of the van for us to stretch out. How the night flew by.

I suspect that the southern Welsh audience wasn't ready for Marillion because the gigs were sparsely attended and the audience in Newbridge seemed strangely aggrieved. We didn't have any lights to speak of and so we were at the mercy of whatever was available in the venues we played. Here there was a single fluorescent tube illuminating the stage, which could be either on or off. We left it on.

We didn't take any more bookings from Terry King or his associates after that; Fish hatched a plan to tour Scotland instead.

Although we grandly titled the seemingly endless trail of gigs as *The Saliva Tears Tour*, it wasn't a tour per se, more a litany of back rooms and pub alcoves where we could set up our gear and play. That didn't stop us having a tour poster though, namely a more polished version of the acid trip mural on the wall at Steve's house. A plant with an eye inside a mouth at the centre of a flower crying into an outstretched hand below, over which the roots of the plant were growing. The tears watering the plant in a never ending cycle. No, I'm not sure what we were thinking at the time either.

These small posters were deployed with the gig date handwritten in a marker pen. We produced hundreds of these and sent them out in advance of our gigs to the venues. Fish and I spent a number of hours per week furtively fly-posting bus shelters and any suitable walls with them too. All legal, of course.

The Scottish tour would be different; this was an *actual* tour. 30 or so dates all booked in advance by our in-house booking agent, Fish. On paper it looked great, but the reality was a mishmash of mostly pubs and hotels, some which had never hosted live music before, never mind a progressive rock band wearing sackcloth and face paint. The only thing these venues had in common was that Fish had either once lived there, had a girlfriend there, had a drink there or knew someone who did.

The other big downside (there was always a downside) was we would have to sign off the dole. It was already getting a bit hairy signing on each week while we became better known in the Aylesbury Vale. It was only a matter of time before we would be caught working (playing music for money, no matter how little, was considered work) while claiming unemployment benefit. Trying to claim while hundreds of miles away in Scotland would be asking for trouble, not to mention almost logistically impossible. This leap into the metaphorical dark of financial insecurity was the reality of becoming a professional band.

We played a support slot to Aylesbury heroes John Otway and Wild Willy Barrett at Friars. Once again, promoter David Stopps turned down our entreaties to manage us. David had never managed a band before and, having dealt with artists and their managers over the years, he knew what sort of challenge he might face if he took us on.

It was early March, and we were back at the Marquee for a sold out show with a new song in the set, *Chelsea Monday*. Fish had been spending more time in London, Earl's Court to be precise, staying with Kay, and this song, set in London, told of young dreamers who are drawn to the bright lights, but are too scared to give up the day job. In this case, almost inevitably, our heroine ends it all in the Thames.

Many years later some wag noted that many of Marillion's songs were about death and water. This was probably the first in a long line where the protagonist either got dunked, ended up dead or both. Musically, it was a simple four chord structure that plays for almost the entire seven minutes with a number of modulations (key changes, you were bound to ask), but it featured a fabulous guitar solo from Steve and a dramatic play-out that makes it worth the journey.

As we added new songs to the set, the older, weaker songs were quietly dropped. *The Madcap's Embrace* and *Skyline Drifter* were already gone and, even though it was a new song, *The Institution Waltz* wasn't going to be around much longer. Fish was starting to assert himself more and have some say in how the music was structured. He felt quite strongly that *The Institution Waltz* should be an actual waltz in 3/4 time. The uninspired outcome was a song that lacked any real spark which resulted from trying to do what Fish wanted rather than following where inspiration might take us.

By mid-1982 there was a lot of talk in the music press, especially *Sounds* and *Kerrang!*, about a 'new wave of progressive rock' or 'neo prog'. Marillion were considered to be spearheading it, with Pallas, Solstice, Pendragon, IQ and Twelfth Night taking up the rear. The truth is it was less of a movement than the success of Marillion helping to spotlight a number of bands, most of whom had been around longer than Marillion but had barely made a ripple in the press. Our publicist, Keith Goodwin, who subsequently took on a lot of those bands, was probably more responsible for this 'new wave of prog' narrative than anyone.

Pallas were making some headway in their native Scotland and were keen to keep that momentum going by playing some gigs south of the border. They contacted us with an offer to team up; they would play with us in the south and we could play with them in Scotland. The timing couldn't have been better, plus Pallas were set up with their own tour bus and lighting rig.

The first gig we played together was in Canterbury. We agreed to go on first so that we could listen to the *Friday Rock Show* and hear our session being broadcast. It's hard to believe today but the first time we would get to hear the recording was on air. There's nothing quite like hearing your music on the radio. We were so excited.

There were also some more pressing matters. Sometime in mid-March Fish, Steve, Mick and I arranged to meet to discuss what to do about Diz. We chose to meet at the Dark Lantern because it was a pub we never frequented and thought it unlikely we would meet anyone we knew. We had only been there a few minutes, pints in hand, muttering darkly and huddled around a table when a trendy looking blonde girl in her twenties appeared out of nowhere and said hello to Fish.

She recognised him from behind the counter at the UBO when she'd been between jobs a few months earlier. Fish, in his usual gregarious manner, got chatting and invited her back to Victoria Street for a drink after we had finished our meeting. She accepted, as I would find out later, because she was interested in meeting me. When I say 1982 was seismic, believe me when I tell you that within four months we would be engaged, living together and expecting our first child. My life was about to become a whirlwind both professionally and personally.

By the time we headed home from the pub we were agreed that Diz would have to go; it was just a case of when. We had a Scottish tour looming and we felt it would be better to make the change before then, rather than spend over a month touring with him, knowing his days were numbered.

The search for a new bass player was on.

The band were open to my suggestion of inviting Jack, the bass player from Chemical Alice, to audition. I called him up, but he declined, citing his girlfriend, job and unpaid for motorbike as reasons. I suppose it takes a certain kind of person to follow their unrealistic, unhinged dreams.

One evening Fish went to a party at the King's Head pub in Aylesbury and local band The Metros were playing their farewell gig. I remember an elated Fish returning home to tell me that he had found us a bass player. I must admit we were all sceptical, if not dismissive, of Fish's newfound fervour. The Metros were a pop band, so it didn't sound promising, but Fish had already invited Pete True (as he was known) for an audition the next day.

Conveniently, Diz and Helen were away for a few days, so Pete came over to Victoria Street and we all piled into the garage behind the house for the audition. Pete had a Rickenbacker, as played by bass legend Chris Squire. A good sign. As soon as he started to warm up Steve and I exchanged looks of approval. Pete was good – very good!

We ran through *Garden Party.* Diz's bass part was mostly an unremarkable one note reading of the song, plodding along to the stuttering rhythm that Mick hammered out over my keyboards. In Pete's hands the part sprang to life with fifths and octaves. It danced and sang with a melody of its own; he literally transformed the song. In fact, every song he turned his hand to was improved by his creative input.

We offered him the gig there and then. I don't think Pete had to think about it for long before accepting. Marillion were already well-known in Aylesbury and Pete saw that we were probably going places. He had been in a number of bands, even some prog outfits. The Metros were just his latest failed attempt to make it big. Marillion was the band he had been looking for.

Like me, Pete wasn't a stellar student and had worked a number of jobs while dreaming about music. Unlike me, Pete started playing from an early age. He was 12 when he took up guitar and bass. He has a very musical brain. His natural ability and enthusiasm also mean he's great to work with too. He can put a positive spin on any musical idea, and then help to bring it to fruition with his musical dexterity.

It was agreed that we would break the bad news to Diz after our show at Milton Keynes because there was almost two weeks with only one gig booked in before we headed to Scotland. It would be challenging for Pete to learn the set but no worse than my frantic initiation into the band.

On arriving at the Starting Gate in Milton Keynes, we set up as usual, soundchecked and found ourselves in that interminable position of hanging around waiting to go on. And then, for reasons known only to himself, Fish decided that we should tell Diz *before* the gig. I tried to talk him out of it, because there was a good chance that Diz would walk out before the show, but Fish was determined. He also insisted that I should be the one to tell him, as it was my idea to sack Diz, which was news to me. With a heavy heart and a little trepidation, I agreed to do it. Fish followed me out to the car park where I found Diz.

Then, like an actor marked for a cameo role who strides on to the stage and proceeds to perform a surprising soliloquy, Fish took over. I hadn't even got past my preamble when Fish told me that I was fucking it up and he needed to deliver the bad news himself. It was gruesome to watch, Fish detailing Diz's shortcomings as a player, telling him how useless he was. It was like he was building up to some sort of confrontation with his old friend. Fish suggested Diz should take a swing at him, but Diz was more forlorn than itching for a fight. He just left asking that we return his equipment, which was currently sitting on the stage.

I was confused and saddened. What the *fuck* was that? It was like Fish had planned the whole thing, teasing out a scenario hinged on confrontation and ire. All the while seemingly able to sit back and take it in, making mental notes that could somehow be assimilated into lyrical form somewhere down the road. It seemed that Fish was riding the emotional highs and lows of his experiences, whether those in the band or in his personal relationships, and using those moments as fodder for his writing. And if life wasn't thrilling enough to feed the machine, then he would happily throw a spanner in the works just to see the mess it would make, and if people got hurt along the way, then so be it.

We played the show as a four piece. I didn't have to wait long for the altercation in the car park to be spun into lyrical form. Fish opened the evening by announcing: "I am the Assassin, with a blade forged from verbal eloquence. This whole set is dedicated to a guy called William Robert Minute who left the band ten minutes ago." I tried my best to cover the missing low end with the organ, but the audience seemed untroubled by our lack of bass player.

Before Diz's departure we had been working on another new song. Not long after moving to Aylesbury, Fish had met with a charismatic, leftie agitator who called himself Brick. Fish decided to make him the central character in the song. He wrote it all down while off his face late at night in St Mary's graveyard. I wrote the main keyboard riff that became the bulk of the song and Steve later added the breakdown section in the middle which had something of a folk rock vibe, reminiscent of Thin Lizzy. It was catchy and quite commercial (for Marillion at least). It bounced along at almost indecent haste, clocking in at a mere five minutes. Lyrically, apart from a nod to the antichrist, it could almost be Radio 1 material.

Market Square Heroes made its live debut at the same gig as Pete, the General Wolfe pub in Coventry. As if Pete didn't have enough to deal with, Fish also dropped an acid tab that night and was having way too much fun when he elected to swap places with Privet during *Forgotten Sons*, mixing the sound while Privet recited the prayer section. It wasn't a quarter as inspired as Fish thought it might have been at the time. What Pete must have made of it all as he looked up and saw Fish poring over the mixing desk and a startled Privet to his right is something he's remained tight lipped about to this day.

We left for Scotland the day before my 21st birthday, stopping to play Scarborough on the way and spending the night with Steve's mum in Whitby. Once in Scotland we based ourselves in North Berwick at Fish's parents' holiday home which they kindly lent us. We drove back there after most of the gigs unless it really was too far, in which case we made other arrangements, like not going to bed at all.

I will always remember sitting on the banks of Loch Lomond as the sun rose in strands of pink, orange and red, the day coming to life over the still water, the trees filling with birdsong as the clear blue sky came to life as a dome above us. Less romantically, but just as vivid, was waiting for a bakery to open one morning to buy breakfast, which was going to be, on Fish's insistence, bridies. This Scottish delicacy resembles a pastie but with more fat, lots more fat. Fish loved them; the rest of us were less keen.

Another memory that cuts through was Fish's birthday. It was 25th April at the Cross Keys pub in Kelso, and Fish and I were horsing around after the soundcheck. We locked hands above our heads in a friendly wrestle. Fish had a height, weight and strength advantage and he used it to twist my arms downwards and back. My right shoulder made a sound like a Christmas cracker being pulled and popped with an excruciating pain as the humeral head was forced out of its usual place in the shoulder socket. With my right arm hanging uselessly in front of me, I was rushed off to hospital. Despite my protests, the gig was cancelled. The next time I would miss a gig from injury was in 2019 in Essen, Germany, after I was hit by a cement mixer truck. But more on that later.

The best stop on the tour was the Kaim Park Hotel in Bathgate. The proprietor, Robin Ingles, was an avuncular chap who loved music, especially progressive rock, and couldn't do enough for us. He gave us all rooms for the night and fed us free of charge. The gig was such a success that he offered us another date towards the end of the tour, by which time we were welcomed like returning heroes. It was rammed with people and we blew the roof off the place.

The only other gig we played twice was the Dial Inn, Glasgow. This wasn't by choice. If you wanted to play, they insisted that you did a lunch time session as well as that night's show. It was weird playing at lunch time, but we had a surprisingly good gig, and the fees were better than we were used to back home.

We managed to play as far north as Inverness, where we met a very young Avril Macintosh, who would, many years later while working with her husband Andy Bradfield, remix some of our early albums.

We got as far east as Aberdeen, thanks to our gig exchange with Pallas. It was their hometown, and we were happy to support them that night.

Glasgow was the furthest west we managed, but it was the beginning of a fervent Marillion stronghold that still exists today.

On the whole, Fish had done a remarkable job putting this tour together from a back room in Aston Clinton, and because it was unheard of for an English band to tour Scotland so extensively, we landed some media interviews along the way that bolstered our profile and audience in Scotland.

One day while driving from North Berwick to a gig we were stopped by the police. It looked like that night's gig was shot as we were driving, quite illegally, with a bald tyre. Fish told us to quieten down and leave it to him. He made a point of mentioning his father's garage, Dick Bros, and the policeman's attitude instantly softened. He went from treating us like a bunch of unemployed hippies in a beat-up van (which he was entirely right about) to upright citizens who had unwittingly found themselves on the wrong side of the law.

"Be careful as ye go", he chirruped as he waved us on our way. Fish later explained that his dad had a good relationship with the police as he was often called up to clear the wreckage from traffic accidents. He was also a freemason. It's not who you know, it's how you shake their hand.

Pete had settled into the band perfectly well musically. He was just what Marillion needed, even if he was finding it hard personally. As is often the case when a bunch of lads spend all their time together, there was a fair amount of good humoured piss taking going on. In his position of new boy, Pete wasn't sure how to take it when Privet and Mick constantly ribbed him. Pete wasn't the most outspoken person, so rather than react he suffered in silence. Some of it crossed a line and both Mick and Priv should have known better, and perhaps we should have intervened, but instead they egged each other on. I don't think it helped Mick's position in the band a year later when he needed all the friends he could get. But, as the saying goes, what comes around, goes around...

Things between Debbie and me were even more fractious than those between Pete and Mick. We saw each other infrequently and, when we did, it wasn't much fun. We'd argue all the time when we were together and said some things we'd both regret. The honeymoon period was well and truly over and the reality of having a boyfriend in a band that lived halfway across the country was starting to get old. She wanted to visit me when we were on tour in Scotland, but I put her off. I had heard a rumour that Susie, the girl I'd met in the Dark Lantern pub, was interested in coming to visit. Stef, Mick's girlfriend, was coming up and Susie offered to drive them both to North Berwick. She was keen and I was excited at the thought of getting to know her.

By the time we were back home from Scotland, Susie and I were an item. The only problem was Fish and I no longer had a home. Unsurprisingly, we weren't welcome to live with Diz and Helen anymore.

I went to stay with Mick and Stef at their house in Waddesdon on the other side of Aylesbury. Fish moved in with Steve and Priv, but their days in the hippy commune in Bedgrove were numbered as their neighbours were up in arms about the noise and late night commotion.

Finding a place to live when you don't have a job is difficult. Landlords are keen that you have the means to pay rent before giving you the keys. Susie, who worked for a carpet tile company, offered to rent a house that we could live together in along with Steve, who would soon also be homeless, and Pete, who was keen to move out of his parents' home. It seemed too good to be true and we all accepted gratefully.

Interest in Marillion was intensifying too. Most of the music press still treated us derisively, but we had a few champions like Phil Bell at *Sounds*, who loved us even after we kidnapped him in Glasgow, took him with us to Inverness and then ditched him there because he woke up late the next morning. And he was one of the journalists we did like! A few years later we stripped Mick Wall, another journalist, naked and thrust him into a lift descending to the lobby of a busy hotel. I'm surprised we received any good reviews.

Around this time, David Stopps finally relented and agreed to manage us too. One of the first things he made us do was go out and buy some stage clothes. I bought a green nylon jump suit. This was certainly an improvement on the sackcloth, and didn't come with an unblinking eye motif, but once under the stage lights I found that it made me sweat like Mo Farah on the home straight, and as it was virtually waterproof the sweat just ran down my body and literally filled my boots.

As our manager, David booked us for our first headline show at Friars. This was to be in the main hall which held about 1,200 people. Meanwhile, our regular sold out appearances at the Marquee were generating a buzz amongst the music business bods who regularly drank there. David did the rounds of all the major labels hoping to secure us a record deal, but it was hard work convincing any of them that our brand of progressive rock might have any commercial clout when The Human League and Dexy's Midnight Runners were what people were buying in their millions.

In making the switch from promoter to manager, David still had a number of shows he was committed to, and they were taking up a lot of his time at what we saw as a crucial period for the band. Fish, with his usual flair for the dramatic, became impatient for results from David and within a matter of weeks was already talking about firing him. I felt that we hadn't given him long enough but didn't put up too much of a fight when Fish wanted to call it a day with David, because we were all nervous that we might miss our chance of the big time if we didn't get signed soon.

I'm sure in time that David would have landed us a decent record deal. And, perhaps, in the longer run we might have avoided some of the unforced errors we subsequently made because of short-sighted decisions that were taken in the interests of the manager rather than the artist. But then, hindsight's always 20/20, isn't it?

A few months later David asked if Howard Jones, whom he had started to manage, could support us at the Marquee. I remember reading something later where Howard described it as the worst experience of his life. Our fans could be predatory with support bands if they didn't take to them. Happily, David went on to have a long and successful career managing Howard. I'm happy to report that I can still call David a friend some 40 years later.

With the clock ticking, or so it felt to us, we set about finding a new manager.

We met with Nigel Thomas, who managed Joe Cocker. We didn't like his dismissive and aloof attitude and we were pretty sure he didn't like us either. A few years later when we told Ian Mosley about meeting with Thomas, he looked aghast as he told us that he was once managed, or should I say mismanaged, by Thomas when he played in Daryl Way's Wolf. No great loss there then.

The next manager to meet with us was Peter Mensch, then the hot shot manager of Def Leppard (and later Metallica). He made it clear that he wanted to manage Fish and Fish alone. To his eternal credit, Fish wanted nothing to do with it or him.

The search was still on. Up next, one John Arnison…

CHAPTER 6

Welcome To The Machine

It's 1999, and Marillion are stuck somewhere between the giddy heights of arena shows and troubling the album charts, an era that defined our earlier career and some way off the renaissance that would see us change the way the record industry did business and packing 'em in at the Royal Albert Hall. This was the commercial hinterland, two steps forward, one step back.

Right now, Rod Smallwood, longstanding Iron Maiden manager, is looking after the band's interests. And that's why we're now performing in what can only be described as a banqueting hall (though Henry VIII might have balked at the word banqueting) playing a short set to the Music Managers Forum. For those not familiar with their work, the MMF is an industry body set up to represent and occasionally celebrate managers.

On this dank Thursday night, they were gathered to honour Rod with the Peter Grant Award. As he was our manager at the time, we were asked to play a short set to the great and good (and mostly stony faced) throng, the prospect of which thrilled us about as much as a root canal with no anaesthetic. Imagine that Dustin Hoffman/Laurence Olivier torture scene in *Marathon Man* in 7/8 time and you're close.

Inspired by our surroundings, I hit upon the great idea of reciting the lyrics to a song titled *More*, written by an old friend called Roy Hill. It shines a light on the work of the music management industry, but perhaps not in the most flattering light.

> *'They wouldn't have got to number one if it hadn't a been for me*
> *They went and blew their seven per cent, I saved my ninety-three*
> *It was all there in the small print, but they couldn't have realised*
> *That running a band's expensive and it can't be subsidised'*

About halfway through my recital, as the sea of faces before me curled a collective lip and a funereal hush fell across the room, that, I thought, as the rest of the band's eyes bored into me, was not your finest hour.

Then again, screw it. The wealthy, cigar-chomping, big shot manager who rips off a naive young band might be a cliché, but, like so many clichés, it's founded in truth. You only have to look back at the foundling years of bands as big as Black Sabbath and Def Leppard to find the familiar stories of bands hamstrung by ugly contracts and underhand deals.

Many people are drawn to work in the music industry for the exact same reasons that people want to be in a band: girls, travel, money, parties, meeting famous people and sometimes even the music itself. That said, if you do love music and can't play or sing, then a job in the music industry is the next best thing. As Frank Zappa once said: "Most rock journalism is people who can't write interviewing people who can't talk for people who can't read."

And that's just Frank on people who wrote about music! Plainly put, a love of music doesn't qualify you to run a record company, promote a concert or manage a band, though that's rarely stopped anyone trying.

Some bands circumnavigate the tricky route of finding the right manager by going in house, that's to say they get a family member on board. The Jam and Paul Weller had dad, John Weller, to look out for them. That said, being managed by your dad does somewhat negate many of the reasons for joining a band in the first place. How Bacchanalian can you possibly be with your dad in the next hotel room nursing a mug of tea and banging on the wall, telling you to turn it bloody down?

Ozzy Osbourne, as singer of Black Sabbath, showed just why he was dubbed the madman of rock 'n' roll when he opted to be managed by his future father-in law, Don Arden. Called the 'Al Capone of pop' (after the notorious, syphilitic, coke-snorting gangster), nobody crossed Don. He was as much fun as broken glass in a lucky dip, once threatening to toss Robert Stigwood out of his office window for trying to take The Small Faces off his hands. After firing Ozzy from Sabbath, daughter Sharon took over, and when 'honest Don' found out, not being one to bear a grudge, he attempted to set the family dog on his pregnant daughter. They wouldn't speak for the next 20 years.

Which isn't to say that all band managers are sociopaths, despots, or complete control freaks with a demeanour like Caligula. Some start out as a mate of the band or a roadie and, as the band grows, they too grow into the role of manager, learning as they go. Or not, as was the case with Guy.

Like cars or dogs, there are different types of managers too. Some approach their role like a lawyer might: doing the deals and looking after the bigger picture. This approach, along with air quotes around the phrase 'bigger picture', is more popular in America or when there's a management company involved. It usually means that different employees of the company are assigned different roles. Like who fetches the coffee and bagels.

Other managers are more hands on, not in the Don Arden hands on your throat way, but looking after the band's day-to-day minutiae, as well as organising the tours and recording sessions. Some do everything from finding lost luggage to locating mandolin strings in the middle of Austin, to talking the artist down off a window ledge at four in the morning.

When we met John Arnison, he was a one man operation with three acts in his portfolio. His most successful was punk poet, John Cooper Clarke. Managing JCC was relatively straightforward as touring involved just one person and a microphone. This was made slightly more complicated by the heroin addiction which had, at that point, taken over his life. He also managed Pauline Murray, the ex-singer from punk band Penetration. His third band were more his mates than they were a serious proposition for making it as arena rock stars, Liverpool band Rage.

John didn't put up too much of a fight when we told him that we wanted him to manage us and us alone. We didn't think he would have the time to manage more than one band properly. He agreed that once Marillion were starting to earn him enough money he would drop his other acts.

John started his musical journey as a DJ. From there he was offered the role of personal manager to a small artist signed to Status Quo management company Quarry. John quickly discovered that he loved touring and all that came with it. Organising the dates, hiring and firing the crew, booking the trucks, the lighting and sound systems, merchandise deals and the after-show parties, and all the excesses that came with it.

He learnt from the masters. Status Quo knew how to party and John was a good student.

By the time we met him he had left Quarry and struck out on his own, although he kept close ties with Quarry money man, Alan Crux, and his merchandise company Bravado. I got a bad vibe from Crux the first time I met him. He was the sort of person who prompted you to count your fingers after shaking his hand.

John used to frequent the Marquee for a drink after work and he knew Keith Goodwin, who told him we needed a manager. A few days later we were sitting across from John in a pub in Earls Court.

We liked John from the start. He was affable and enthusiastic about us and our music. He also seemed knowledgeable about the music industry. Saying that, he knew more than we did, which was next to nothing. He told us we should play to our strengths, which meant getting out on the road in front of as many people as possible.

We agreed to a three month trial period working with him, and if we weren't happy after that, we could walk away with no strings attached. It's true that the tightest grip is an open hand.

Our handshake deal was simple and fair. John wanted 20% of our income, which is pretty standard for most managers. We argued that John would be like a sixth member of the band and should receive an equal share, which equated to 16.6%. This was rounded up to 17% The actual deal when written down was more complicated than that, like advanced trigonometry and young love is complicated, but we'll get to that.

John was one of the lads, more like a mate than a business partner. Which is hunky dory when there's no band conflict and everything is out in the open. But managing Marillion was soon to become more byzantine, as John would find out.

John set about trying to land us that all important record deal. Another Marquee regular was Tony Stratton-Smith, an ever popular, larger than life character who had signed Genesis to his Charisma Records label in the '70s. So, when he showed an interest in signing Marillion, we were keen to be on the same label, even if that label's best years were behind it.

Strat, as he was known, sent his financial director, Brian Gibbons, up to see us at Retford Porterhouse with instructions to sign us up to his label. Gibbons, thinking he would get us for next to nothing, offered us pretty much that for a two single deal.

Clearly, he had no idea what we were about; we saw ourselves as an albums band and felt insulted by the offer. We turned him down and John carried on looking.

It was festival season and we had played a hot and sweaty gig in Bath at Moles Club. We had heard that Peter Gabriel was launching the first ever world music festival, WOMAD, down the road in Shepton Mallet and thought it would be fun to just drive down there and try to wrangle our way onto Sunday's bill.

We arrived at the backstage entrance at about 1am and the security guard let us in after Fish convinced him we were booked to play. Parked up in the artist car park, Fish and I decided to go exploring while the rest of the band tried to get some sleep.

Outside the backstage area there was a bit more going on and we found a campsite with some people sat around a fire. In no time at all, Fish was purchasing some LSD from our new friends. After a short discussion we agreed we'd have two tabs each. If something's worth doing, it's worth overdoing, right?

Knowing how dreary other people's drug stories can be, I'll keep this short. A few hours into the trip I thought I was losing my mind. The sky was a full spectrum of colours as the sun rose while the rock strewn car park suddenly felt like we were walking on the surface of the Moon. The journey back to the van and our bandmates became a Herculean endeavour.

I'm not sure how Fish and I must have looked as we stumbled towards the van, probably like two extras from *The Living Dead*, but the rest of the band sized us up the way a mum might when her youngest drags mud through her clean kitchen, and told us to get in. We were going home like two naughty schoolboys. I think Fish protested that he would be fine to perform, but I was grateful to be in the relative safety of our vehicle, even though I was both embarrassed and strung out at the same time.

And yet, my spangled adventure wasn't quite over. When we arrived home, Susie was waiting to greet me with her older brother whom I'd never met before. He was a policeman. With Steve and Pete as cover, I made for the stairs and the safety of the bedroom, mumbling something about being sick. That was the last time I took LSD.

Back on Earth, John went to see Ashley Goodall (brother of composer Howard Goodall), A&R at EMI. Ashley was interested enough in Marillion to book us into the 16 track studio located in the basement of EMI's offices in Manchester Square, London. (The Beatles can be seen looming over one of the building's balconies for their respective blue and red best of album covers.) He wanted to hear what we could do in the studio. We recorded three songs, *Chelsea Monday, Market Square Heroes* and a revamped version of *He Knows You Know,* replete with a keyboard solo and a new picking guitar part that replaced the heavier riff in the verses.

But the recordings failed to capture the live excitement that was Marillion. They were flat and uninspiring. I don't think Goodall ever heard the recordings because he left EMI shortly after meeting with John. Rather than play them to Goodall's replacement, Hugh Stanley-Clarke, John persuaded him to come and see us play live at the Marquee instead.

This was a masterstroke; he knew that Stanley-Clarke would be impressed by the audience's reaction even if he didn't get the music, as music didn't seem to be his forte. He was a rich kid dabbling in the music business. We ripped the piss out of him (behind his back, because, like music, humour wasn't his strong suit either) when he complained that we should respect him more because "His family owned half of Bristol".

I think he expected the audience to be a bunch of ageing hippies reliving their 1970s' youth, but instead found the place rammed with crazed teenagers mesmerised by Fish's charisma and who happened to be singing along to every word. Even if he couldn't hear it, Stanley-Clarke was smart enough to *see* this was the start of something big. We were offered a five album deal by EMI.

Remember that half a million quid record deal, which I know has been on your mind since I flagged it up a chapter ago? Well, let's unpack that shall we? Deep breath…

The five album deal was really a one album deal, with options for four further albums if the first one sold well enough. There was an advance of £17,500 for the first album plus £10,000 tour support. An advance is a sum of money that the label will recoup from your record royalties. Tour support is sometimes provided by the label to make up losses incurred while touring, also recouped from future royalties. If we entered the UK top 40 album chart an additional £2,500 was payable. That makes a total of £30,000 for the first album.

For each subsequent album we would be paid ever increasing amounts as long as the record company was still making a profit from the arrangement and decided to take up the next option. In the small print, and this is important, there was a provision for something called 'overcall albums'.

This colourful language is used to describe additional albums that the label could demand at any time during the lifetime of the deal. That meant they wouldn't have to increase the advance in line with the agreement but could pay the same advance as the previous album. There were three overcall albums written into the deal and our second album, *Fugazi*, was deemed an overcall album. So, in reality it was an eight album deal. John had effectively negotiated our careers away. No wonder the combined advances added up to £500,000.

It gets worse. The royalty rate was only 10% and we had assigned the recordings to EMI for life of copyright, or forever in layman's terms. There was also a provision to reduce the royalty by 50% on 'cut price' records which, in time, all records become. As EMI were making much more per copy than we were, and even though they paid for the recording costs, they were in profit long before we recouped the advances. This is exactly where record companies want their artists, unrecouped but profitable. It was 1982 and we would remain unrecouped long after we left EMI in 1996.

At the time I don't think we (the band) even read the agreement and we couldn't wait to sign it. John wasn't experienced in negotiating record deals and certainly not one of that size. But to be fair to him, while it wasn't a great deal, it could have been worse and, apart from the sheer number of albums, was standard for a major label contract in 1982.

Over the August bank holiday weekend, we played our first two festivals. We opened the Theakston's Festival in Wakefield and got off to what can best be described as an underwhelming start when I discovered my organ wasn't plugged in properly for the opening song. Steve's guitar wasn't audible either because in the rush to get set up somebody had put the microphone on the wrong amp. We had never been on such a big stage before and even though it was sparsely attended, the big field below still held thousands of mostly bemused or curious looking people.

To make matters worse, I looked over to the side of the stage and saw Ian Anderson, singer of festival headliner Jethro Tull, watching what felt to me like a bad dream. I figured out why the organ wasn't working, fixed it, and we launched into our first song. My hands were shaking so much I could barely play. I don't think I've been that nervous before or since.

Our Sunday afternoon slot at Reading Festival was much better. We played a short but well-received set. Theakston's had felt like a warm-up for this. From the stage Fish announced, "On Thursday night we were told we have now signed with EMI Records for the world" to a small cheer from the crowd. Most of them had never heard of us.

Meanwhile backstage, Strat nearly choked on his Pimm's. He couldn't believe that Gibbons had failed to sign the band. He had been out of the country and hadn't been keeping up with the fast moving events of the previous few weeks. He whipped out his cheque book and wrote a cheque for £5,000 as an advance for Marillion's publishing rights. John accepted, feeling that he owed Strat something. I like to imagine that Strat walked away whistling, given the bargain he'd just landed.

In case you're wondering why we signed two terrible deals in such quick succession, please understand that, like thousands of young bands that went before us, we were stone broke, in debt, our gear was on its last legs (our faithful van Margaret died for good a few months later) and were horribly inexperienced.

Try to look surprised when I tell you that our publishing deal was even worse than our record deal. Publishing is what songwriting is commonly known as. Before the invention of recorded music songs were published on manuscript as musical notation. Royalties were paid per copies sold, like books. We were paid 60% of any income the publisher, Charisma, collected. They kept the rest. Not a bad deal for them when you consider they did little more than collect the money, most of which came from EMI, and pay us our share, which we split equally after John took his 17%. At least we were splitting everything equally, for now.

Back home, Susie discovered she was pregnant. Becoming a father wasn't part of my plan, but, as a man who can heft a hod almost as easily as mastering the widdly-widdly parts of most of Marillion's early catalogue at short notice, I was nothing if not adaptable.

I was almost completely occupied with the band, and having a baby couldn't have been further from my thoughts. Susie was a few years older than me and, although still young, felt ready to start a family. Now she was pregnant and, though the timing was far from perfect (sharing a house with half the band and a musician boyfriend), we were giddy with love and optimistic that everything would work out fine.

John took me to one side after a gig one night and confided that Fish had told him that it was John's job as manager to make sure I didn't get married. I cast my mind back to that car park and the final stand-off between Fish and Diz. For the first time since joining Marillion I was feeling insecure about my position. Was our singer secretly writing a song about me? Was I going to feel the assassin's blade next?

On 8th September we showed up at EMI's offices to sign our recording contract. The territory covered was the Earth and its solar system. Which didn't leave much wiggle room. After the customary photo call, we all got stuck into the free booze and sandwiches.

Hugh Stanley-Clarke was put out that Steve passed out drunk on the sofa during his rousing speech about EMI and Marillion doing great things together. He would later show how miffed and misguided he was when he urged John to sack both Steve and Mick from the band. John agreed that Mick might have to go but didn't think the timing was right.

One of the first things we did with the recording and publishing advances was buy some new equipment. The gear we had was literally falling to pieces after hundreds of gigs with no flight cases to protect it. I splashed out on Roland's flagship polyphonic synthesiser, the Jupiter 8. I also upgraded my lead synth to a Pro-One and added a Korg CX-3 to replace the clapped-out Farfisa.

At Hugh Stanley-Clarke's insistence we also spent five grand on an Emulator One to replace the Mellotron. This was the first 'affordable' sampler. With a total sampling time of four seconds. Motivational speaker Peter Bregman contends that four seconds is all you need to regain self-control, establish direction in your life and achieve your goals. I was lucky if I could capture the sound of someone coughing in four seconds, let alone turn my life around. Regardless, it was at the bleeding edge of what you could do with digital memory in those far off days.

New toys aside, and from a far more practical point of view, John started us on a monthly wage of £350 each. Not a fortune, but enough to live on and keep the band on the road.

Before we knew we'd be signing a record deal and recording a single at headlong speed, the plan was to tour Scotland again in September. We only played a few of those gigs, including Glasgow, because of a planned radio broadcast which took us to the city. After the show we were taken out to dinner by the label to a restaurant called The Ubiquitous Chip, considered fine dining in Glasgow, which leaves me to think that 'fine dining' is code for 'I'm not sure I can finish this' north of the border. They even splashed out on a night at the Holiday Inn and flew us all back to London the next day. It was my first time travelling by air and, as Hamilton appeared intermittently through the banks of clouds below as we headed south, I felt briefly buoyed by the idea of possibilities.

We played yet another sold out show at the Marquee on 25th September before heading down to Parkgate Studios in Battle near Hastings to begin work on our first single. Two days later the whole band (excluding me because I drew the short straw and agreed to work) headed back to the Marquee to watch Genesis play a warm-up gig for their *Six Of The Best* reunion show. This was a hastily organised, money raising event to bail Peter Gabriel out from the mountain of debt he had accrued from his financially disastrous WOMAD festival.

I can't remember who suggested bringing in David Hitchcock to produce our first single, but it probably wasn't the ideal choice given that EMI were looking for a hit single from the band. That said, we were delighted because Hitchcock had produced *Foxtrot* by Genesis, a seismic prog album whose contents had never worried the singles charts one iota.

The fact that he had done little of note since the mid-70s and was – how shall I put this? – a bit rusty, didn't deter us. We had already decided we didn't want a normal 3 minute single with a forgettable flip side. We would make a statement with our first release by putting the 17 minute epic (the word 'epic' does a lot of heavy lifting in this sentence) *Grendel* on the B-side. Hitchcock had produced *Supper's Ready*, so who better to produce its poor relation? *Grendel* was already feeling worn in places because most of the music predated myself, Fish and Pete. We didn't want to drop it entirely because it was a live favourite. Our solution: make it a B-side.

Budget allocated, the studio was booked to record a single and its flip side. We planned to record 28 minutes of music in that time. What's the saying, tell God your plans and make him laugh? I'm almost certain I heard him chuckling as we loaded our gear in that afternoon.

Just to add to the pressure, and to give you an idea of my giddy optimism at the time, Susie and I set a wedding date for 4th October. Leaving us very little time should the recording overrun.

Despite the exhausting schedule, I loved recording. Playing live was something I got used to but have never felt totally comfortable with. By contrast, the studio felt like home to me. No matter how many times we went into a studio in the years that followed, nothing matches the excitement of starting a new album or single in those high, brightly lit rooms rammed with gear. Since making the eminently practical (and economically sensible) move to equipping and working from our own studio, the Racket Club, I have missed that thrill. Not to mention the catering.

No matter how thrilling the experience, we weren't entirely happy with how the recording sounded. It was a clear step up from anything we had achieved before, but it wasn't where we wanted to be as a band, and we knew we could do better yet. Also, while nobody discussed it openly, it was obvious that Mick was struggling to lay down a drum part that he or we were happy with.

Nowhere is this more obvious than on *Market Square Heroes*. Mick plays a lumpy tom-tom pattern through the first two choruses and then switches to the verse pattern for the third and yet another pattern for the final fade chorus, none of which work very well. It was leaden and ate into our studio booking. Almost inevitably, we ran out of time. On the last day we worked through the night, and bleary eyed I caught the 5am train back to Aylesbury to get married.

With no prospect of a honeymoon, I joined the rest of the band for the mix at Wessex Studios in North London. By this time poor David Hitchcock was so exhausted that he fell asleep at the wheel driving home on the last day. His injuries put him in hospital for months and he decided a change of career was overdue. He retrained as an accountant.

EMI wanted to get the single out before the charts became crowded with the usual flurry of Christmas releases, so they turned *Market Square Heroes* around in a matter of weeks. The cover art began a long working relationship with artist Mark Wilkinson and introduced the jester that became a significant part of Marillion's folklore.

There was some wrangling over the design as Hugh Stanley-Clarke tried to push us into heavy metal territory with a more angular looking logo (I can only imagine he spotted an Iron Maiden banner somewhere in the EMI offices and a lightbulb popped somewhere above his head), whereas we wanted something that was a bit more subtle. The label designer, Jo Mirowski, had also performed a sleight of hand by ignoring our original choice of artist and substituting Mark in his place. We only found out much later, by which point we couldn't have been happier with Mark's work.

We toured the UK for much of November, filming the promo video for *Market Square Heroes* at the Guildford show. About halfway through the tour we were on the north-east coast in Redcar. Fish and I went for a walk alone and stopped in a seaside café for a cup of tea. Again, my thoughts raced back to the car park with Diz and I imagined either getting my marching orders or dunked in the brine or both.

Quite the opposite in fact: Fish laid out how he saw things with the band. He said he and I were the core of Marillion and we should stick together. He also said he was prepared to do what Stanley-Clarke wanted and get rid of Mick and even Steve to keep the record company onside. I didn't like the sound of that at all, but I nodded in agreement, while urging him not to make any changes before recording our first album.

My head was swimming. It felt like the world and my dreams were being dashed against the rocks just metres from where we sat. As my ambitions were on the verge of being realised, I could see them spiralling away. Marillion were a band and firing Steve and Mick at this stage would most likely damage us beyond repair. I kept my thoughts to myself for the most part. It occurred to me that my position wasn't as precarious as I had first thought, for now at least. I had survived getting married. Would I survive having a child too?

The tour finished with a sold out show at the 1,000 capacity Venue in Victoria in London. It felt very far from the Marquee. Within a few months, and before we had even released *Script*, we would sell out the Hammersmith Odeon too. From the outside, our trajectory must have looked like a shooting star ascending, cutting through the sky, burning brightest before it crashes and burns.

CHAPTER 7

Charting The Singles

It's dark in Soho by the time we turn on to Richmond Mews to unload the van. It's not our first time on this West End backstreet unpacking gear. Here's where we used to load into the Marquee Club, the black-painted fire doors swinging open to reveal the dark interior of the venue somewhere beyond. The hard work we put in at those shows has, fittingly, brought us back here to the Marquee Studios to record our debut album. The studio door sitting a few yards up from the backstage entrance, for a moment it feels strange to not be walking into the gloom of the venue and heading to the stage to set up.

Instead, we're in the studio control room. The console desk in front of us, the main space beyond the glass, the soft glare of studio lights, the screens to baffle sound. I could not be happier. That said, something was missing: David Hitchcock. David was still in hospital and, as we felt we needed to get our first album out, we had started casting around for a new producer.

Hugh Stanley-Clarke wanted us to work with Martin Birch, Iron Maiden's producer. You may remember that he was also keen that we adopted a more pointed, heavy metal, Iron Maiden-like logo. In retrospect, Stanley-Clarke was either a closet metalhead or just really, really liked *Run To The Hills*. In hindsight, I think Birch may well have been a good choice. But at the time we were opposed to working with a heavy metal producer, wrongly believing that he would make us sound like Iron Maiden. I mean, who wants to sell that many millions of albums and T-shirts?

In truth, a good producer, while certainly having an influence on how a band might sound, wouldn't be able to change their music to that extent unless he worked like Trevor Horn and literally replaced the entire band with his studio team, as he did with Frankie Goes to Hollywood. We finally settled on Nick Tauber after meeting him backstage at the Venue in London, the final gig of the November tour. He was introduced to us by Jon

Crawley, who worked for Charisma. The Charisma office was on Richmond Mews, in the same building as the Marquee studio where Nick Tauber liked to work.

On the face of it, Nick seemed an unlikely choice having just finished working on a Toyah album, but we liked his vision. He was a pop producer but with rock band nous, having produced Thin Lizzy's second and third albums.

Before we get going, let's clear up some misconceptions. Record producers are not the same as film producers. They are more like film directors, though without the loudhailer, thankfully. It's the producer's job to extract the best performance and the best arrangements of the best songs the band can come up with. They work in different ways. Some are very much hands on. They will do everything from twiddling the knobs on the mixing desk to placing the microphones (which they often own) to doing a bit of playing and singing if needed. They might even contribute to the songwriting if that's what's required. Which is why producers like Def Leppard's Mutt Lange, who knows a hook when he writes one, could once afford to live in an actual Swiss castle.

Nick was what you might call an old school producer. He rarely touched the desk and didn't play or sing. He steered rather than pulling an oar himself. All the grunt work was done by Simon Hanhart. Though relatively inexperienced, Simon was a solid engineer. Nick would say what he wanted and Simon did his bidding. They were a good team and perhaps more importantly, for us at least, relaxed and fun to be around.

We were still new to all of this, so they suited us well. Nick's pop sensibilities guided us away from some of Prog's excesses. Some of the parts I was attempting to play were technically a bit out of my reach and Nick gently guided me to play simpler but just as effective parts. Nick and Simon spent a lot of time with me looking for sounds too, including exploring the range of keyboards that were available for hire such as the German made PPG Wave 2.2. Not as friendly as its name suggests, this extraordinary piece of kit with a price tag to match was all over the first three Marillion albums. We ended up shelling out £6,000 to buy one because every time they quoted the hire charge at least one of us would gasp or swear out loud.

In case you've got your calculator out and you're keeping tally, the PPG Wave, Emulator and Jupiter-8 came to the princely sum of 14 grand. To give you some context, I paid £23,000 for my first house in Aylesbury in the summer of 1983. And the Emulator didn't even have somewhere I could park my car.

I felt blessed to be working with Nick and Simon. I loved the whole experience of making *Script For A Jester's Tear*. I was like a kid in a candy store. Nick was a big fan of keyboards and the early eighties was something of a golden age when it came to keyboard innovation.

When we finished the album and had a playback to a select few, Keith Goodwin was there. He said to me he was looking forward to hearing a Mark Kelly solo album. This boosted my confidence immensely. So much so, that it only took me 40 years to get it done. I regret that Keith didn't live to hear it.

———

Mick was struggling to keep up in the studio. His timekeeping was about as reliable as a pub bought Rolex. After hundreds of gigs, we couldn't have been better prepared to record our first album, but the studio can be an unforgiving mistress and, with that level of scrutiny, Mick's timekeeping, or lack of it, was laid bare for all to hear.

With careful coaching and not a little patience, Nick and Simon managed to coax a passable performance from Mick. Simon was a master of "dropping in" on recordings too. "Dropping in" or "punching in" is the technique of correcting a mistake by playing along with the track and at precisely the right moment the engineer hits the button and seamlessly records over the mistake.

This was made more difficult by the fact that there was a short delay between hitting the button and the machine responding. Drop in too early and you erase some of the previous take you want to keep; too late and you will have to try again. Not a trick for the faint hearted. This was easy when recording vocals (just wait for a gap between words), but more difficult with guitars or keyboards. Unfortunately for Mick it was virtually impossible with drums. Because of the long decaying sound of the cymbals any drop in is easily audible.

The only option is to physically cut and join the tape, keeping the sections you want. A 24 track tape is two inches wide, so it's unwise to have too many edits in a song. The upshot of this was that Mick had to deliver a good enough performance in as few sections as possible. This took time.

You can imagine our delight when I tell you that after that it was up to the rest of us to play along with Mick, speeding up a bit here, slowing down a bit there to mask the unevenness of his performance. Being the bass player, Pete was at the sharp edge of this. Thankfully, in Pete we had a great player who could stick to Mick like glue, and when he didn't quite hit his mark, Simon was always ready to drop Pete in for another attempt. By the time we were finished, you would never know that we had gone through more tape than a 100 metre sprinter. That, you'd surely muse to yourself, is a solid rhythm section.

When it came to recording *Script*, I don't think Steve had such an enlightened experience as I did. Over the years I've found that producers, often unwittingly, favour different instruments. Nick was a keyboard guy, whereas Chris Kimsey (producer of *Misplaced Childhood* and *Clutching At Straws)* favoured the guitar. Conversely, Chris Neil (*Holidays In Eden)* was very much focused on the vocals. As far as he was concerned, everything else was only there to support the singer. Which, oddly enough, is how a lot of singers feel too.

Steve was still exploring what sort of guitar sound he wanted. Achieving the perfect guitar tone can be a life's work and Steve was very much at the start of his journey in that regard. Eventually, with his dexterous playing and rich, warm tone, he managed to create a sound that can make grown men weep like a teenage girl who has just discovered her older sister has stolen her boyfriend. That, though, was some way off.

In 1982 he was still in the discovery phase and Simon's tendency to record hard, brittle sounding guitar (typical of the early '80s) met with little resistance from a young Mr Rothery. This was something he would later regret. Especially when it came to *Fugazi*.

Fish, like the rest of us, pretty much did what was asked of him. He turned in an excellent performance overall. We were all so inexperienced that Nick had an easy time of it getting us to do what he wanted. There were only a few sticking points. One was when Fish arrived at the studio with the brainwave of reciting a Shakespearean soliloquy at the start of the album. Quick as a flash, Nick suggested that he write something himself, in the hope that Fish wouldn't get around to it. Nick surmised that opening our debut album with Fish reciting Shakespeare might put a kink in the listening experience, as well as cause irreparable damage to our commercial clout.

Apparently, however, Fish lit up at this news, made a mental note along the lines of 'challenge accepted!' and returned a few days later with his own soliloquy. Now we truly had a problem. Had Nick just said no and nipped Fish's idea in the bud that probably would have been the end of the matter. Nick told Fish he could record it when everything else was done. On the last day Nick asked me to stay late so that I could tell Fish the bad news. Thanks, Nick.

Fish took it quite well and simply said that he would use it on the next album. The opening verse of *Incubus* was the result. Not a bad outcome all things considered.

The next time Fish had a brainwave – yes, another brainwave – was when Kay decided to end their relationship during the *Script* sessions.

Fish wanted to record a personal message to her in the title track. Again, rather than just saying no, Nick rather diplomatically recorded it and then asked Simon to insert it backwards and bury it in the mix. Fish got what he wanted and so did Nick.

It wasn't all work and no play either. Nick and Simon were a pair of practical jokers too, so they never missed a chance to yank our chains. Their inventiveness and our naivety meant we didn't stand a chance.

While recording my piano intro to *Script,* they played me a click track from the tape to keep time to. As I played, they gradually sped the tape machine up until I was struggling to match the pace. When I went back into the control room to tell them how difficult I was finding it, the pair of them were falling about, laughing like idiots. And I thought Mick was having problems keeping up in the studio… In my defence, playing to clicks was new to me and the tempo change halfway through made it less obvious that we were off to the races. And that's my story and I'm sticking with it.

Less happily, and not so harmless, was Nick's fondness for cocaine.

I imagine I'm not alone in telling you that the first time I tried cocaine was when I was flagging in the studio. It was past midnight at the end of a long session when Nick casually asked if I wanted a line.

Before you go wagging your mental finger at Nick for leading an easily influenced young musician astray, please keep in mind that if he hadn't asked me, before long somebody else certainly would have and I wouldn't have said no. Also, you've come this far in the book and will remember the magic mushrooms by light of the golf course and the acid that made me think I was traversing the surface of the Moon, so I hadn't exactly been clean living up until this point. Through good luck rather than willpower I never became addicted to any of the drugs I dabbled in. I even found quitting smoking easy once I decided to. But I drew the line at trying heroin; it sounds a bit too moreish.

In the 1980s, drug use, especially cocaine, was rife in the music industry. There was a dealer who did the rounds of the London studios and Nick was a loyal customer. Simon never touched it. Somebody had to operate the equipment. The dealer called himself Stewart, though I'm betting his mum didn't. He posed as a tape salesman. Like someone from a spy novel, he rented a flat for cash (unfurnished, except for a phone and answering machine) somewhere in London that he never visited. He would dial in to collect his messages, which were always people placing orders for tapes. A C60 equalled a gram, a C120 was two grams and a two inch tape a whole ounce. Drug dealers these days don't know they're born with their pay-as-you-go burner mobile phones.

Like almost anything, a little bit of coke now and again can be fun, but that's rarely enough for most people. Under its influence certain individuals like the sound of their own voice a little too much and combined with alcohol it can lead to paranoia and late night plotting in hotel rooms. Though we had all that to look forward to, right now it was fun.

We broke from recording for Christmas and to set up our equipment next door for our three last ever gigs at the Marquee as Marillion. Subsequently we would play there twice more but under assumed names, as our success meant we had outgrown the venue.

The first time we performed as the Skyline Drifters, after the song of the same name. That was in May 1983, and we would return for the last time in October that year as Lufthansa Air Terminal. Which nearly landed us in trouble with the airline. John got a call, which, unsurprisingly, he thought was a prank, from a lawyer at Lufthansa ordering us to cease using their name or the whole thing would end up in court. At one point, mustering all of his Teutonic sensibilities, the lawyer demanded to know if we were also using pictures of their aircraft or logo. We weren't.

Script For A Jester's Tear entered the UK charts at number seven in March 1983 as we embarked on a 28 date tour of Britain. We were expecting that we might enter the top 20 after the minor chart showing by *Market Square Heroes* but entering the top ten felt like an enormous achievement.

Our opening act on the tour was Peter Hammill with just guitarist John Ellis as backup. Fish had approached Hammill to open for us but was not expecting him to say yes. He was a big star to us. But as is often the case when a singer departs his band, the audience doesn't necessarily follow. Besides, Van Der Graaf Generator had split up five years before and I think he saw touring with Marillion as an opportunity to reach some younger fans. Fish and I were both thrilled to have him on tour with us. I was less thrilled when I found out that he was urging Fish to dump the rest of us and go solo.

On the second night of the tour in March 1983 at Reading Top Rank we launched into the recently rewritten and still unfamiliar *Charting The Single*. Unlike the record, I started the song with a sweeping synth and Mick, Steve and Pete joined me after a few bars. It was apparent something was wrong. Fish was confused and couldn't figure out what had happened as he looked for a way into this now unfamiliar sounding song.

The answer was behind him: the beat was the wrong way around. A snare hit where a bass drum should be and vice versa. It would have been a simple matter for Mick to fix it, but he doggedly stuck to his inverted rhythm and kept going. After the gig, Fish was furious with Mick for making him look like an idiot. I'm guessing, but that was probably the point when Fish made up his mind that Mick was out, although we didn't actually talk about it as a band until we got to London.

After the gig in Newcastle on 25th March I was driven home because Susie was very close to giving birth. The 26th was a day off and right on cue she went into labour that night. The hospital was just up the road, but as first time parents we wasted no time going there. They sent us home as the labour was only just getting started. By mid-afternoon the following day the baby still hadn't arrived, so I reluctantly left for Bournemouth where we were booked to play that night.

Looking back now I find it hard to understand why, when booking the tour, John didn't consider starting the tour in April after the baby was born. I didn't ask because I didn't think I should make a fuss or give anyone, especially Fish, a reason to think that by getting married and having a baby I was going to be an inconvenience or get in the way of Marillion's meteoric rise to stardom. There was now this culture, driven by Fish, that girlfriends weren't welcome in the studio or on the road. He was single, having been dumped by Kay, and expected everyone else to behave as if they were.

During the gig, as if it was part of that night's entertainment, I went backstage to call the hospital from a payphone while Steve led the band in a country and western jam to keep the audience entertained. I returned to the stage, shook my head in an exaggerated 'no', the audience heaved a disappointed groan and we played on. Immediately after the gig I was driven back to Aylesbury to arrive at the hospital just after midnight. Freya arrived 20 minutes before I did, and I was back on tour the next day.

As we were playing theatres there was more money coming in and we had moved up to staying in hotels every night and travelling between cities in a minibus, driven by Paul Lewis our tour manager. It was Paul's job to be John's deputy. He made sure we got out of bed in the morning and were at soundcheck on time. He also collected the money from the box office at the end of the night. He checked us into the hotels and paid the bills when we checked out.

Paul made a point of making sure we carried our own bags. He believed that it would keep our feet on the ground, though he didn't let on to us until years later. It's a habit that stuck and we always carry our own bags in and out of hotels even up to the point of wrestling our suitcases from the white-gloved hands of overzealous bell boys in some of the more expensive hotels we've stayed in.

This had disastrous results when arriving once at a hotel in Barcelona on a sweltering hot day. We had to trudge down a cobbled side street too narrow for the bus, dragging our suitcases behind us. As we arrived at the hotel, Ian yanked his suitcase away from the concierge, clipping the edge of the glass door at the entrance, which made a sound like a thunderclap and shattered into tiny fragments all over the lobby. Without looking back, Ian strolled up to the desk and grinned, "Mosley to check in", as chaos erupted behind him.

I liked Paul. He was like a member of the band (but with better timekeeping) who was first up and last to bed. He accompanied us to the side of the stage when we went on and was waiting when we came off. Like parents at a school gate, but with towels and a cold drink. Always there, prepared to sort out problems, lend us a fiver or party until dawn if that was what was required. He was good to talk to, always ready with an anecdote about touring with Van Halen. He didn't gossip or create problems and he rarely complained.

Which isn't to say he was perfect. He sometimes forgot to collect the fee at the end of the night or left behind the bin bag of expensive stage clothes meant for washing. His sense of direction and map reading skills were awful too, so he was always getting lost, which earned him the nickname of U-ey Lewis. I sometimes forgot that he worked for John, not us, even though we were paying his wages. He was John's eyes and ears and as John's man, was as diligent at keeping us in the dark about the tour finances.

Although we were now staying in hotels, we still shared rooms. Pete and Steve roomed together, I was in with Mick, and Paul shared with Fish.

None of the band wanted to room with Fish because, not unlike Andrew W.K., he liked to party hard, every night. Nobody could keep up with him. Paul would often go to bed and just leave the door ajar if there was only one key.

Even though we carried our own luggage, shared rooms and travelled in a minibus, there were signs that our success was starting to affect Mick. After the Aylesbury gig a fan asked Mick for a drumstick as a souvenir. Mick replied, "I'll get my roadie to bring you one", instead of going himself. This raised both eyebrows and hackles.

Hammersmith Odeon was my favourite venue to see bands when I was younger. It held nearly 4,000 people and we had sold it out before the release of our first album. This was highly unusual and showed how much of a buzz we were generating. We added another night at Hammersmith, which promptly sold out. On the last night, after the soundcheck and when Mick had wandered off into the venue, Fish, perhaps keen to get going on another lyric about an ex-bandmate, brought up Mick's shortcomings as a drummer for the final time. He had been waiting for the right time and we all agreed that after the last night of the tour we would oust Mick and start looking for a new drummer.

Wasting no time, the next day we all met up and went together to see Mick at his home. As soon as he opened the door and saw the four of us standing there, he knew we weren't there to bring him flowers, but he invited us in anyway. The now familiar scene unfolded but, unlike Diz, Mick wasn't going quietly. He became angry, telling us that Marillion was his band, and we would never find a better drummer. We let Fish play to his strengths and do the talking and by the time he was finished Mick was no longer in the band he had founded. Mick went back to his old job of fitting kitchens for the next ten years until a chance meeting led to him forming a new band, Arena.

Mick still hates Fish (or Derek as he insists on calling him) to this day and I suspect he still blames me for my part in his being fired, believing that as his roommate and friend I should have warned him during the tour. I felt bad about Mick, but we had gone as far as we could with his playing. Steve tried to make peace with Mick and even played a few solos on the first Arena album. Pete's and Mick's relationship had not really recovered since Scotland, so Pete wasn't too sad to see him go.

The tour had been a huge success, although the music press was completely divided on what they thought about us. We were divisive like Marmite is divisive. Some loved us and others loved to hate us.

We had a few days off before starting the search for a drummer and I got to know my beautiful new daughter, Freya. Susie had moved back in with her parents while I was away, and we stayed there on and off until we had enough time to find and buy our first house. Now that we were a family, living with Pete and Steve wasn't something we or they wanted to do any more.

The band set up in Nomis rehearsal studio in Shepherd's Bush and began the surprisingly arduous task of finding a new drummer. We had all invited various drummers we knew or had worked with in the past. It quickly became apparent that while they may have seemed like good players to us at the time, we had all improved and they hadn't.

By chance, we bumped into Andy Ward, Camel's former drummer, who was collecting his drum kit from storage. We invited him to audition and pretty much offered him the gig almost unheard as we were all big Camel fans. So far, so very Marillion.

Had we bothered with due diligence (or even just called someone who knew him) we might have had second thoughts. Andy suffered from bi-polar disorder, although he wouldn't be diagnosed until many years later. His time with Camel ended with an attempt on his own life that left him with damaged tendons in his left wrist. His grip was weakened but he was still a formidable drummer. His illness manifested itself with heavy bouts of drinking and depression. We met him not long after he had been discharged from a psychiatric ward, but, perhaps understandably, he kept that to himself.

Andy's playing was fluid and natural. Pete kept quiet about Mick's shortcomings as a drummer, but as the bass player it must have felt like a breadth of fresh air playing with Andy. Also, he was relaxed, funny and something of a hero to us.

When I got to know him a bit better, I asked him what led to him leaving Camel. He told me that he and Andy Latimer met as teenagers and were close friends until after the success of *The Snow Goose*. He was in their manager's office one day and he happened to see a large cheque made out to Latimer. When he asked about it, he was shocked to learn that it was for publishing royalties. Until that point, he hadn't even been aware what publishing was or that money was earned for songwriting. Andy believed they were all in it together and he told me that, after that, things were never the same for him with Camel.

I know there's more to Andy leaving Camel than disparity of income but it's a familiar tale: bands often split up over money. Some bands get it right from the start and split everything equally. Like Coldplay, for example, who split their songwriting income equally, even though Chris Martin writes all their songs. Or like Queen, who we toured with in 1986. Queen were highly unusual in that every member of the band had written a number one song, so maybe splitting everything equally was easier for them. The truth is that trouble usually raises its ugly head when there's far too much money sloshing around or far too little.

At that time Marillion spilt everything equally, including songwriting income. I believe that's how things should be in a band. If somebody writes songs for other people to record, that's a different matter. If two people divide the task of writing a song between them, one writing the lyrics and the other the music, then I'm sure most people would think a 50/50 spilt seems fair. Writing for a band you are a member of is different. The songs you write and record together will only be worth something if the band's rendition of those songs sell and the band succeeds. If the band is agreed they are equal members, then why not include songwriting income in that too? It's an egalitarian thing, or at least it is to me.

John Arnison treated our songwriting income differently from the beginning. He decided that it should be like a bonus. The icing on the cake. All of our income from other sources such as recording advances (we were a very long way from receiving actual royalties), merchandising income and gig fees were added to the Marillion pot and spent as needed, including on our wages. Publishing advances (and royalties) were immediately shared out after he took his 17%. We liked this for obvious reasons, but, ultimately, it was lighting the blue touchpaper that would later blow up in our faces.

As was the Marillion way, we dropped Andy in at the deep end. After a few days' rehearsal we played a gig at the Marquee under the Skyline Drifters moniker. This was to be a warm-up for two festivals we were booked to play in Germany but before that we had a BBC TV appearance performing *Forgotten Sons* live on *The Old Grey Whistle Test* and filming a video for *Garden Party,* our next single.

As Marillion promotional videos go, *Garden Party* wasn't too bad. It was a fun day where we all got to dress up and behave like kids, not a Herculean stretch for most of us, though Steve elected to play the part of a priest. The previous video, *He Knows You Know,* was a more serious affair with a padded cell and drug-induced hallucinations. (And we were worried that Fish quoting Shakespeare might dent our marketability!) Freya, then a mere three weeks old, makes a cameo appearance.

Garden Party (with a quickly recorded "I'm miming" to replace "I'm fucking" to make it radio friendly) was released in June 1983. Thanks to the fans' excitement over any new Marillion records and EMI's willingness to exploit that by playing the format game and releasing a cut-out picture disc version (jester, phallic cucumber, all very tastefully done and above board) alongside the regular single, we charted at number 24.

We were invited on to *Top Of The Pops,* the BBC's flagship music programme. In the 1970s and '80s *TOTP* was where the country's youth got their weekly music fix. It was huge, with an audience of 15 million viewers. It looked exciting and glamourous through the camera lens, but in real life it was about as much fun as being hit by an out-of-control car.

The entire day was more boring than a regular day on the road. Most people don't realise that life in a band involves a lot of hanging about. To paraphrase the late Charlie Watts: "I worked five years and spent 20 years hanging around."

TOTP took hanging around to a whole new level. They insisted on acts arriving at 10am, an ungodly hour for any musician, never mind the fact that you're going to be scrutinised by 15 million people later that day.

It wasn't just *TOTP* that was a disappointment. Our first ever TV appearance, performing *He Knows You Know*, in January on the *Oxford Road Show* got off to a bad start. Pete, Steve and I were hanging around, sat on the edge of the stage when the presenter, Peter Powell strolled up and asked us when the band were arriving. Without Fish around nobody had a clue who we were. We were slightly insulted that we had been mistaken for the crew. Though I'm sure the crew would be insulted to hear me say that. That said, in time, being the faceless members of Marillion and not Fish would become a blessing.

It was the same with interviews. At first, we all wanted to be there, sat with our tongues hanging out, hoping the interviewer would toss a question our way, like expectant seals waiting for a kipper. After a while we would try to find something to do instead of being interviewed. I always had the perfect excuse at gigs: fixing the latest keyboard problem.

I had begun to notice that the more famous the interviewer, the more inane the interview. If the person interviewing you actually knew something about the band that was an indication that their audience was small. If they asked an intelligent question, then we were probably at a local radio station with an audience in the thousands as opposed to the hundreds of thousands.

I would always play the game and tailor my answers to fit the question. I can talk drivel with the best of them. Both Fish and Steve Hogarth wouldn't suffer fools gladly and often got annoyed with the interviewer, especially if their questions made it clear they hadn't bothered to learn anything about the band. I was always of the attitude that they can ask what they like as long as they play the record.

Where were we? Oh yes, TV Centre and *Top Of The Pops*. Why so calamitous?

From a distance, the *TOTP* studio looks impossibly glamourous, teeming with vibrant kids as far as the eye can see. From the stage, it was like standing in a shoe box, a typical square studio with a small stage on each wall. This was to facilitate quick changeovers between bands. They would have four 'live' bands interspersed with pre-recorded videos in the 30 minute show. I say 'live' but it was always mimed. They weren't set up to broadcast a real live performance, so everyone had to mime. Just like the lyric in our newly minted, radio friendly single.

The audience was tiny, no more than 30 people who were herded like cattle from stage to stage as each artist performed. There were professional dancers placed at strategic points around the room, usually on raised platforms or stairs. Carefully placed cameras completed the illusion of a happening gig full of people dancing and having the time of their lives.

Happily, even the professional dancers couldn't dance to the stuttering beat of *Garden Party*, which finally gave us something to smile about.

Though, for all our remonstrations, that never ending day in west London did the trick and *Garden Party* crept up the charts the following week to the number 16 spot. This was our highest chart showing yet and wouldn't be beaten until *Kayleigh*, though that was some years away. As a band we still had some growing to do before then.

CHAPTER 8

Kill The Pape

Like Alice's White Rabbit, I was in a hurry. The promise of my own personal Wonderland, or a US tour of supports slots and club dates, which sounded wonderful to me, was hanging tantalisingly before me. Tarry and I'd be late, and by late I mean I'd be standing stupefied on the tarmac at Heathrow as the rest of the band took off for the land of the free.

I needed a passport, and I needed a passport now. Having never been abroad (except for Ireland), I sent off my application for a UK passport. This was returned to me with a polite note explaining that I didn't qualify for a British passport as I was Irish. It went on to suggest, in a tone that a mother usually reserves for her dimmest child, that I could apply for naturalisation, but it could take up to six months. As I stood there ruefully thumbing the manila envelope, I knew how that unenlightened child felt.

I honestly didn't even think about applying for an Irish passport. If asked, I would say I'm Irish, but I've spent most of my life in England, and back then already felt as much English as I did Irish. I'm like the opposite of The Pogues' Shane McGowan: the middle-class Englishman posing as a working-class Irishman. That's not where the dissimilarities end either: I've also got my own teeth and can get up from a chair unaided.

Fortunately, I was able to get myself an Irish passport within 24 hours by visiting the Irish Embassy in London. In 2019 I was finally naturalised, and I now hold dual British/Irish citizenship. I am not in the slightest bit nationalistic and am happy being a citizen of the world. I find the whole being proud of your country schtick rather jingoistic, and it seems to only lead to unhappiness and conflict. Equally I think if I identified with my Irish heritage more, I might have found some of Fish's lyrics offensive.

Forgotten Sons, which Fish always maintained wasn't pro-British or anti-Irish, is clearly written from the point of view of British soldiers and their families. Or the occupying army, as many Irish people described them. Fish often used to call me 'Pape', an insulting term used by Glasgow Rangers' Protestant supporters to describe rival team Celtic's Catholic fans. As I'm not a football fan or religious, I would shrug it off, apart from when Fish leapt on me in the lounge of the tour bus, punching me in the head while shouting "Kill the pape!" after a few too many drinks. Then it was less easy to ignore.

But before America, there was something more pressing. We had a new album to deliver. With almost undue haste, we set off for Gwynedd in north Wales to begin writing. The location chosen was as far away from civilisation as possible. A rehearsal studio with very basic accommodation in a small cottage on a hillside. I remember green hills and an almost endless white sky and getting very little done.

Being deposited in the middle of nowhere was less than ideal for me with a new baby, but I didn't complain. I was trying to show the band, especially Fish, that just because I was a dad now, nothing had changed. Though, naturally, everything had and Susie was back living with her parents with a sparing visit or two from me.

Her days weren't the only ones that felt long and drawn out. Writing was slow going. Fish had plenty of lyrics already written but we had no music. We had already decided that *She Chameleon,* which had been through more changes than Spinal Tap had drummers, wasn't cutting it musically.

Like most bands, writing our first album took over two years if you count the early versions of songs like *The Web* and *Forgotten Sons.* When someone in the band came up with a promising sounding idea, we worked on it. If we didn't have any new ideas, we didn't worry. Now, for the first time in our lives, faced with the demands of a major label wanting the next album, we had to write one to order.

We had a few weeks in Wales interspersed with making videos and playing German festivals before our debut tour of the USA and Canada. We would have a few months more to play with in the autumn and then we would be expected to start recording our sophomore album.

The only genuinely good idea we had was a riff Steve had written, which became the foundation of *Assassing.* Fish wanted the song to have some eastern influences because he was channelling whirling dervish assassins in his lyrics. Steve had become the proud owner of a GR-300 guitar synth made by Roland. While interesting sounding, it was only good for slow parts and drones owing to the delay between plucking a string and the

Like butter wouldn't melt. My best beatific smile in 1963.

Love's young dream: Mum and Dad in Cardiff in 1958.

Saddle up! Me and brother Mike at Phoenix Park Zoo in Dublin in 1964.

Family portrait - the gathering of the Kelly clan in 1967.

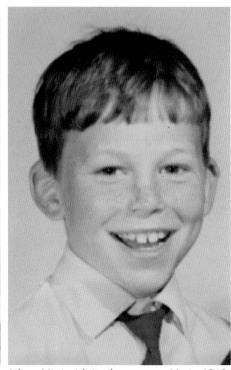

Man of Steel: the uncompromising and notorious Dick the Gunman in 1968.

Like a Mini with its doors open. Me in 1969.

Practising my best Blue Steel smoulder in 1971.

By 1976 prog rock was starting to shape my world view and even my haircut.

Hello, ladies! And art college. Freshman in 1979.

"I said it's in 13/8!" Chemical Alice rocking my world at Chaffords Sports Hall, Essex in July 1981.

The eyes have it! The suave and sartorially compelling Marillion at the 101 Club in Clapham, south London on 28th January 1982.

Giving it my best Rick Wakeman at the Marquee on 19th May 1982.

A return to kaftans and loonpants

Marillion
Marquee

MARILLION (NOW there's an original name) hail from Aylesbury and have been regularly playing SRO (sold right out) showcase gigs at the legendary Friars boozer, which believe it or not is in Aylesbury.

Marillion recently took London by storm, and gave Aerosmith rip-off merchants Girl a bit of a scare. It's not often a support act gets an encore at the Marquee, although to be fair to Girl Marillion had brought down rather a large contingent of ageing hippy 'eadbangers. No denim and leather here mate, more like kaftans and loonpants.

A trip back to the mid seventies maybe, but at least Marillion aren't jumping on the NWOBHM bandwagon. Instead they're more at home borrowing licks from the old school of Genesis, Styx, Yes, Canuck rockers Zon, and wait for it Trillion, just a few names that spring to mind.

Onstage Marillion come across very bizarre, not dissimilar to Agony Bag. Whatever happened to them? Lead singer Fish, a rather tall and mysterious Scot, stalks around the stage in jerky movements and at times reminded me of Gene Simmons, although Fish's make-up coulda been more outrageous.

The rest of the band look like some weird religious sect, wearing what looked like old potato sacks, each one with a bright coloured eye painted on the back, giving that mythical look. Perhaps the Band have been reading too many Stephen King novels.

Marillion have a very tight sound. Songs like 'He Knows You Know', 'Garden Party' and 'Charting The Single' are all long workouts, well crafted, not too much guitar, and synthesizer drifting in and out. Fronting this rather complicated sound is Fish, who does have a good voice, and sings pretty off the wall lyrics. So what a surprise when they encored with an old Scottish jig classic, 'Loch Lomond', a real show stopper.

The sooner Marillion get signed the better. Now if someone could tell me what the big eye on the back of those potato sacks means, I'll join the sect.

XAVIER RUSSELL

The big time! Marillion's glowing review in Sounds *magazine.*

Thanks a Marillion

MARILLION, now sporting **Mark Kelly** from Chemical Alice on keyboards, have lined up a club tour of the south and west of the country to check out support for the pomp rock revival.

They start at Chadwell Heath Electric Stadium on January 6 and then play Cambridge Great Northern Hotel 9, Leystone Green Man Club 11, Luton Mad Hatters Club 12, Treforest Polytechnic Of Wales 15, Tonypandy Naval Club 16, West Hampstead Starlite Ballroom 18, Luton Technical College 22, Chadwell Heath Electric Club 23, Chadwell Heath Electric Stadium 27, Clapham 101 Club 28.

I had arrived! Even if Sounds *couldn't spell the name of our band.*

The smell of the greasepaint, the roar of the crowd. Fish rocking Dacorum College in Hemel Hempstead on 25th March 1982.

"Test one, two…" Privet Hedge helps us to set up and soundcheck at Luton Technical College on 22nd January 1982.

The Saliva Tears tour poster. Who could walk past that and not want to pop their head into the venue?

Get the flock out! Mick Pointer and Stef Jeffries in 1982.

The ever adaptable Pete Trewavas rocking a short lived beard at the Marquee on 19th May 1982.

Steve Rothery, still persisting with the sackcloth, at the Marquee on 19th May 1982.

At the same Marquee show, my shirt making me hard to miss.

Steve takes flight at the Marquee on 7th March 1982.

At the Marquee on 2nd July 1982 sporting my legendary jumpsuit, which made me feel like a piece of broiled fish each time I came off stage.

Market Square Heroes. The kings of Aylesbury in 1982.

Moving up to Marquee headliners, 29th December 1982.
Note my eye-catching outfit. (It's hard not to.)

Blue Steel II at Aylesbury Friars on 18th March 1982.

"Do you remember?" Fish and Kay at my wedding reception on 4th October 1982.

MARK KELLY

MICK POINTER

FISH

PETER TREWAVAS

STEVE ROTHERAY

Blue Steel III. We were all at it: 1982 Marillion promotional photo.

"Yes, but this one goes up to 11." Me, Pete and Nick Tauber searching for the lost chord at the Marquee Studios in 1982.

So here I am once more...
Recording Script at the
Marquee Studios in 1982.

"Fish, you've got something on your face." With Mick Pointer in 1983.

Welcome to the world. Freya and her proud father in 1983.

Phew, rock and roll. Dad duties at Whipsnade Zoo in 1983.

With Andy Ward in 1983 during his brief stint with Marillion.

A state of Utopia. On tour with Todd Rundgren in 1983.

Pete and Privet cuddle up and bro down at Mountain Studio in 1983.

The world is completely Fugazi… *Simon Hanhart, Pete and me, recording our second album at The Manor in 1983.*

resulting sound. Steve used it to great effect for the intro of *Assassing* while also ticking a few bagpipe/eastern scale boxes to boot.

Even the novelty of a new drummer wasn't enough to get the creative juices flowing. Moses might have come down from the mountain with ten commandments, but we left Mountain Studios in Wales with only one song to show for our efforts.

The US tour started off with some dates opening for Todd Rundgren. I was very excited to see Todd live as I had become a fan after first hearing him warming up for Led Zeppelin a few years earlier at Knebworth Park.

At Knebworth he was on fire, but headlining to half full venues he felt more like a damp squib than a prog rock colossus. His audience, what there was of it, regarded us with a look that was quizzical at best. Our own headline gigs were in small clubs and bars mostly half empty too. Admittedly, the bars were bigger than the ones we left behind in the UK, but it was a humbling experience all the same.

Most people, when they think about a band touring the USA, imagine a purpose-built tour bus, gleaming chrome and tinted windows, airbrushed murals adorning the sides, the freedom of the open highways, the air filled with possibilities.

On planet Marillion in 1983 it wasn't quite like that. We travelled in an eight seater minibus, with Paul up front driving and Ian 'Clutch' Ritchie, shirtless and passed out from the heat, in the back. Clutch was our 'merch man'. He travelled with us because there was even less room in the crew van, and they usually departed the hotel earlier than we had to. Although the minibus had air conditioning, it wasn't powerful enough to cool the whole bus, so it was like the fifth circle of hell towards the back. Without being asked to, but following tour etiquette, Clutch graciously chose the back seats.

It's early, the kind of early where you wake and make a sound like you've been shot. That's how it was on the road that summer. You woke, the shuttered sunlight still hurting your eyes, crawled into the van and then sat cramped gasping for the AC unit as it made a sound like an old Cortina starting on a hill in the middle of winter, emitting about as much cool air as your average asthmatic. You'd sit like that for anything from 4 to 14 hours until you reached the next stop on the tour.

The longest drives were usually on non-gig days, so even though they were marked down as days off on the tour itinerary, in reality they were more endless miles down America's highways. On those days, we noticed Andy would leave the minibus noticeably the worse for wear. We didn't understand how he was getting pissed en route until somebody saw him secretly topping off a can of Coke with some vodka.

We didn't exactly approve of Andy's behaviour, but we could hardly condemn him either as there were nights when we couldn't make out the numbers on our hotel room doors through the hazy fug of post-gig booze. I say post-gig, but one night Steve and I were sat in the bar waiting to go on stage when we chanced upon a drink we had never tried before called a Long Island Iced Tea. Tea, I thought, how welcoming, a taste of home right there in the glass.

Four or five drinks later and it was time to go on stage. I was so wasted I spent the entire gig propping myself up against the keyboards the way a drunk relies on a bar for leverage. I'm being kind when I say our show was shaky that night. Steve swore he would never drink before a gig again after that. A promise I believe he has kept. Note: A Long Island Iced Tea has nothing to do with tea. It's vodka, gin, tequila, rum and Triple Sec topped off with Coke! I recommend it, unless you're operating heavy machinery or trying to play the *Garden Party* solo.

Things came to a head with Andy when we were driving into New York for our final gig opening for Todd. We had a relatively short 3 hour drive from Rhode Island to Manhattan, but as it was a day off Andy started drinking early. By the time we were driving through Harlem, Andy was drunk enough to think that throwing his empties out of the window was a smart idea. It only got worse when we were all in the hotel lobby waiting for our rooms. Andy was somehow both erratic and subdued: that uneven pendulum swing of the drunk. By the end of the day, following an emergency band meeting in John's room, we decided to cancel the rest of the tour and fly home.

We played our final gig of the tour to an especially hostile Todd Rundgren crowd. After *Garden Party*, only the second song of the set, Fish was hit square in the chest by an overripe peach. Fish, as calm as the surface of a pond, said into the mic, "I'd like to say thank you for the peach somebody threw onstage. It got damaged on the way in. If they want to get it back, come backstage and I'd love to give it back to you personally, except I might not be able to get it out of my hand which means you would get a clenched fist right between your fucking eyes, cunt face! To the rest of the crowd, I'd like to say hello."

We arrived back in the UK earlier than planned, which was just as well because we needed to find a replacement for Andy. John Arnison put the feelers out and found us a drummer at short notice. John Marter was a competent, no frills drummer who learned the set in a few days.

We played a warm-up show in Liverpool with him the day before we closed the summer with a triumphant return to the Reading Festival stage. In fact, Reading had two stages, side by side. This set-up was to facilitate a smoother, faster change over between bands. We were closing the Saturday night on the B stage with only Black Sabbath to follow us on the adjacent A stage.

The crowd were restless, and the air was thick with campfire smoke and projectiles flying in all directions. It was too late to reconsider our choice of opener with its slow start, *Grendel*. As Steve began playing the gentle picking intro, eyes closed and focused, a two litre plastic bottle that once contained Coke, but may now have held a different, less sweet liquid, came tumbling through the air in a gentle arc, clear yellow droplets cascading from the neck and catching the light as it turned end over end. Time stood still as I watched in fascinated horror as the bottle completed its journey, bouncing at Steve's feet and somehow missing the row of guitars behind him. It flew off the back of the stage with a clatter and into the darkness. Steve played on without missing a note.

Fish had the audience in the palm of his hand, all 35,000 of them. That said, about halfway through the set he started getting irritated. The audience were all looking to their right at Stage A. What was so interesting there? We found out later that Black Sabbath's comically huge Stonehenge stage set (the inspiration for the miniature one in the movie *Spinal Tap*) was on fire. We played on while their crew tackled the flames. That Ian Gillan led incarnation of Black Sabbath would go up in smoke not so long afterwards too.

Andy Ward had turned up backstage earlier in the day. We invited him to join us on stage playing along on percussion. It felt like a positive note to end to his time with the band.

In September we were back in New York again, this time to open for Canadian prog trio Rush. Five nights at the prestigious Radio City Music Hall. We died a death every night like Christian slaves tossed to the lions in a Roman amphitheatre, shown no mercy by the braying mob. One particularly passionate and possibly drunk Rush fan in the front row stood on his seat, pulled down his jeans and pants and yelled "Kiss my ass!", helpfully pointing out his generous derrière in case we missed it.

Every night we trudged back to the Mayflower Hotel bar on Central Park West to drown our sorrows, and every night we had to listen to John Marter drone on that if we gave him the producer gig on our next album, he would do a brilliant and comprehensive job. By the end of the week, he had talked himself out of the gig, not only of potential producer, but as our drummer too.

Going to New York wasn't a total waste of time though. One evening we met with a 20 year old drummer from Boston called Jonathan Mover. He'd heard word we were looking for a drummer and came to try to persuade us to let him audition. We were unsure, mainly because we didn't want him to waste time and money flying to the UK only to be turned down. He was sure he wanted to try anyway and it was hard not to be impressed with his tenacity and determination. It reminded us of ourselves a few years earlier before being flashed by Rush fans had ground us down.

Back at Nomis we had another round of auditions, saving Jonathan's until last in order to give him a fair crack as he had travelled so far. Unwittingly, we had saved the best until last as he impressed the hell out of us. He was technically brilliant with incredible precision and timing. And all at 20. Part of me wanted to choke him.

As was the Marillion way, we dropped him in at the deep end. Though this time it was akin to going off the top tier of a diving board into a bottomless sea. We asked him if he would like to come to Germany for his first gig, which would be recorded and broadcast live on radio.

Talking of taking things to new extremes, Fish broke the news to John Marter that he wouldn't be needed in Germany with even more cruel glee than he had when sacking Diz and Mick. It was like the old joke, I say joke: "All those coming to Germany, take one step forward. Where do you think you're going, Marter?" John had obviously forgotten (or forgiven) this when Fish asked him to play drums on his *Fellini Days* album in 2001.

We left for Germany the next day and that evening I talked Jonathan through the entire set in our hotel room while he tapped out the parts on a practice pad on his bed.

We were interrupted by a knock on the door which I answered. I fell backward into the room spinning around to protect myself as a blast of dry powder hit me square in the face. The room filled with a choking white dust and we made for the windows to let some air in before we were asphyxiated.

Our level-headed manager John Arnison was the culprit. Mistakenly, he was convinced that I hadn't spotted him. He hurried back to his room and jumped in the shower. I like to imagine he was whistling happily with not a care in the world as he reached for the shampoo. Once we could breathe again, I grabbed a fire extinguisher and went to John's room. He answered the door dripping wet with a towel around his middle, an inquiring and innocent expression across his face.

I was having none of it and without hesitation squeezed the trigger. There was a 'whump' sound, an explosive cloud of white and the dry powder not only covered his entire room but stuck to his wet skin and hair. Other members of the band joined in the fun and pretty soon the entire hotel floor was covered in a thick layer of white powder. Thank God an actual fire didn't break out just then.

That said, the actual fire brigade was called when somebody mistook the white clouds billowing from our open windows for smoke. The police arrived too. When they discovered what had really happened, they lined us all up against the wall and asked who was in charge. John, still half naked, covered with only a towel and tell-tale sodium bicarbonate, sheepishly raised his hand.

I got the impression that Jonathan wasn't too impressed with his first night with his new band. At least we didn't charge the thousand pounds cleaning bill to his room. And despite having had no rehearsal and only one day's notice, Jonathan played a stellar gig. It was a success.

By mid-October we were back in Wales, this time at The Old Mill House in Monmouth. This eight bedroom residential rehearsal studio was part of the famed Rockfield Studios, which was situated just down the road.

Black skies weren't just forming over the Welsh hills. I invited Susie (and Freya) to come and visit because we were seeing very little of each other, which wasn't good for our relationship. She didn't stay long; it wasn't easy being the only married guy with a child in a band of unattached young men.

Meanwhile, Fish had already informed EMI that *Punch & Judy* would be the first single from the new album. He probably failed to mention that it was about domestic violence or that there was no music just yet.

Easy, all we had to do was come up with catchy tune to go with it. Fish was fixated on the idea of a Bo Diddley type beat, so we tried to incorporate that with something a bit more scintillating. I had a lot of fun working out the 7/8 keyboard intro with Jonathan. I found his playing a bit intimidating because he was so good. If he thought that I wasn't up to his standard (which I wasn't), he was tactful enough to keep it to himself. The basic chord structure was also mine.

We also started work on *Incubus* with the music written by Steve and a rhythm from Jonathan that would later be developed by Ian Mosley and used for the intro section. Fish had been working on the lyric from the soliloquy he first put forward for the *Script* intro.

John Arnison was less than delighted to learn that the second part of the lyric was inspired by a spell Fish spent as his guest at his flat in Blackheath, referred to as a Blackheath cell in the *Fugazi* lyric. Sleeping in the room next to John and his girlfriend, Fish sat through the night listening through the wall, notepad in hand, scribbling away.

> *The darkroom unleashes imagination in pornographic images*
> *In which you will always be the star (always be the star)*
> *Untouchable, unapproachable, constant in the darkness*
> *Nursing an erection, a misplaced reaction*
> *With no flower to place before this gravestone*
> *And the walls become enticingly newspaper thin*
> *But that would only be developing the negative view*

As Diz had found to his cost, you had to be careful around Fish in case you unwittingly became the starting point for his next song. As Fish once said, "I assimilate experiences like a bucket filling up with water. After a couple of weeks, I overflow and I have to write something down."

John was also the inspiration for another Fish lyric. I say inspiration, he's actually quoted word for word in *Lady Nina*.

In the movie *Rashomon*, the characters provide subjective, alternative, self-serving and contradictory versions of the same incident. Similarly, when bands dump members, every person you ask has a different slant on the way things went down. When it was Jonathan's time to go, Fish blamed his technical ability, that Jonathan didn't fit into the band's social infrastructure and, what's more, he was American. For his part, Jonathan said he was fired because he argued with Fish over the idea of recording a concept album and because he was Jewish.

I don't remember the concept album argument, but that wasn't the reason Fish wanted him out. Fish made it clear to the rest of us, almost from the start, that he disliked Jonathan. I don't think Fish is anti-Semitic, but he wouldn't hesitate to insult Jonathan's faith to upset him. As far as Fish was concerned, this was war. He wanted Jonathan out and he would use whatever means necessary to get rid of him. Which was easier said than done.

Jonathan was a determined and ambitious young man. He was serious and didn't have time for fooling around. He didn't drink and most of his conversations revolved around music. Fish was also ambitious, but still wanted to have fun and saw the band as both a musical vehicle as well as a group of friends with whom he could socialise. Jonathan, brilliant drummer as he was, couldn't and wouldn't be Fish's mate.

This shows how important the chemistry between the members of a band is, it needs to work on and off the stage.

One night we all sat around the big kitchen table, half empty drinks set before us. Jonathan, as was usual, had retired to bed early. Fish delivered an ultimatum: either Jonathan was out of the band or he was. We reluctantly agreed to fire Jonathan. This was one of the last times we would capitulate to Fish's demands.

I felt much worse about firing Jonathan than either Mick or Diz because this time I wasn't a willing accomplice. I didn't think it was for the greater good of the band. I remember Jonathan crying as he left the house.

Sentiment was quickly put aside and we didn't waste any time bringing in a replacement. Schedules demanded we move as quickly as possible; the writing sessions were already lagging behind. Luckily, we had somebody in mind. A session drummer who would come in as a hired hand and at least help us finish the writing.

Ian Mosley was eight years older than me, but he came highly recommended by Paul Crockford, a show promoter who John knew. We found out later that Ian had asked Crockford to put in a good word for him as he really wanted the gig.

Ian had been touring with Steve Hackett and had wanted to audition previously, when we were seeking to replace Andy Ward, but couldn't make it to Nomis a few weeks earlier due to a drum clinic he was already booked to play. His priorities might have been off, but it was hard not to like Ian.

He was relaxed and confident but not cocky. Imagine an Easter Island head in Aviator shades and you're close. His playing was excellent, and he brought experience and insight to the job. Years of session work had taught him that it was more important to play what was needed rather than showboating. Ian was comfortable with the sometimes complex nature of our songs, but he knew when to keep it simple. Jonathan was technical but didn't swing. He was like a machine, precise but lacking in emotion. Ian had the feel to go with the technique.

Ian drank occasionally and smoked a bit of dope but never while working. He knew how to have fun but only when the work was done. Ian's dry sense of humour suited the band perfectly too.

Even though Ian ticked all the boxes, we were wary of making him a full-time member right away. We had got our fingers burned with Andy, John and Jonathan in quick succession, so less haste, more speed seemed the best option. The inscrutable Ian Mosley quietly got on with everything we asked of him.

We launched into the writing with new enthusiasm. Pete finally had somebody who would complement his playing. For my part, I was feeling less sure about my ability to keep up with this newly confident rhythm section. Steve and I were struggling to come up with enough good music for a whole album, but by the time we left Monmouth we were only short of music for the album's title track and the middle section of *Incubus*. Interestingly, the two best tracks on the album.

We were booked to record the album at The Manor Studios near Kidlington, Oxfordshire. Owned by Richard Branson, the first album recorded there was Mike Oldfield's *Tubular Bells*. No pressure then. The Manor, unlike the Marquee Studio, was a residential set-up. A big sprawling country house with a swimming pool in the grounds. It was priced accordingly, costing somewhere north of a thousand pounds a day to hire.

Time was going to be tight recording *Fugazi,* but that didn't stop John putting in a few 'warm-up' gigs before the sessions plus some dates during Christmas week to finish the year with a bang (and a bag of cash).

The warm-up shows were a good idea. They gave us a chance to try out the new songs in front of an audience. There's nothing like playing new material to people to expose the weaknesses in your writing. *She Chameleon,* like its namesake, went through a number of changes as we wrote and re-wrote the music throughout 1982 and '83. The music for the most recent version was mostly written by me, but we were never entirely happy with it and never played it live again after recording it.

The Christmas gigs were meant to be both fun and an easy payday. The only way to avoid eating into our recording time further was to play them from 27th until 31st December. John didn't consider that I might want to spend Christmas and New Year at home with my family because the rest of the band could easily invite their girlfriends to any gigs they liked. Inside the band there was a culture, driven by Fish, of life on the road being for boys only. One time Susie took Freya on the tour bus for a moment's respite from that night's show and Fish came aboard and asked if we had become a band of travelling gypsies. It was classic Fish: both passive and aggressive.

We started recording in mid-November amid the usual hubbub of excitement and anticipation, but almost from the start things started to unravel. An overly confident Nick Tauber had decided to record the album in 48 tracks. This was ambitions because it involved using two 24 track machines running together. A piece of kit that should never have left the lab was used to read the timecode from the master machine and vary the speed of the second, slave machine to make it match. In practice, it took 20 to 30 seconds for the slave machine to catch up and stabilise, which meant that every time you had to stop the machine, rewind the tape and go again it wasted valuable time. Over the course of a day this resulted in many lost hours.

We only had about 8 weeks booked at The Manor and the first few were spent finishing off the arrangements and writing the music for *Fugazi*, the title track.

Whenever things weren't going well, which was most of the time, Nick consoled himself by having another line of coke. As Nick spiralled into a paranoid wreck, Simon took on the responsibility of getting the album finished. At one point, in a half-hearted attempt to make up for lost time, Nick asked if anybody would be willing work on Christmas Day. Apart from being a ridiculous idea, we were starting to wonder if Nick's reason for recording at a residential studio was because he didn't want to go home.

Things came to a head just before Christmas. We had an emergency band meeting with Hugh Stanley-Clarke and resolved to send Nick home, effectively firing him from the project. Simon agreed to finish the album alone. Instead of just packing up and leaving on being told the news, Nick refused to leave and, like a spectre at the feast, he carried on turning up each morning in the studio control room. Things at home must have been worse than we thought.

In happier news, we decided to invite Ian to become a full-time member of Marillion in January 1984. He was very happy to accept on one condition. He said he couldn't live on £350 per month, so could we all have a wage rise to £500? John agreed, as he thought we could afford it. I have to admit that I didn't take any interest in our accounts and John never offered to show them to us. As long as we got paid every month, then what was the problem? That was something that would come back to haunt me a few years down the line.

But for now, we were fighting the clock, hobbling on until, inevitably, we ran out of time at The Manor and spent most of January moving between any studios in London that had free days available. In all we worked in eight different studios, most of which are no longer in business, which, to be clear, had nothing to do with us. Angel Studios in Islington finally closed its doors in 2019.

Nick had the grand idea of recording the organ part for *She Chameleon* at Angel Studios because, being a church in a previous life, the studio still had a real, working pipe organ. Quite why we were still taking advice from him at this point still puzzles me to this day, but I was very excited at the prospect of playing there. However, the experience was a disappointment. The organ was old and poorly maintained, which made it difficult to play (although luckily the part was pretty simple). It also didn't sound that great, but time constraints meant we used it anyway.

With the tour booked, sold out and looming on the horizon we took the decision to speed up the mixing by splitting into two camps. With Steve and me in one camp and Ian, Fish and Pete in the other, we also brought in another engineer. On Stanley-Clarke's recommendation we hired Tony Platt, fresh from working with EMI stable mates Iron Maiden, who mixed *Incubus* at Abbey Road. His approach to recording was completely different to Simon's, so the first thing he did was attempt to make the drums sound like they would have done had he recorded them himself. Which irked us, but we said nothing because he was doing us a favour. As Fish wasn't there, I took the opportunity to ask him to cut most of Linda Pike's backing vocals, which neither Steve nor I liked.

The backing vocals I actually did like were at the end of *Fugazi* and sung by Carl Wayne, lead singer from '60s band The Move. Though he was never credited because the artwork was already at the printers by the time he came to record his part.

With virtually no rehearsal and the mix still not finished, we toured the UK starting at Leeds University on 11th February 1984. We were booked to film a show for the BBC series *Sight And Sound In Concert* at Chippenham Goldiggers on 8th February, but we weren't confident we would be good enough, so we moved it to the end of the tour in March. Which was a shame because, while we were certainly tighter as a band, Fish's voice was pretty ragged by that point.

Despite everything, the tour was sold out and the album entered the UK charts at number five, topping the position that we had managed with *Script* the previous year.

Given our relative inexperience, we were delighted with this news and convinced that our plan for world domination was still on track.

What we didn't know was that EMI were disappointed with the lack of a hit single. *Punch & Judy*, even with an appearance on *Top Of The Pops* and kids TV show *Razzmatazz*, only managed to reach number 29 in the singles chart before dropping like a stone the following week. They were also unhappy about the huge studio bill run up by our late album delivery (which wouldn't be the last time that would happen). *Fugazi* cost over £120,000, almost twice as much as *Script,* while failing to match its sales.

Back in London, storm clouds were gathering over Manchester Square. EMI had pored over the paperwork, added up the numbers, and were now considering dropping Marillion altogether.

CHAPTER 9

Do You Remember?

There's a good reason why people single money out as the root of all evil. It's because they don't know what the Bible actually says about money. The Bible doesn't harangue cold hard cash (God's no idiot; churches cost a fortune to build, and all those cornices won't pay for themselves), but reserves its ire for those who *love* money and sully their hands with the stuff.

I'm with God and renowned wit Dorothy Parker on this, and, on reflection, it sounds like they were both singing from the same hymn sheet at one point: "If you want to know what God thinks of money, just look at the people he gave it to." That was Dorothy; I doubt even God would talk about himself in the third person. Not that we were worried about people being given money, more about the ones trying to take it from us.

There's a scene in Danny Boyle's *Shallow Grave* where the three protagonists have been gifted a mysterious suitcase full of cash. The less recalcitrant of the trio balks as the other two begin a spending spree; he admonishes the pair: "We don't know how much it cost us yet. For you two to have a good time, we don't know the cost of that yet." And, as we the audience discover, a sudden influx of cash comes at a price.

When you've almost nothing to go round it's easy to agree to share everything equally. The real test comes when the money starts coming in, as we were about to find out.

Americans have a reputation for being more litigious than most and in this respect Jonathan Mover was about to revert very much to type. Not long after *Fugazi* was released we received a communication from Mover's father, who just happened to be a lawyer. Mover was demanding a share of the publishing royalties for songs on *Fugazi*. We must have been feeling guilty for firing him (or were suffering from a momentary lack of reason) because why else would we then agree to give him 10% of *Punch & Judy*?

As the drummer, it was his job to play the drums. He had direction from Fish for the sort of beat to play (remember the whole Bo Diddley thing?) and the 7/8 time signature came from the music I wrote. That leaves very little, if anything, for the drummer, no matter how inventive, to have 'written', but it does beg the question: what constitutes songwriting in a band situation?

There are a number of examples that might help answer this knotty quandary that has perplexed band members since time immemorial. An infamous case concerns The Rolling Stones and their song *The Last Time*. Basically, the Stones borrowed the chorus from *This May Be The Last Time* by the Staple Singers, who had, in turn, adapted it from a traditional gospel song that was long out of copyright. Even if we did know who wrote it, as long as the writer's been dead for at least 70 years, then the song would be considered to be public domain or, in layman's terms, royalty free.

In those cases, where a new arrangement of a 'traditional' song is created, the arranger is free to claim the songwriting royalties. Led Zeppelin used this to great effect on their debut album. This little nugget of information also came in useful for organist Alan Price when he registered himself as the arranger of The Animals' hit song *House Of The Rising Sun,* and then sat back as that little nugget became a full blown goldmine. Unfortunately, he had omitted to tell the rest of the band, which caused the kind of resentment that men usually reserve for first wives. It was something that The Animals never fully recovered from.

Where the Rolling Stones' story gets interesting is when their then manager Andrew Oldham commissioned composer David Whitaker to write and/or arrange (depending on how you define them) orchestral versions of some of the Stones' catalogue. The orchestral version of *The Last Time*, while having little in common with any of the previous versions, had a catchy theme that was subsequently sampled by The Verve for their 1997 monster hit *Bittersweet Symphony.*

Unfortunately for them, former Stones manager Alan Klein held the copyright to the song and refused to grant The Verve a licence to use it (after it had already been released and become a hit). Reportedly, Klein said he was a reasonable man and wanted a 50/50 split, 50 for Mick and 50 for Keith. 100% of the publishing royalties went to Jagger and Richards, leaving Verve singer Richard Ashcroft feeling bitter, not sweet. Though, many, many years later, Klein relented, and The Verve got a sliver of songwriting royalties, for which I'm sure they're eternally grateful.

Less famously, when Rick Wakeman was haunting the streets of Soho as a session musician, he was paid £10 to play the piano on the smash hit hymn *Morning Has Broken* by Cat Stevens (now known as Yusuf Islam or more recently just Yusuf). At short notice,

Rick was asked to knock out a new intro for this old tune. Thinking on his feet, Rick repurposed a piece he had written for his first solo album.

Cat liked it so much he wanted more but Rick explained it was already taken so he would have to settle for a few bars. Anyone who's ever heard *The Six Wives Of Henry VIII* will recognise it instantly from the track *Catherine Howard*. When the song charted in the top ten in multiple countries around the world, Rick was brassed off to learn that he wasn't even credited with performing, never mind co-writing the track. It's a shame Rick's dad Cyril wasn't a lawyer.

Almost there, promise. The point I'm making is that apportioning songwriting shares when there's more than one person involved in making a record is almost as complex as the *Sunday Times* cryptic crossword, but only if you don't opt to share everything equally. We were just about to find out how complicated.

A lot of the praise for our first album went to Fish and his lyrics. Journalists usually only wanted to talk to Fish. He was always great for a headline, exceptionally garrulous and enjoyed talking about himself and the essence of our songs. Understandably, and he's not the first singer to fall for this, he started to believe the hype: that Marillion's success was down to him. To paraphrase sci-fi writer Philip K. Dick: the problem with introspection is that it has no end. And our singer was spending a lot of time looking inwardly.

There's an argument to be made that Marillion would still be playing pubs without Fish, but that's not the same as saying that Fish *was* Marillion, because it ignores the fundamentals, not to mention the importance, of the musicians and performers in Marillion. We weren't merely his backing band. It takes a hundred different factors, including the fortunate roll of the dice, to succeed in music.

After the *Fugazi* album was finished, I received a phone call from John. Fish had been bending his ear about publishing. Putting it bluntly, Fish felt he deserved a bigger slice of the publishing pie, a 50% slice to be precise. Which, no matter how you cut it, is a lot of pie. John told me that he had managed to persuade Fish that everyone in the band deserved to get some 'bunce' from the songwriting, and if Fish were to take 50%, there wouldn't be a lot left for the rest of us. Fish agreed that 50% should be divided equally between the five of us and the remaining 50% be split equally between the lyric and music writers.

This meant that as the lyric writer Fish would always get 35% and any band member who didn't contribute to the writing would get 10%. This was a radical change from equal shares, but, according to John, Fish was adamant. John advised us to accept it. In the interest of band harmony, we folded like cheap deckchairs in a storm. Are you seeing a familiar pattern here between band and singer: Fish asks, we acquiesce?

So, from *Fugazi* onwards we started splitting the publishing income (and advances) unequally. To add to the fun, this meant that we would have to sit down and agree who wrote what. Fish always wrote the lyrics, so that was the easy part. He also usually came up with the vocal melodies, known as the 'top line' in the business, which most publishers would agree also constituted writing. Thankfully, Fish wasn't aware of that, or if he was, he didn't push for a share of the music writing royalties too, so he never got a bigger cut than 35% for each song while he was in the band.

Apart from Jonathan sticking his hand out, we also had a case to settle with Mick. He had been busy getting advice on what he could squeeze us for financially. He was on his 20% record royalties for his performance on *Script* and 20% of the songwriting royalties, but he felt he deserved something for the band name, which he had dreamed up while staring intently at the spine of a Tolkien novel called *The Silmarillion*. Inspiration can strike at any time, right? After some haggling, we settled on a one-off payment of £10,000.

Just when we thought we could stand down the lawyers, along came Brian and Diz wanting a share of the songwriting royalties from the first album. "Where there's a hit there's a writ", as the old adage goes. We were finding that you didn't even need a hit, just a few disgruntled ex-members.

I have some sympathy for Brian's claim. He did come up with some of the music for *The Web*, *Forgotten Sons*, *He Knows You Know* and *Garden Party*, but, as far as I could tell, Diz was less deserving. But, like World Wars, they came as a pair, so we agreed to pay them both the same share each, which amounted to most of mine and Pete's 20%.

The upshot of all this was that from *Fugazi* onwards Fish would be on 35% and the rest of us would have to go through the awkward and arbitrary process of deciding who wrote what on each song when an album was finished in order to split the remaining 65% between us. Inevitably, this was put off for as long as possible because we wanted to avoid the unseemly spectacle of having to say things like "I thought I might have written that part?" or "Doesn't my playing on that song deserve a little more than 5%?". It was shaping up to be like a Noel Coward farce without any of the bon mots.

We needn't have worried, because being robustly British in our approach each of us would be politely suggesting that this person or that person should surely get more, not less. Happily, we never once argued over how the songs were split and agreed to let it go and get back to being friends in a band together again. That all changed when Fish left: the only manners we had then were bad ones. We had an explosive and expensive legal battle over the publishing amongst other things, but let's jump off that bridge when we get to it.

We ended the *Fugazi* tour with the now traditional sold out shows at Hammersmith Odeon, three this time. Backstage there was a small bar up on the top floor where the band and their guests could meet after the show. Fish and I headed up there to steady our nerves before the final gig. The bar was empty as we didn't allow guests backstage before we played. After a few minutes standing at the bar, we noticed a small figure in a long, dark coat, a trilby and round glasses sat alone at a small table by the door. Curious, we walked over and said hello.

Like he was born to play a walk-on part in a Truffaut movie, Robert Fripp introduced himself. He motioned for us to sit down and after bit of awkward small talk he said in a conspiratorial voice that he was planning to sack his band, King Crimson. And he was doing so, and I'm quoting here, to keep them on their toes. Fish and I swapped quizzical glances as we headed to the dressing room, all the while with me wondering if Fripp's unique leadership style might have given Fish some ideas.

Fugazi was released the following day. Better late than never.

The failure of *Punch & Judy* to set the charts alight was partially blamed on the lack of a promo video. Given the subject matter, I'm not exactly sure how we would have pitched it to the label or production team. For *Assassing*, the next single, we discovered green screen technology and spent a tidy sum making a load of twaddle that not even Fish understood. This was a mimed performance, thrown together with lots of meaningless computer graphics, a pretty girl and some James Bond bad guys, topped off with a Ford Cortina.

The highlight of the day was when the Cortina stunt driver confidently assured the film crew that he would have plenty of stopping room after mounting a ramp and sailing through a paper green screen, only to crash into the wall on the other side of the warehouse. He gave a shaky if somewhat embarrassed wave to assure us all that he was alright.

In a rare week off in April, John took us all to Tenerife to meet his business partner, Alan Crux. He had something he wanted to show us. Apart from his interest in Bravado, the merchandise company John had employed to manufacture and sell our T-shirts, Crux was involved in property.

When we got to Tenerife, still amazed by John's generosity, we discovered Crux was trying to sell us a timeshare. It was like being in an episode of *Only Fools And Horses*, I kept expecting Del and Rodney to pop up from behind the bar and offer me some knock off merch from the back of their Reliant Robin. Though instead of some dodgy Fred Perry tops, this was a few units with views of the beach, apparently. I didn't know whether to be appalled or unsurprised. I assiduously avoided his smarmy sales patter and worked on my tan until it was time to go home.

We headed into a summer filled with various European festival appearances and an idea that we might yet again attempt to conquer the USA and Canada.

The first gig on the continent was in Copenhagen on 4th May. We planned to take a ferry there from Yarmouth docks, so John added a date in Great Yarmouth that we could play on the way. The gig itself was uneventful, but there were lots of people hanging around afterwards. I didn't suppose much ever happened in Great Yarmouth, so a band like Marillion playing was a big deal and the locals wanted to party. Fish took a fancy to a young lady who was with her boyfriend. The boyfriend was so upset about Fish's advances, and his girlfriend's obvious delight at the attention she was getting, that he resolved to end it all and marched into the sea.

Fish, clearly fearing for the poor lad's safety, went after him and with a right hook broke his jaw to stop him drowning himself. This resulted in the police being called and Paul Lewis having to leave two young ladies unattended in his hotel room while he attempted to save Fish from spending a night in the cells. Paul left his attaché case, containing the night's takings, a cool £10,000 in cash, in the room. But he wasn't worried because he had handcuffed it to the TV pedestal stand just like he'd seen the mafia do in movies. On returning to his room, he discovered the TV on the floor, the stand carefully dismantled and his attaché case and handcuffs missing. The mafia would have no doubt tossed Paul into the sea in a concrete overcoat, but we were a little more forgiving.

The police were called for a second time that night (probably their busiest night all year). They said that the two missing suspects were known to them, and they would have no trouble tracking them down. They were as good as their word; they found the case broken open in the back of a car belonging to one of the ladies. There was only £50 missing. We decided not to press charges and headed for the continent.

Somewhere along the road, and God knows how, our singer had acquired a set of conga drums. Is there a more chilling sentence in the English language? He felt he needed something to do on stage during the instrumental parts of the set. The congas are traditionally played with the hands, but Fish was having none of that and used a pair of Ian's sticks to bash the crap out of them. He might have had a certain flair for the congas, and he was certainly good at hitting things, as the lad in Great Yarmouth had discovered, but hitting things in time was a whole other skill.

Fish, being Fish, insisted that his less than metronomic strike rate be mic'd up for all to hear. The crew dutifully did as they were told and carefully positioned a microphone in front of the congas. The cable leading from the mic was then carefully tossed under Ian's drum riser. This is what's known in the trade as an 'air patch'. If you saw us around that time, then you're welcome.

Not so easily put off, Fish upgraded his onstage percussion to something that was so loud it didn't need a microphone to be heard above the band: timbales. This annoyed Ian the way dragging nails across a blackboard can sometimes set people on edge, so he instructed the crew to leave them on the truck. Fish gave up after that.

Ian has a presence (Easter Island head plus sunglasses, remember?) about him that commands respect. Even Fish was wary of crossing him. Ian brought a professionalism to the band that went beyond deciding who was allowed to hit things (in time or not) on stage. Steve, Pete and I felt like we had to take playing on stage seriously. Ian set a standard and he expected the musicians in the band to meet it. I'm sure this work ethic served to keep the three of us (but especially Pete and me) straighter and more sober than we otherwise would have been over the years. Fish, being the singer, wasn't so easily swayed by Ian's influence and started to gravitate away from us and towards socialising with the crew, who were a little less fickle about setting parameters on their partying. Don't get me wrong, we all liked a drink, just not as much as Fish.

The North American tour the previous summer wasn't a complete disaster. For some reason we were doing quite well in Canada. In fact, the French-speaking province of Quebec was even better for us than the English-speaking Ontario. We decided to go back there for some more dates in an attempt to build on our fanbase.

We also played a few shows in the USA including one at The Lost Horizon in Syracuse, New York. I slipped down a flight of stairs chasing after Paul Lewis (I can't recall if he was clutching a briefcase full of our cash at the time) in some drunken after gig antics and ended up in hospital with my shoulder dislocated for a second time in as many years. The doctor had little trouble relocating my shoulder because I was virtually horizontal. He also refused to give me painkillers as I was already 'medicated', like Hunter S Thompson was occasionally medicated. Thankfully, this time I didn't miss a gig and I'd like to say I'd learned my lesson and vowed to be more careful, but I think you know me well enough by now to know that's not true.

While we continued to play shows through the summer, John was trying to convince EMI that they should take up the option on our next album. He suggested that we could produce a live album as a stopgap. That this would be made very cheaply and sold at a low price is how I imagine he sold it to them. We could use it to tour some more and hopefully recoup some of the losses from *Fugazi*. EMI liked the idea and *Real To Reel* was born.

Blissfully unaware of this, we got on with mixing the album with Simon at Rick Parfitt's home studio in Surrey. Parfitt had recently separated from his wife, Marietta, after the tragic drowning of their 2 year old daughter, leaving her the house and studio. Marietta was hiring it out to earn some money. Unsurprisingly, there was a pall over the place.

Nick wasn't invited to join us. Most bands when mixing live recordings replace, repair, overdub or completely re-record their songs before mixing. Thin Lizzy's *Live And Dangerous* set the standard by which subsequent live albums would forever be judged. They managed to capture the essence of an amazing live show while simultaneously recording 75% of it as overdubs in the studio. This is something Thin Lizzy have always denied, but my money is on producer Tony Visconti's account when he claimed that everything except the audience and drums were replaced in the studio.

I can see why Visconti kept the audience's roar for that album because it does sound both live and dangerous. Some bands liked it so much they have added it to their own live albums when they found their own audience sounded less ecstatic.

For our part, the songs for *Real To Reel* were recorded at Leicester's De Montfort Hall and The Spectrum in Montreal earlier in the year. We've always been a bit coy about what we got up to in the studio with that album, and I'm here to tell you, hand on heart, that we didn't go that far. It certainly wasn't like we took the metaphorical halves of two separate cars and welded them together, but there were a number of repairs.

Some were because of bad recording such as the bass, which was badly overloaded as it went to tape in Leicester. Others were plain old bum notes or out of tune vocals. It's one thing to experience a song in a hall with a few drinks inside you and a rowdy crowd singing along and quite another to hear the same mishap over and over again on headphones from the sterile and sober comfort of your living room chair.

With that job done, and while waiting for the album to be released so we could tour again, we booked ourselves into a residential rehearsal studio in Surrey called Barwell Court.

This was another country house similar to the Old Mill in Monmouth, but noticeably more upmarket. It had recently been opened by bassist John Giblin and his wife, Eveline. Although John was a sought after and well-respected bassist, he wasn't earning the sort of money to buy a place like Barwell Court. No, the house was a family property inherited by Eveline and they were filling some of those big empty rooms with music to make a crust.

It was time well-spent. Barwell Court was idyllic and atmospheric, and we laboured away utterly ignorant of how close we had come to being dropped by EMI. Indeed, we were growing confident and bullish about our relationship with our record label. We decided there and then that we were done with trying to please EMI. We were going to make a concept album.

We spent our days in the brightly lit room (a nursery in a former life), with a brand new plush carpet underfoot, only stopping for lunch and dinner, and making music we were all enjoying. Rothers was on fire, coming up with some great music. One part was a motif he had played for the first time to his girlfriend, Jo, a few days earlier to demonstrate to her how he wrote. It consisted of four simple chords, B minor, A major, F sharp minor and G major, with a picked melody and rhythm. He must have liked it enough to remember it when we got to Barwell Court.

When he played it to us, we all liked it and agreed it sounded like a verse, but we needed a chorus. I remembered that for a while Steve had played a descending chord sequence in D major at the end of one of the early versions of *She Chameleon* which never made it on to the album version. For some reason it occurred to me that it could be a possible chorus. I asked Steve to play it and the major progression worked beautifully juxtaposed against the minor verse.

That verse and chorus was the most important piece of music we ever wrote.

I still marvel at the fact that a simple melodic phrase or set of chords (the same notes and chords already used countless times before) played in a particular way can become an inspired and original piece of music that transcends time.

I also love the fact that, once created, a song, symphony or hymn exists forever. Even after every human on this planet has died and the sun has exploded in a supernova and fried the Earth to a crisp and there's nobody left to play or sing the music anymore, it still exists, echoing through the universe and the ages.

It's impossible to predict when that magic might happen, but on that day the stars aligned.

Kay had split up with Fish for good, so by the time we were at Barwell he was well into pouring it all out onto the pages of his notebook. He started singing, 'Do you remember...' over the verse and we all knew we were onto something.

When it came to the chorus he sang 'Kay – Leigh' and I winced. It felt a little bit too real, too close to Fish.

"How would people be able to relate to you singing about Kay?" I asked. "Can't you try something else?"

Fish glared at me.

"What would you like me to sing?" he barked. "'Maybe?' 'Baby?'"

By the end of the afternoon, we had a guitar solo leading to a dramatic key change up into the second verse but surprisingly we were able to keep the final chorus in the original key. That might not be important to you, but it meant it wasn't too high for Fish to sing. It shouldn't have worked but it did. The guitar solo was straight in after the first chorus too, which was hardly Writing Hit Records 101, but we didn't give a damn about that because we weren't writing a single. *Kayleigh* was going to be just one part of a much longer, more considered piece, so we put the solo where it suited us. Fuck EMI and fuck Stanley-Clarke too.

After a few weeks of incredibly enjoyable and creative endeavour, we had written all of the first side of *Misplaced Childhood* apart from *Lavender*.

Unfortunately, we had to break off because *Real To Reel* was released and we had another tour booked to play. John was beginning to wonder if we were wasting our time in the USA and he made a conscious decision to concentrate on Europe where things were starting to happen for us. With that in mind he had booked us 40 shows all over Europe, finishing in time for Christmas back at Friars in our hometown of Aylesbury. We were so pleased with how the writing was going we took the decision to play our new music on the tour, not something we'd dare do these days as it would end up all over the internet.

Fish introduced it as: "The new direction, unlike the direction a lot of people would like us to go in. This is part of an album which will be out next May or next June. And the album will be roughly a 46 minute concept album with two tracks, one called side one and the other one called side two. This, what we're about to play for you tonight, is part of side one of an album which will be called *Misplaced Childhood*."

I mean, if that didn't get the crowd fired up and punching the air then nothing would. Plus, we knew exactly what we were doing and that had energised the whole band. Ironically, this new conceptual, fuck 'em all bent of ours would turn out to be our most commercial and best selling album by far.

Before we went on tour Pete found time to marry his long-time girlfriend, Fiona, on 6th October. They managed 3 days in the Channel Islands for their honeymoon, the unremitting glamour of it all. Finally, I wasn't the only married member of the band. There's safety in numbers.

After the 1984 Christmas break, we went to a small recording studio on the Bray film studios site in Berkshire to finish writing *Misplaced*. In a flurry of creative activity, we were able to complete the album with demos by mid-February. All we needed to record it was a producer.

We approached a few respected producers, including Glyn Johns and Rupert Hine, but none of them were interested, especially when they got wind of our plans to record a concept album. That sort of talk in 1985 was bordering on heresy. Eventually someone suggested Chris Kimsey, who we knew little about apart from the fact that he had worked with The Rolling Stones and engineered for ELP early in their career.

He was invited down to Bray where we played him some of the album demos. He quickly understood where we were coming from and made some insightful observations about the music, which instantly struck a chord with us. We liked his personality too. On the back of the meeting, it was agreed that Ian and I would fly out to Berlin to see Hansa Ton Studios. Chris was doing what was known as a tax year out. This meant that he could only spend 60 nights in the UK in a 14 month period or he would have to pay income tax in the UK. Clearly, working for the Stones hadn't done his bank balance any harm.

Ian and I, the most sensible members of the band (though I'm not sure how Rothers would take that news), took a look around the studio. It was a beautiful old ballroom on the first floor with a control room containing an old Neve mixing desk and primitive speakers that looked like they had been knocked up by the studio's intern. The desk was badly in need of a service as Geordie Walker from Killing Joke (Chris's most recent production job) had let off a powder fire extinguisher in the control room causing the knobs and faders to crackle every time they were adjusted. They had also painted the grand piano in the studio silver. Luckily for me, Thomas Stiehler, our excellent German engineer, had managed to blag a loan of a nine foot concert grand from Bösendorfer for the entire session, which they kindly delivered *gratis*. Thomas's sense of humour dictated that he called me Pfennig throughout the session, which he found highly amusing.

To say we were underwhelmed by Hansa's equipment would be putting it mildly. We retired to a nearby bar to consider our options. The barmaid suggested we drink shots of tequila and that if we had ten each then we would get one free. A complete no brainer (which described our later state, as it happens). We were quickly warming to Berlin.

Because EMI were paying, we were staying in the glamorous Kempinski, one of the best hotels in Berlin. Still, it must have been difficult to enjoy the luxurious surroundings when you've spent the night clinging to the bathroom floor. That said, Ian (stoic, reliable Ian) made the best of those smooth, cold tiles. We both returned to the UK the next day blinking like men who've never experienced sunlight before, but still decided that we should record the album in Berlin. Besides, we didn't have much choice because our recording budget was on a tight rein and Hansa was about half the daily rate of studios in London.

We returned to Berlin with the rest of the guys a few weeks later and checked into the Hervis Hotel. This was nothing like the Kempinski. Not even the bathroom floor. It was a short walk from the studio along the Berlin Wall in an area known as Kreuzberg near Checkpoint Charlie. Run down and literally cut in half by the wall it wasn't the most prestigious place to stay in Berlin, but it was suffused in modern history and our home for the next few months.

Berlin, before the Wall fell, was a microcosm of anarchy and unrestricted freedom, something we embraced with reckless abandon. We would work every day from around noon until about 7pm and then break for dinner, which usually meant going out to a restaurant and eating and drinking for a few hours. We would then return to the studio and, depending on our alcoholic equilibrium, do some useful work or fool around recording music that was destined to be erased the next day.

We'd then venture out again until the early hours, bouncing from one club or bar to the next. There was plenty of drinking but no drugs as far as I knew, although I was to learn years later that Fish was becoming ever more adept at finding drugs and the people who could supply them.

After a few weeks of recording, we were starting to worry that the music didn't quite sparkle in the way we had hoped. The home-made speakers weren't exactly flattering our songs and Chris didn't seem bothered by it. We had an emergency band meeting and considered pulling the plug on the whole album, firing Chris, flying home and starting all over again with a new producer. We phoned Stanley-Clarke and told him our plans; he was on the next flight out to Berlin before the phone had settled back in its cradle. We decided to come clean with Chris and tell him our concerns.

He took it surprisingly well and with a smiling demeanour explained that he liked to record everything without any effects or 'fairy dust', as it's known. The so-called bells and whistles would be applied in the mix. He took us upstairs to the mixing suite (which had a decent set of speakers) and did a quick mix of some of the album. We heaved a huge sigh of relief. It sounded great. We got back to work, confident that Chris was the right choice.

When a breathless Stanley-Clarke arrived, he wanted to hear what we had been working on. We took him out to dinner and got him pissed before playing him anything. Now it was his turn to fall asleep. We weren't any more forgiving than he was when Steve crashed out on his couch. When the album playback ended, he asked if we had anything else because he wasn't hearing a hit single. We played him *Lady Nina*, the B-side we had written and recorded in an afternoon. *Lady Nina* was the name of an establishment Fish had frequented a few times and provided the inspiration for that song. Hugh loved it and wanted it to be a single. We refused to put it on the album, let alone release it as a single. Had he insisted I'm not sure there was much we could have done about it, but thankfully he dropped the idea before he had even got back to London.

Talking of Fish's Berlin haunts, one night he took me to a cocktail bar called Annabelle's. He was obsessed with one of the waitresses who worked there and so he returned night after night, filled with longing. The feeling wasn't reciprocated. She wasn't interested in him in the slightest, but Fish persevered. She didn't speak a word of English, and although Fish claimed to speak some German, it was schoolboy level stuff. He probably could have asked her where the museum was in her native tongue, but it was hardly the language of love.

Towards the end of the session, with *Kayleigh* confirmed as the first single, we planned to shoot the video for it in Berlin before we left. A model was booked to play the part of Kay and the boy, Robert Mead, whose image appears on the album cover, was flown in from the UK to be in the video too. On the morning of the shoot the model called in sick. Fish had invited Tamara Nowy, the girl from Annabelle's, down for the day to watch. An aside: Nowy is pronounced Novy, which made me wonder if they would double barrel their surnames when they got married a few years later and be called Novy-Dick. And much like Ahab and his hunt for the great white whale, this voyage also looked doomed and likely to sink without trace. Besides, Tamara hated Fish's last name and refused to use it because 'dick' translates as 'fat' in German.

That said, she was interested enough to show up and Fish didn't waste any time persuading her to be in the video in place of the sick model. Luckily there wasn't any acting involved, just mooning about and looking pretty, which she managed without too much difficulty, although if she had been asked to emote or look happy, I think she might have fled the set.

A month after we returned to the UK *Kayleigh* was released and charted at a reasonable number 16. We had a few dates to play in Spain and Portugal, so after appearing on *Top Of The Pops* and popular TV magazine programme *Wogan*, we set off on tour. When we arrived back in the UK, Marillion was a household name. We were number two in the singles chart and number one in the album chart.

Wogan was the appearance that put us in front of millions of people who would go out and buy *Kayleigh*. It transpired that they would not only buy the single, but would also name their unborn girls after the song and even come and see a progressive rock band play when they didn't even know they liked progressive rock.

That summer we got used to miming *Kayleigh* in TV studios all over Europe, sometimes doing two or three different pre-recorded shows in a day. One time in Italy, miming on some very shoddy equipment, Ian stabbed his drumsticks through the skin of the snare in disgust as he got up to leave the set. A few hours later at the next TV station, we arrived to find the same equipment. Ian's sticks were as he left them, poking through the broken skin of the snare drum. Another time, to relieve the boredom of miming, Pete and I swapped instruments.

We were off the launch pad and reaching escape velocity, and come September we were planning to play in excess of 50 sold out shows all over Europe, starting with my home city of Dublin. What could be better?

We arrived in Dublin and Fish was in a party mood. We were there for three days of production rehearsals before the first gig, and Fish was having so much fun he somehow forgot to sleep. By the time the first show came around his body was having none of it. His throat or more specifically his vocal cords decided enough was enough and promptly shut down. We struggled (as he croaked) through two more shows, a second night in Dublin and one in Belfast, but the game was up. The medical advice was that Fish needed to rest his voice, and if he didn't follow the advice to the letter, he was in danger of doing more damage, and permanent damage at that.

I threw my clothes into my suitcase and let my eyes linger on Belfast's cityscape below. We cancelled the entire sold out UK tour, trudged out to the airport and disappeared into the sky and towards home.

CHAPTER 10

Too Big To Fail

We came blinking into the sunlight of success like new-borns. Imagine being that person who nips into their local newsagents for something and on the off chance picks up a scratch card and, in that moment, changes their life forever. It could be you... And it was. Not the rewards, not the riches, not the parade of press and the giant cheque. This wasn't about the money; this was something much bigger. In that brief, glimmering moment, we had won at life's lottery. Scratched at the silver foil and the numbers had aligned. In the parade of a million young, hopeful musicians, we had been the ones to make it.

We had done what every band dreams of; from the day they begin to scrape around in a rehearsal room and feel the spark of writing their first song until, almost certainly, they finally call it a day. Real life gets in the way: the realisation that they're spending too much time and money pursuing a fantasy. Maybe their lives have moved on from the free and easy days of being a bunch of mates without jobs or responsibilities, playing the music they love, a carefree band of brothers. Maybe girlfriends and parents are pestering them to get a proper job.

Or, perhaps even more cruelly, they were one in a thousand, a band who landed a major recording contract only to suffer disappointment after disappointment as their single sales dwindled, their audience, like Spinal Tap's, had become more selective, and they were back playing the same small gigs they played on the way up, yet now they were going down. Dreams die, though who wants to wake up to that?

Think about it: we were playing music that people, at their kindest, were describing as unfashionable and scaling the charts with a concept album, and this was all happening in the mid-1980s.

We were high on life (and the odd pharmaceutical) as we set off to Europe in October 1985 to pick up the rest of the tour. We were also able to reschedule the cancelled UK dates and move them to January '86, even moving some of the shows into larger venues as we went. We were up to seven sold out shows at Hammersmith Odeon by then. That adds up to a whole week of sold out shows in one venue and still makes my head spin.

So, naively, we had worked out a simple equation for success: you simply wipe out on the wave you're riding and then another, more helpful, bigger wave comes along to raise you up again. This kind of thinking, if it can even be described as thinking, was a summation of our collective thoughts as we spiralled ever higher. What's the phrase, we were too big to fail? And with that in mind, and I'm sure this will come as no surprise to you, we had learned absolutely nothing from the episode in Dublin and the subsequent cancelled shows. It's said that someone who won't learn from their mistakes is doomed to repeat them. We should have had that legend printed on T-shirts and worn them every day.

As soon as we were back on the road it was party time again. Travelling in a tour bus of our own meant we could sleep in comfort, or, as was usually the case, we stayed in hotels unless the journey to the next show was especially long. One time we stopped in a motorway services and a young lady approached our table to ask for an autograph. We each signed the piece of paper in turn and passed it around. Pete signed last and offered it back to the girl. "Can you write Iron Maiden at the top?" she asked. Pete, with a shrug of his shoulders, did as he was asked. After she left, we fell about laughing.

Notwithstanding cases of being mistaken for the men who brought you *Run To The Hills*, we were rarely stopped for autographs except when we were together in a city we were playing that night. Fish, being taller than most bungalows, was hard to miss, plus he was the singer, which usually helped single him out. After the success of *Kayleigh*, the chances of being asked if I was Mark Kelly in the street increased significantly, but on a sliding scale we were some way off Beatlemania.

Germany was especially good for us and the gigs were getting bigger, including the 7,500 capacity Philipshalle in Düsseldorf. Not content with selling it out, our German promoter, Peter Rieger, oversold it and then to cram all the additional people in turned the house lights down early so that the fans would all surge forward making room at the back to let even more people in. Idiotic as well as dangerous and almost certainly illegal. It was distressing to stand up at my keyboards and see the pained expressions on the faces of the people crushed against the barriers at the front begging the security guards to haul them out to safety.

John Arnison was complicit in this kind of cash grab and it caused some friction between him and the band. Not troubled too much by his conscience, if at all, he had a tendency to put profit above all else. He even tried to persuade us to play Sun City at a time when artists like Little Steven and Bruce Springsteen were calling out the hypocrisy of playing that gig in the Artists United Against Apartheid song *Sun City*. Not that it had reached John's ears, but he argued that Queen and Status Quo had both played there and the money would be worth any critical brickbats we might receive. We could have used the cash, but apartheid was still in full effect, so we refused.

But back to Rieger. When he wasn't stuffing poor souls into oversold venues, he was more rock 'n' roll than most of the bands he promoted, enjoying the fruits of the rock star lifestyle. It won't surprise you to hear that he got on with Fish and John like a house on fire. Also, unsurprisingly, he burnt out too soon, and died aged 63 in 2017.

Germany turned out to be the gift that kept on giving. Around this time we also acquired a new travelling companion, the happy-go-lucky Tamara Nowy. After years of being told women weren't welcome on the road, Fish was now pleading that we make an exception for his new girlfriend, Tammy. He claimed that she needed rescuing from a life of depravity in Berlin. It seems she had fallen in with a bad crowd, some of whom had very dubious habits. We were sympathetic but there were double standards at play here and Fish knew it. You can imagine the good natured ribbing I got at home when I dropped that particular bombshell with Susie…

On tour excesses aside, the success of *Misplaced Childhood* didn't bring the trappings of fame one would usually associate with rock stars. Our lives carried on at relatively the same pace: living the Thatcherite dream of owning a small house with a big mortgage in Aylesbury.

Around this time John invited us all to his new house in Fleet, Hampshire for a dinner party.

Self-awareness wasn't John's strong suit (I'm not sure what was), but the glaring disparity between our income and his was writ large in bricks and mortar as we pulled up to his home. Palatial might be overselling it a bit, but you could have wedged my living room into his kitchen and still had space for a dining table. We gently teased him about it, and, clearly uncomfortable, John tried to explain it away by claiming that he bought it with the money he mostly earned before managing us. I'm not across John Cooper Clarke's earnings, and no disrespect intended, but I'm not sure he did seven nights at Hammersmith Odeon even when he was clean and at the height of his powers.

Our money was going somewhere and I'm guessing at least some of it was in John's new gazebo.

By now, I'm sure you're wondering what happened to the sixth share I told you about. Not being complete idiots, we pressed John to agree to take his 17% of touring income from the net rather than the gross. He went some way towards this by agreeing that he would take his commission after PA (sound system), lighting hire and trucking costs were covered. This sounded reasonable to us, but he had easily outmanoeuvred us because back then we didn't know that the biggest expense on tour by far is hotels and crew wages, a cost we would bear in its entirety.

It's a story as old as time, or at least Black Sabbath when they started to make it, but we started to get an inkling that whenever we went on tour John made money, sometimes lots of money, while we often did little better than break even. Exactly how much he made was kept from us and we were kept too busy to ask.

The sales of *Misplaced*, approximately 1.5 million units in the first year, were enough to recoup our losses from the previous albums and tours. But don't forget, touring the USA was expensive and the £50-100k shortfall per tour went on our balance sheet.

Kayleigh was one of the best selling singles of 1985 in the UK, even though it didn't reach number one. It was held at the number two spot for a few weeks by Gerry and the Pacemakers who released a charity single in aid of the Bradford City football club fire disaster which killed 56 spectators. It would be churlish to feel any resentment about that. *Kayleigh* was a few thousand sales short of half a million sales; not easy in 1985 when singles sales were waning compared to their heyday in the '60s and '70s.

Our royalty rate had increased slightly to 11% (*Fugazi*, as you might recall, was an overcall album, so that was at the same 10% rate as *Script*), so it was going to take millions more sales before we would start to earn even decent royalties. According to John, Fish wanted more money, so instead of pushing EMI to pay us a better royalty rate now that we were finally in the black, John opted to ask for a bigger advance for the next album.

I won't lie, we were all happy to get a bigger advance and the trickle down effect of another wage rise, but it was incredibly short-sighted because we would have to repay the advance at the low royalty rate we were still on and we had to commit to even more albums, which extended the deal even further.

I'm surmising here, but it's possible that John was wondering if Fish would decide it was time to show him the door soon. In which case it made sense for John to opt for the cash up front because he might not be around to collect his share of the royalties. I was blissfully unaware of any of this at the time because for one thing, I wasn't wearing a T-shirt that told me that we were doomed to repeat our mistakes and we were having the time of our lives on tour thinking it would last forever. None are so blind as those that won't see, and we were myopic at best.

Back home things had settled down into something of a rhythm and we had another baby on the way. Susie had grown used to being a rock 'n' roll widow. We were eyeing a bigger home because we were outgrowing our small two up, two down in Aylesbury and my credit rating was on firmer ground. Which is to say that I finally had a credit rating.

Apart from playing more and bigger venues in Germany, France and the Netherlands, we were moving into southern Europe and venues in Spain, Portugal and Italy for the first time. In December we also debuted in Japan. This was a window onto a new world. The gigs were small and full of what can only be described as businessmen in suits and ties. They had come straight from the office to watch us play at 7pm. The atmosphere was reserved, like a classical concert where you could hear a pin drop when we weren't playing. They would wait a respectful second or two (to make sure we really had finished, which was fair given the litany of false endings in our songs) before politely clapping. It was endearing, but we felt like were being scrutinised, which made for less bum notes or offbeats.

Japan was a strictly no drugs society, so for the first time in months there was no "class A" culture surrounding the band. That said, it didn't stop the crew letting off a bunch of fire extinguishers in the hotel. For once, we weren't involved. The hotel manager lined everyone up, band and crew, in the lobby and our Japanese promoter was there too, ashen faced. It had been explained to us beforehand that his honour was at stake as we were his guests in Japan. In order to preserve said honour, it was imperative that whoever was responsible for letting off the fire extinguishers owned up. After a tense silence, Privet and a few other crew members stepped forward. There were no consequences as far as I could tell. Honour was restored.

The crew were no better at keeping out of trouble beyond the confines of the hotel. Sporting new satin tour jackets and being loud and boisterous at the bar of the Lexington Queen in Tokyo, Smick and Robbo (our guitar tech) attracted the attention of a belligerent Brit spoiling for a fight.

Robbo took a big bite of his glass and started chewing. Through broken glass he enquired of his new acquaintance: "Do you think you're hard?" The guy made a gulping sound like Scooby Doo when he spots a ghost, before assuring Robbo that he really didn't want any trouble.

We arrived back home on 8th December and my son Kai was born the following day. I was present at the birth but didn't get to spend much time at home because the next day, thanks to Marillion's relentless schedule, we were back at the Marquee for a live broadcast on the BBC's *Old Grey Whistle Test*. This was followed by another seven gigs around the UK, including our biggest indoor show to date at the NEC in Birmingham, before stopping for a much needed break for Christmas.

In January 1986 we hit the ground running with the cancelled UK dates from the previous September. The final night of our run of seven Hammersmith shows was played in aid of Pete Townshend's Double 'O' charity. We donated £17,000 to help drug addicts and alcoholics. Which is only fair, as I'm sure a few of them were in our entourage.

John Otway and Robin Boult (Pete's old school friend guitarist) opened the night. Peter Hammill played a short set too. Then, following the usual charity gig format, we invited various guests to play with us on stage. Mike Oldfield, his keyboard player, Mickey Simmonds, and singer Roger Chapman performed *Shadow On The Wall* with us.

Steve Hackett also joined us to play a version of Genesis's *I Know What I Like (In Your Wardrobe)*. My memory of the chords was sketchy at best and I wanted to make sure I didn't embarrass myself in front of one of my heroes, so I asked Steve how it went. He said he didn't really know. "But you wrote it", I persisted. He raised a laconic eyebrow, "Yes, but I only know what *I* play and I'm not really a guitarist anyway; I'm more of a harmonica player." Which, in truth, was his first instrument. If he'd stuck at it, I'm sure Hackett could have given Larry Adler a run for his money.

Luckily, Mickey had more of an idea about the keyboard parts and we ended up playing it together, back to back. Following the gig, Mickey would strike up a friendship and later a working relationship with Fish. It was the blue touch paper being lit, inspiring the thought in Fish that maybe he didn't need Marillion after all. That said, caught in the moment, sharing my riser and keyboards with Mickey was fun.

After a few weeks' break we flew back to New York in style. John had booked the entire upper deck of a Virgin 747 just for us. We had our own waitress and lounge. Marillion was playing on the TV. We felt like true rock stars. Meanwhile in cattle class our crew were causing havoc. Privet had fallen asleep reading a newspaper and another crew member, clearly high on life, had thought it would be fun to set the newspaper alight. Luckily the fire was extinguished before it really got going. That's the kind of thing that can get you arrested once you land at the other end or a fiery death somewhere over the Atlantic.

Flame free, we arrived at JFK, though not without casualties. It was clear that John was in a sorry state having had more than his fair share of the free bar. He was barely able to stand and made his way to our helicopter like a man who had just been shot. There was no way we could be described as remotely close to sober, but even we were embarrassed. This was the man who was meant to be in charge of our careers.

John was acting less and less like a manager and more like an out-of-control rock star. Even Fish was becoming impatient with him, which was ironic considering his alcohol intake even outpaced Arnison's. Though to his credit, Fish *was* a rock star and he never appeared drunk. Ever.

We had been invited to open for Rush again, this time by the band themselves. What were they thinking after their fans had flashed us in New York?! We were ready to say no thanks, but a message came through that the band really liked us and thought we would do well with their audience, especially outside New York City, which is notoriously hard on support acts.

So here we were again touring the USA. This time we had a much better time of it, playing a mix of support shows with Rush and sometimes headlining shows to our own much smaller but dedicated audience. There were no peaches being thrown in our general direction on these dates.

Things hadn't really happened with *Kayleigh* and *Misplaced Childhood* in the USA the way they had all over Europe. The album had only reached number 47 in the *Billboard Hot 100* and *Kayleigh* fared even worse in the singles chart. We had a decent number of radio stations around the country playing *Kayleigh* and it should have grown exponentially when we were touring with Rush, but things came to an abrupt end early in the tour when Capitol Records promotion man Walter Lee was secretly filmed by NBC News walking with mobster Joe Isgro on their way to a Hollywood restaurant.

This was part of an investigation NBC were conducting into payola (paying for radio play). The mob had become big players in the radio plugging business and the major labels were willing participants. They paid the mob for 'promotion' and the mobsters made sure you got played on the radio by bribing the radio DJs and station owners with whatever it took – drugs, money, hookers and even cars. Conversely, if you didn't pay, the mob would make sure you didn't get played.

The major labels didn't mind this arrangement too much at first because it kept the smaller independent labels out of the game. But they had created a monster and the cost of paying the mafia for radio play soon spiralled out of control. Even though all the majors were involved, it was Capitol that were caught and, to avoid looking guilty by association, radio stations quickly dropped any Capitol artists from their playlist, which, of course, included Marillion.

Regardless of radio play, we were enjoying touring with Rush. From the first show they made us feel welcome by leaving a chilled bottle of champagne and a note welcoming us to the tour in our dressing room.

I enjoyed watching their show every night and would sometimes sit down backstage for a pre-gig dinner with Alex Lifeson and occasionally Geddy Lee. Drummer Neil Peart was a much more private person. Neil travelled alone outside of the band, and I rarely saw him off stage. Both Fish and I were becoming follicly challenged and from the tell-tale plug marks along his hairline it was obvious that Alex had been the recipient of a hair transplant. Fish wasted no time in asking him about it over dinner one evening. I squirmed in my seat, but Alex seemed happy to talk about it.

Emboldened by Alex's openness and off the shelf thatch of blonde hair, when I got back to the UK in May I started to look into what I might do about my thinning barnet. With some encouragement from Susie, I ended up in the Svenson Hair Centre in Wigmore Street (Wigmore by name, Wigmore by... ah, you get it) in London. After being subjected to more than an hour of the hard sell I signed a cheque for over a grand and was soon to be the (not so) proud owner of a new head of real hair. Admittedly somebody else's hair, but still.

By the time I got back to the car, the salesman's spiel had worn off and I came to my senses. I had just made a down payment on a wig (yes, the thousand pounds plus didn't even cover the full rug)! I hurried back to Wigmore Street and demanded my cheque back. They reluctantly returned it to me and I tore it in half. I shrugged and said goodbye to my hair forever.

In summer 1986 we played several big open air shows second on the bill to Queen. Below us were Level 42 and Gary Moore. These were some of the most enjoyable gigs we had played so far. Riding high on the success of *Misplaced* we felt like we had earned our place up there on the same stage as these giants of rock. The audiences were totally on our side too, although we never went down as well as Queen. I fondly remember a dinner with Queen in Paris the day before the June 14th show. Like a bunch of over eager schoolboys, we arrived at the restaurant before anybody else. The place was completely empty apart from us as Queen had booked the entire place.

Eventually, fashionably late, the doors burst open and in strode Freddie Mercury wearing a bright yellow military jacket with the entire Queen entourage following behind. It was very much like a monarch and his courtiers. Freddie came straight up to us, took a cigarette from my packet on the table and held it between his lips, waiting for me to light it. I didn't keep him waiting. He was like a force of nature. He looked around, chose a place to sit, patted the seat next to him and said, "Mr. Fish, you sit next to me." I remember one of the band muttering under his breath: "Could be your lucky night, Fish."

Brian May celebrated his 39th birthday on July 19th in Cologne and we invited him to join us on stage for a song. On hearing that Brian was planning to join us for a number his guitar tech snorted with derision, never going happen he grinned. As Brian made his way to the stage his tech suddenly panicked as he realised Brian was actually going to play and he quickly tuned up his iconic fireplace guitar and flipped the switch on his huge stack of Vox AC30s which were piled high behind me.

Brian hit the first big D major of *Market Square Heroes* and I saw white spots darting before my eyes and felt like my head was being squeezed in a vice. It was the loudest thing I think I've ever heard. Once my senses returned, I almost certainly enjoyed the rest of the song. It was certainly an honour to have Brian May play with us and Freddie returned the favour by inviting Fish on stage to sing *Tutti Frutti* with him during Queen's set.

Queen were the perfect gentlemen but knew how to have a good time when the occasion arose. We had a party after the gig at the hotel and by the early hours the few of us who were left standing (including Brian and Roger Taylor) were crowded around the piano on which Spike Edney (sometimes referred to as the fifth member of Queen) bashed out a bunch of pub singalongs including a version of Tommy Steele's *Little White Bull* complete with their own X-rated lyrics that they all seemed well-versed in.

We even headlined our own open air show in the UK at Milton Keynes Bowl in late June. This was the largest headline slot we had ever played, if you exclude our festival shows. It was a big financial risk because, unlike festivals where each band is paid an agreed fee by the promoter, Milton Keynes was our gig.

There was some jostling for position between Gary Moore and Ian Anderson. Moore wanted to be second on the bill, but we had agreed with Ian Anderson that would be

Jethro Tull's slot. Anderson took the pragmatic view and agreed to be third as long as his fee remained the same, so we paid him £50,000 to go on third while Gary Moore was only paid £35,000 to appear second.

In the end we sold enough tickets (around 30,000) to make a small profit, so we considered the event a success, enhanced by a great party afterwards. I knew it was a great party because there were still people in the hotel bar when I came down for breakfast the next morning.

At the end of the tour, Queen threw a party to end all parties at the currently defunct Roof Gardens in Kensington. It was pure rock 'n' roll Babylon: unlimited supplies of champagne, tables groaning with fine seafood, waitresses naked apart from a coat of paint applied to look like clothes. The guest list was wall to wall famous faces, and if there had been midgets with silver platters of coke balanced on their heads wandering around handing out straws, I wouldn't have been surprised. (There wasn't.)

The house band was called Dicky Hart and the Pacemakers, AKA Queen. Famous faces joined them on stage to jam along. This was only slightly marred by Sam Fox (who let her in?) pleading with Freddie to sing her song. To his credit, Freddie looked as though he had suddenly found something stuck to the bottom of his shoe. In case it had slipped your mind, Sam had scored a minor hit with something best described as a bit of old tat called *Touch Me*. Something that even Fish or infamous lothario Roger Taylor managed to resist.

In case you were wondering if all this success was going to our heads, we were brought firmly back to earth with a thump when we witnessed what can only be described as a mass brawl between members of the audience at St Helen's rugby ground on Merseyside in late July. We had unwisely agreed to play Soap Aid, a badly conceived follow up to Live Aid. Various soap stars took it in turns to embarrass themselves on stage until, as the headliners, we trooped on to play. During *Garden Party* a fight broke out which got so gallingly bad that Fish asked us to stop playing while he attempted to pour oil on troubled (not to mention soapy) waters.

On 1st August Steve married his sweetheart, Jo Salmon. Steve and Jo had been together for a few years, and we all wished them well as they went on honeymoon to the Caribbean for a few weeks.

Two days later we had a small gig to play to curry favour with Roland (the musical instrument manufacturer), so we asked Pete's old friend Robin Boult to stand in. Robin did a great job covering for Steve, but it cemented the thought in my mind that there's only one Steve Rothery.

Tammy was finally won over (some say worn down) by Fish's persistence and she made the move to Gerrard's Cross to live with Fish. Both Ian and Fish lived in this expensive commuter belt village in generously sized detached houses. Susie, Freya, Kai and I were now living in a large four bedroom house in Wendover around the corner from Susie's parents.

Friendships in a band are as important as musical chemistry if you want to survive in the long run. In the early days we always socialised together; the five of us would meet up for drinks or dinner even if we didn't have band business to discuss. When everyone has a partner, then they usually come along too. Susie and Fiona Trewavas became firm friends very early on, and Jo is the sort of person who is easy to get on with but was probably less of a party person than Susie and Fiona.

When Tammy arrived on the scene there was already some residual resentment after Fish insisted on her being on the road with the band. One night things turned ugly, like the monsters in *A Quiet Place* are ugly.

This put Fish and me on the back foot. Our friendship was already worn thin from the events of the last few years, but we had agreed, on the surface at least, that if Tammy and Susie fought like cats and dogs we wouldn't get involved. I'm not sure if we were lying to ourselves or each other, but the lines in the sand were drawn. We were both of the view that the other's partner was poison. In all honesty, it was hard to know who was telling the truth, but I knew my loyalty had to lie with Susie and experience had taught me that I couldn't fully trust Fish. Plus, I didn't know Tammy at all, but my instincts told me she was trouble.

And that's where the singer and keyboard player of Marillion were in September 1986; completely at odds as the band were trying to pull together and show a united front as we headed to Stanbridge Farm in Sussex to write our fourth and final album together.

CHAPTER 11

Going Under

Somehow, somewhere between our songwriting sessions in Barwell Court and Bray Studios and in the long days and even longer nights spent in the wood-panelled rooms of Hansa Ton Studios in Berlin, we had captured lightning in the bottle: that elusive marriage of art and commerce. Perseverance and inspiration had culminated in something quite magical for our band. It was a brilliant moment spent on the creative higher ground and now we were coming down again. The obvious question remained: could we ever reach those peaks again? Simply put, how do you follow that?

We had to start somewhere, so, earlier in 1986, the four of us (without Fish) had met up at Steve's house to work on some new songs. We wrote the music for *Hotel Hobbies*, *Warm Wet Circles* and parts of *That Time Of The Night*. I say we, but it was mainly Steve. Energised by the sessions with Chris Kimsey, the whole *Misplaced Childhood* writing and recording experience had helped bolster Steve's confidence and he was on a creative roll.

Like the proverbial dynamo, Steve had also written the music for *Sugar Mice* during a session at Bray Studios earlier in the year. The demo we recorded there was going to be hard to beat. I was feeling frustrated at my paucity of ideas. Artist Chuck Close said it best: amateurs look for inspiration; the rest of us just get up and go to work. The problem was that I was getting up to go to work and still finding nothing when I got there.

I have no idea why or where my musical ideas come from, so when they don't come, all I can do is helplessly wait for them to appear. It's not like you can throw back your head and implore the heavens to rain creativity down on you. I mean, we'd all do it if it were that easy. I can flex my creative muscle by sitting at the keyboard and playing, but I can't force the issue. The muse will come, but rarely when called upon. You can't mark a date with creativity in the calendar.

Yet, we persisted and tried writing at Nomis for a week or two in September. There were one or two bouts of creativity, and we came away from it with an early version of

Torch Song (another of Steve's ideas) worked out and the beginnings of *Just For The Record* (one of mine).

We even spent a week or two back at Barwell Court trying to rekindle the creativity and excitement of the *Misplaced* writing sessions, but, like first wives, it's never good to go back; nothing's the same the second time around. As if to cement that fact, Chris Kimsey came down to check on our progress and reported back to John Arnison that thus far we weren't delivering the goods. Cheers, Chris.

There's been much speculation over the years about the 'lost' *Clutching At Straws* sessions. The story, because that's what it is, goes that we wrote a whole concept piece that was rejected by the record company for sounding too much like *Misplaced Childhood*. Can you imagine EMI rejecting something that sounded like our biggest and most well-received album to date? Most people at record companies have so little imagination that repeating a previously successful formula is *exactly* what they want you to do.

What actually happened was we wrote and arranged *Hotel Hobbies*, *Warm Wet Circles*, *That Time Of The Night* and some other bits and pieces into a proposed side one for the album. After Kimsey's visit we didn't abandon it and start again, we just trimmed the excess fat.

Stanbridge Farm had recently been opened as a residential rehearsal and writing facility for bands wishing to get away from busy London just over 30 miles north as the crow flies. I'm not sure what we were trying to get away from as we already lived in rural Buckinghamshire. The hills and fields from our windows at home didn't look too dissimilar to the hills and fields we were now gazing out upon, though this vista was rented, but we planned to stay at Stanbridge from October until December 23rd. Still chasing the dream that you could make a date with creativity, we thought this would be enough time to finish the writing and rehearse for the upcoming Christmas shows.

Stanbridge consisted of a Tudor style house with a smaller cottage nearby and a large barn. There was enough space for the band and a few of the crew, who we paid to sit around for months on end just in case we needed someone to go to the shops. This casual and expensive idiocy was becoming more common with Marillion, primarily as John was controlling the purse strings and didn't really care how we spent our cash.

This is conjecture, but I think he figured out it was easier to just let us have what we wanted – like five Veruca Salts at the pick 'n' mix – and then go cap in hand to EMI for more cash, which they were willing to give us since *Misplaced Childhood* and the rest of our catalogue was still selling well. This put the chance to renegotiate our contract ever further out of reach, but you probably realised that, as you've almost certainly been paying more attention than we were at the time.

On a rare evening that was reminiscent of the early days, Fish and I watched a film together in the cottage, a comedy called *The Supergrass* by the same team that made the Comic Strip series. We drank a bottle of Jack Daniels, passing it back and forth until it was empty. We laughed and talked, occasionally pausing to watch the movie. I think Fish was slurring a bit by the end of the evening, but I couldn't be sure because at that point I could only see out of one eye.

Alcohol was a common denominator, consumed with dinner every night and then imbibed until bedtime. There was plenty of dope too, principally for the crew and Fish, but Ian indulged too from time to time when the boredom became too much. As far as I remember there wasn't any cocaine about, but in hindsight I suspect that there was, and I just didn't know about it.

Personally, I've never enjoyed the feeling of being stoned. When I used to indulge, I liked my drugs to make me feel like doing something rather than lay me out. During one of the late night drinking and jamming sessions, Steve started playing a rocky riff in the style of The Who. I joined in with some of my now trademark widdly-widdly Minimoog and the music for *Incommunicado* was born, although Fish didn't finish writing the lyric until many months later in a taxi on the way to Advision Studios, much to Steve's annoyance.

Apart from those rare flashes of inspiration, we spent a few months plonking away on keys and plucking at strings in a desultory fashion, punctuated by eating, drinking and playing pool until we were released from our self-imposed prison in time for Christmas, like a convict let out early for good behaviour.

We played five gigs starting in Aylesbury and finishing up on New Year's Eve 1986 at Barrowlands in Glasgow for the now traditional Marillion Hogmanay. We played *White Russian*, *Warm Wet Circles*, *That Time Of The Night* and *Incommunicado* every night.

1987 should have been a banner year for the band, and in some ways it lived up to that billing. We still had an album to record, but it was already written. We also had a tour booked that would last from the summer and take us through to the following spring, taking in some of biggest indoor arenas in Europe. The size of a tour is usually a reflection of the previous album's success, and the tickets were all sold before anyone had even heard a note of *Clutching At Straws*. We were finally going to make some real money this year too, though Her Majesty's Revenue & Customs would take most of it as the top rate of tax was still an eye watering 60%.

Come January we were ready to go into the studio again with Chris Kimsey. We didn't even consider working with a different producer after our previous success together, but the engineer was a young man called Nick Davis rather than our German friend Thomas Stieler. Nick was an excellent engineer and we got on very well with him, but things felt significantly different. We chose to work in London, at Westside Studios. Chris was not keen but went along with it. We had had enough of being away from home and logic dictated that we could drive back from west London to our families at the end of each day. We were wrong. The sessions often ran on well past midnight and driving home bleary eyed and through the night was bordering on madness.

Chris was the sort of producer who spread good vibes, adept at bringing out the best in us and also capturing that performance on tape. He was untouchable when we recorded *Misplaced Childhood*, but *Clutching At Straws* was a less happy time for him. Musically, Steve had written some of our best music to date but lyrically Chris wasn't feeling it at all. He told John Arnison that he thought Fish had 'lost it'.

You could see Chris's point; the whole album was about Fish's excessive drinking and drug taking and his feelings of isolation exacerbated by our success and his lifestyle choices. This was then compounded by the rest of the band closing ranks and shutting him out. It was dark territory we found ourselves in and its pervading gloom spread throughout the sessions, not least because Fish was wrestling with his demons and Chris, Pete and I were barely clinging to sobriety.

It might have said something about our psyche at the time, but Chris became transfixed by *Going Under*, a track earmarked as a B-side. Perhaps he identified with it or liked its honesty. Whatever the reason, he spent a disproportionate amount of time working away at it, coming back to it again and again, often late into the night.

One night in March, the snooker player Jimmy White turned up at the studio to watch the world heavyweight title fight between Mike Tyson and James 'Bonecrusher' Smith. I don't know who invited this legend of the baize, and I didn't get the chance to ask as he spent the whole fight sticking industrial quantities of coke up his nose. I say up his nose, but he was so frazzled that most of it went on the carpet, so by the final bell it looked like he had been doing the 'shake 'n' vac' and had yet to run the hoover around.

In an environment of diminishing returns, a particularly low point for me came when early one morning I arrived home from the studio. I was doing my best to undress quietly and get into bed when Susie woke up and seeing me there, half-dressed assumed that I was getting out of bed, not in. Embarrassed about how late I was getting home, I played along and put my clothes back on and went downstairs to face the day with no sleep.

I don't think I was a bad father; but could I have been a better dad? Absolutely. I wasn't ready for kids and there was too much happening with Marillion for me to think about what I was missing at home. With the hindsight of fathering three more children in my forties, I realise now that one of the greatest periods with your kids is watching them grow and develop in their first decade. That golden age when they're discovering things for the first time. It's magical seeing them learn to speak, read, draw, write and start to understand the world. Playing games with them, discovering nature and sports. Regretfully, and it is a real and profound regret, I missed most of that with Freya and Kai.

I was spending so much time away from home, as we all were, that from my perspective my relationship with Susie was beginning to wear and I felt that despite our children we lived in different worlds.

There was a table tennis table in the lobby of Westside, and we all enjoyed playing from time to time as a way to let off some steam during the recording sessions. I can't remember who my opponent was, but on this particular occasion I went for a ball with what I like to think of as real gusto, but was destined to never reach, and with a clear and quite distinct popping sound, my right shoulder dislocated once again.

A doctor was called, who tried to put it back in place using a technique I suspect he learned from shoeing horses. I say doctor, he could have just been passing and had borrowed someone's white coat. He had me lay on the floor and put his foot in my armpit while pulling on my arm. I could almost see him tapping his teeth with a pencil, like a mechanic looking under the bonnet of your car and not liking what he sees. He suggested that I needed to relax so that the shoulder would slide back into place. I countered through gritted teeth that maybe he should fucking relax and perhaps hospital would be the better option.

I waited so long in the hospital corridor sat on a gurney that I did start to relax, and my shoulder went back in by itself before a doctor was available to see me. When I eventually saw the doctor, possibly because of his tardiness, he quickly offered me an operation to make the shoulder muscles shorter. I might be a layman, but it seemed pretty drastic to me, so I politely declined and decided to take up strength training instead, as that would have the same effect without leaving a Frankenstein like scar looping from the top of my shoulder to my armpit.

Back in the studio, recording for *Clutching* went pretty much to plan. Despite the charged atmosphere at Westside, we were reasonably happy with the results. Chris chose to mix at Advision Studios in the West End (not far from the Marquee). In a few short years we had learned a lot about working in the studio and were less willing to automatically accept decisions made by the producer, even one we liked and respected. Which is what happened when Chris decided he wanted David Jacob to mix the album.

We all liked working with Nick and had assumed he would be coming to Advision with us. Chris had been impressed with Jacob's work with the Pet Shop Boys, but we found his mixes sterile and uninspiring. He was also one of those people who relied more on maths and meters than his ears, more mechanical than emotional. Despite our protests, Chris got his way, but I think he was having second thoughts about Jacob too by the end of the mix session.

I celebrated my 26th birthday during the mix, but we carried on working. At one point a young lady in a long coat came into the control room, Chris introduced her as his manager's wife. Without me really noticing, everyone left the room until I was alone with her. I was more than a little surprised when she removed her coat to reveal that she was completely naked. Of course, the whole band and Chris were outside, faces pressed up against the glass like a troupe of Garfield car window dolls, to gauge my reaction. I found the whole thing rather awkward which I suppose was the point, right?

After the stripper left everyone called it a night with the mixing and we started partying. Which is when something switched. I'm still not sure how or why, but coke and booze certainly played their part. Steve and Fish had a blazing row, which ended with Fish pinning Steve up against the studio wall and threatening to punch his lights out, while accusing him of saving his best ideas for his solo album. Not only ugly and unnecessary, but manifestly untrue as Steve had written most of the music for our latest album. I'm not sure what Fish thought Steve might be hiding. In truth, I think Fish was angry that Steve was talking to EMI about a solo album, and he expected that he would be the first member of Marillion to make a solo album, not Steve. The cracks in the band's veneer were getting harder to ignore.

Understandably, Steve was done with Fish and by association with the band too. He decided to quit and was only talked out of it some days later by the ever pragmatic Ian.

But the die was cast; things between Fish and Steve were never quite the same again after that.

That said, the night's drama wasn't quite over. Pete, drinking more and thinking less, chose to drive himself home and was involved in an accident on the way. He crashed his car into a railway bridge that crosses the A413 near Amersham. The gods must have been smiling down on him that night, as the car was written off but by some miracle Pete walked away unharmed from the accident and there was nobody else involved.

Meanwhile, John booked us to play some warm-up dates in Poland. In 1987 nobody toured Poland because it was a communist country locked away behind the Iron Curtain. John's logic was that it would be a good a place as any to smooth out the kinks in our production before we started the tour proper in Italy.

We were treated like kings. It was if the Beatles had reunited and decided to kick things off in Krakow. The fans went crazy everywhere we went. I'm not sure I liked it; there's something scary about your bus being surrounded by a mob, any mob, even the amiable kind. I was equally in fear of one of them getting squashed by our over eager bus driver, who seemed in a hurry to get home for his dinner. The tour was promoted by the Polish government who paid us in hard currency, US$100,000 for the six shows. They also gave each of us a daily spending allowance in zlotys. (According to a schoolteacher I spoke to it was equivalent to a month's wages for him.)

We were told that we couldn't take zlotys out of the country, so we had to spend them before we left. That was hard because there was very little to buy in the shops. We all came home with chess sets and miniature leather-bound wooden chests. The rest of the considerable pile of banknotes we amassed during our stay were collected together by Fish at the airport and handed to some unsuspecting old woman pushing a broom around. She took them almost without stopping, before stuffing them inside her apron and resumed cleaning as if it was the third time this had happened to her that day.

We started using the *La Gazza Ladra Overture* by Rossini as a show opener on the *Misplaced Childhood* tour after Fish heard it accompany the 'ultra-violence' rape scene in *A Clockwork Orange*. It segued beautifully into the opening piano part of *Sláinte Mhaith* or *Slange*, as we called it.

Meanwhile back in the UK, *Incommunicado* was stuck at number six in the singles chart for the second week running. We decided to go with *Incommunicado* because it was a rock song. We were worried that having had two hits with *Kayleigh* and *Lavender* meant that we were in danger of alienating our hardcore fans. *Incommunicado* was intended to put that right. In hindsight, from the point of view of sales and commercial success, it was probably a mistake.

Following the success of *Misplaced* and *Kayleigh* there was a strong appetite for the next Marillion album and single at radio stations. Radio 1 got properly behind it and put *Incommunicado* into its playlist the week it charted at number six, which should have resulted in it climbing up the charts, but it didn't budge. The song wasn't right for the Radio 1 audience, who were more used to lighter pop. Radio 1 lost interest and moved on to the next thing and we started the slow slide downwards.

Warm Wet Circles was and is a much better song, I love the music and lyrics, especially the lush chords that Steve wrote for the guitar solo section. I think its radio play may have been hampered somewhat by the title, which Fish refused to contemplate changing despite requests for something more radio friendly.

The album was certified gold the week of release with sales well in excess of *Misplaced Childhood*'s first week sales, but we were held off the number one spot by an even bigger seller, the commercial behemoth that was Whitney Houston.

Fish managed to outlive the doomsayer doctor who predicted that he wouldn't reach 30 if he maintained his lifestyle, but his voice was barely hanging on.

Even though he was only 29, Fish's voice was shot. The previous three years of almost constant touring together with serious cocaine and alcohol abuse and 60 cigarettes a day had taken their toll. Instead of doing something to prevent further damage, Fish's solution was that we take a backing singer on the road to hit the high notes he could only now dream of.

Enter Cori Josias. Having a person who wasn't in the band sharing the stage with us was a bit of a departure. Cori was a good singer, but her vocals only worked when they echoed the female voices on the album versions, in a song, say, like *The Last Straw*. (Session singer Tessa Niles sang it on the album.) Covering for Fish's lack of range didn't really work in practice.

I liked Cori and I have her to thank for getting me started on something that continues to benefit my health today: running. When we got to Boulder in Colorado in September, she invited me to go running with her. It nearly killed me, but, for some reason, I wanted to do it again. Since then, I have always run from time to time, but I only started running regularly in 2009 when training for my first marathon.

The second gig in Italy on 1st July was a washout, literally. There was a huge thunderstorm, and the stage and lighting rig had no cover to speak of – very Italian. Rain soaked all the equipment and lightning struck the rigging a few times. We decided to cancel as onstage electrocution seemed like the only other option. The audience was having none of it and we were rushed out of the venue in the back of a truck to avoid getting lynched by a bunch of agitated Italians.

It was unsettling and we were scared for our own safety, even though we now had our own security. Yes, security guards. Like Mick Jagger and the Queen have security guards. This was at Fish's insistence and another example of John's indifference or weakness when it came to standing up to the general profligacy that was evident everywhere in Marilloland. We hired two German security guards who followed us around everywhere. In practice, this meant that everything we did took longer than before.

They even ran in front of our vehicle as we left the venues in the way only pumped-up bodybuilders can. Their legs unable to easily pass each other due to their bulk. They were trained killers, and life might be cheap, but they weren't. They followed Fish around to every bar and nightclub he visited, so they were kept busy. By this stage the rest of the band tended to avoid socialising with Fish, so it was usually just him and his pumped-up friends out on the town together. I think he liked their company more than the protection they afforded him, as he was more than capable of holding his own.

The whole security guard thing didn't sit comfortably with the rest of us, and not just because of the cost. We all felt like the fame had gone to Fish's head or, as Ian would put it, he was becoming 'big time'.

Another extravagance that we had managed without until that tour was somebody to look after our wardrobe. For anyone who's watched us over the years I think it's fair to say that most of what we wore on stage was unlikely to trouble a catwalk anywhere. We might have dabbled with sackcloth, and who could forget my nylon jumpsuit that helped me lose half my bodily fluid each night? But we were hardly fashionistas pushing the aesthetic envelope at every nuanced turn.

Though Fish thought he might be. He had some expensive items made in hand-painted silk that quickly ended up looking like rags. One particularly striking item was a silk kimono (nothing pseudo about it) he acquired when we went to Japan. By the 1987 tour Fish had four different costume changes that our new wardrobe girl, 'Toots', looked after. In case you're wondering, and you probably were, her nickname had nothing to do with drugs, she was big on trains as a toddler, true story. But back to Fish and his many dazzling personas. There was the Bay City Rollers tartan suit, the shiny black suit with flames licking at the sleeve and trouser leg. And who could forget the furry pyjamas and the harlequin suit? Believe me, we tried.

It wasn't only Fish who was finding new and inventive ways to squander cash. We were all spending at a rate of knots and John didn't have the incentive to talk us out of it as his commission was ring fenced regardless. Had we been as big as, say, Queen it wouldn't have mattered. For example, they had their own party coordinator on the road with them.

As well as having our own man-tanks, the security around our shows had tightened up considerably since our previous tours, as I found out the hard way one evening in Germany. I went back to the hotel for a nap after the soundcheck and woke up later than planned. On rushing back to the gig, I realised I had left my backstage pass in my room. I spent nearly 30 minutes pleading with a stony faced security guard behind a locked metal gate to let me in. Eventually, becoming desperate, I spotted one of our crew across the yard and shouted for him to get Paul Lewis, who was becoming anxious as to my whereabouts. I had just enough time to get in and get ready for the show.

We finished that round of shows at a beautiful open air spot on the Rhine called Loreley, before heading back to North Berwick in Scotland for Fish's wedding to Tamara on 25th July.

Fish and Tammy agreed to forgo their honeymoon and flew to LA instead so that Fish could begin promotion for the US leg of our tour.

They stayed at Rod Smallwood's LA home. This was a beautiful house in Hollywood, once the home of Peter Sellers and James Cagney before him.

John had asked Rod to help manage us in the USA as he felt out of his depth and seemed to be getting nowhere in his dealing with Capitol Records. There is some bullshitting in the UK music industry, but the level of BS in the USA was another whole world of deceit and skulduggery. Iron Maiden were a real force in the US, so at least Rod could bring that to the table.

Unfortunately for Fish, Rod and John had somehow failed to tell him that the promotion which the newlyweds had given up their honeymoon for was off. The trip to the USA had been a complete waste of time. Fish, understandably for once, was furious with John and made up his mind that John would have to go. John blamed his snafu on the imminent birth of his new baby, but that wasn't the whole story. John was drinking and snorting coke like Scarface; he was matching Fish's intake ounce for ounce. When we saw John, he was almost invariably off his face.

A few weeks after Fish returned to the UK, we were all back on a plane together on our way to LA for the US tour. John was at home awaiting the imminent arrival of his first child. During the flight, Fish proposed that we should fire John and have our production manager, Andy Field, take over. He had gone as far as to alert the solicitors and accountants in the UK that there was going to be a change of leadership.

While we all knew that John was fast turning into a liability, we were deeply worried about the idea of effectively handing control of everything over to Fish. Andy was a good crew boss and nice chap, but he wasn't up to the job of managing Marillion. Besides he had drunk the Fish Kool-Aid and would do exactly as Fish dictated. None of us wanted to have to deal with Fish on a day-to-day basis. The bond between Fish and the rest of the band had completely eroded and John, as ineffectual as he was, was the only thing that stood between us and our singer.

We had all experienced Fish's attempts at manipulation. Telling each of us what he thought we wanted to hear, after which we would compare notes, so we had a full picture of what was really going on. Fish had attempted to fire Paul a few months earlier; we had resisted him then and we did the same now regarding John.

Paranoia, mind games and intra band politicking were our watchwords as we set foot on US soil for the last time with Fish.

Fish wasn't the only one getting 'big time'. We had all insisted that we wanted to ship everything with us from Europe for the US tour. If anybody tried to tell us we were crazy, the staggering cost of it all and that most of it wouldn't fit in the venues we were booked to play, then we didn't listen. I suspect by this stage in the game that John had enough of his own problems to even notice a minor thing like tour logistics and our crew were just following orders. Which resulted in us arriving at The Coach House in San Juan Capistrano, California to commence the tour with not one but two articulated trucks full of gear. This was a 600 capacity club. The owner couldn't believe his eyes. Needless to say, most of it remained on said trucks for much of the tour.

Even though we were back to playing smaller venues, they were mostly sold out, and when we got to Canada, we played some bigger places including Le Colisée de Québec in Quebec City, which we had played a year earlier as openers for Rush. At least we were able to unload both trucks and use everything we were carrying that night.

We had gone up another level in the UK too. This time it was three nights at Wembley Arena to start the European tour and two nights at the NEC in Birmingham to finish it, both venues 10,000 capacity and sold out. There was also the 16,000 capacity Bercy in Paris, the largest indoor arena in Europe at the time. We were big, but we were miserable and enduring the least enjoyable tour of our careers.

There were some lighter moments in among the gloom. We met Prince Edward backstage at Wembley. We donated the takings (£36,000) from the third night to a muscular dystrophy charity and the youngest son of the Queen drew the short straw and was in attendance. I was with Iron Maiden's (that band again) drummer, Nicko McBrain, and his wife when I met Edward. We were briefed in advanced how to address the prince and told not to ask questions. Nicko obviously didn't get the memo because he addressed the Prince with a genial, "Alright, mate", and stopped just short of clapping him on the back. Edward was obviously miffed and replied by asking Nicko if he met his wife after he became famous (an obvious dig as she was very beautiful, and Nicko is very much not so). Nicko wasn't bothered in the slightest; he was clearly enjoying the banter.

The band resumed touring in Aberdeen in January 1988 after a short break for Christmas. Over the years we had an ongoing difference of opinion with John about what he should be doing when we were on the road. We wanted him with us so that he could keep us in the loop about what was going on. He argued that he didn't need to be there as it was an additional expense for us, and he would be more effective back in the office. This was probably true, but he always seemed to be around when things were going well or there was a party to be had. However, when we were having a tough time, he was nowhere to be seen.

The fact that he came to the Aberdeen show was probably a sign that he was feeling unsure about his position and wanted to show his face. After all, why else would he make the journey all the way north? Aberdeen was hardly a Marillion stronghold. Whatever his reason for being there, it probably didn't have the intended effect. During the soundcheck he sat on the high walkway that ran across the back of the stage and threw up all over it.

It seemed to me that both John and Fish needed to make some lifestyle changes, but only John would take steps to do something about it.

After only four gigs, Fish was in trouble again. His voice was struck down by a mysterious virus, or at least that's what we told our fans. We cancelled the next three shows and struggled on through the next few weeks with a further three shows cancelled in Italy, Germany and Austria.

We should have been on top of the world, but as we moved into the summer of 1988 it was clear that, instead of this being a new chapter in the band's life, we were quickly approaching our endgame.

CHAPTER 12

Marillion Require Vocalist

What feels like a gentle breeze at street level is a whole other proposition when you're this far from the ground. The ground was much on my mind, not least how far away it was, and what kind of damage it could do if I should happen to lose my footing on this slick ledge and plummet to the rain-washed paving stones below. The wind picked up, the heavy droplets of rain striking me in the face. A far away idea floated in the back of my mind. This, I thought, would be a funny old way to go out.

There's a short story by Stephen King called *The Ledge*, where our hero has to take a bet to circumnavigate the five inch ledge of a grand apartment building or be framed for a crime he didn't commit and ruined forever. I won't spoil it for you, but an errant pigeon plays a pivotal part and there are moments where your stomach flips forward as you feel our leading man might slip, lose his footing and be lost to the inky darkness and the streets far below. Thankfully, there was no pigeon here and no one was expecting me to creep around the building's high perimeter clinging to it like a lusty teen holding on to a partner for the last dance.

As my drunken equilibrium attempted to right itself, I realised that I was in all sorts of trouble. The view from here was something else, but so would the damage be to my frame and face should I tumble from my vantage point. I was perched on the window ledge of a hotel room on the ninth floor in Luxembourg looking down at the tops of the sodium lights illuminating the wet pavement far below. Like the character in the Stephen King story, I had no intention of jumping, but there was no two ways about it: I was stuck.

The window behind me was sealed shut. Inside the room, and an entire world away, were John Arnison and Dwayne Welch. Dwayne was John's new business partner, who had recently left EMI to join All Round Productions, John's management company. Dwayne, the son of Bruce Welch, bass player with The Shadows, was a confident, friendly and ambitious young urbanite, who John hoped would help to grow his management operation outside of Marillion. John had seen the writing on the wall and was planning for a future beyond our band.

Dwayne, a tumbler in his hand, looked up as my shivering frame came into focus: "Isn't that one of your artists out there on the ledge?"

John, as drunkenly hazy as me, bolted into life: "Shit! Yes. I'd better let him in."

Welcome to the world of Marillion circa 1988.

We had survived the biggest and most successful tour of our careers. John told us that we would all be getting a £20,000 bonus from the tour, which was very welcome by me as I seemed to be permanently in debt. Susie had hired a nanny to help with the kids while I was away, adding to our already overstretched domestic budget. The tour grossed over £2 million and so John's commission was considerably more than £20k. We never found out exactly how much more because he had become pretty adept at sidestepping our enquiries to see the tour accounts. We sometimes caught glimpses of how well John was doing because he often let things slip when he was drunk, which earned him the nickname 'Torn Pocket'. Such as the time when he boasted that he had paid off his mortgage and had a cool half million in the bank. Nevertheless, we had more pressing matters on our minds, namely John's deteriorating condition and Fish's general malaise and self-destructive bent.

John had hit rock bottom. He had even attempted to end it all, albeit half-heartedly. One night while drunk he jumped out of his bedroom window. He landed in the flower beds below and, falling like only a drunk person can (as if he had been skilfully deboned before exiting the building), he managed to escape injury. Unfortunately, he didn't have a front door key. So, muddy, wet and pathetic, he rang the doorbell. His wife, Ginny, on seeing this broken man standing there in the rain, just scolded him and told him to go inside and change his clothes. As one might a boy who had been playing football in his school uniform in the park.

This might have been the last straw. Ginny persuaded John to get help. He checked into a private clinic in London and stayed there for six weeks. We went to visit him and were dismayed and saddened by this incongruous, pale figure in a hospital gown. He might have lost his fire, but he still knew where to point the finger of blame when it came to the situation he now found himself in.

John insisted it was the stress of managing Marillion that was to blame for his drinking and drug taking. I'm not sure I buy that. I think some of those proclivities were very much in place before our paths crossed. However he justified his conduct, he did somehow manage to clean up his act and rehabilitate himself. He was like a new man when he finally left the clinic. Dry and drug free. Of course, he still had the stress of dealing with Marillion, but he managed to cling steadfastly to the wagon.

In one of his regular AA meetings, John described his previous life to a circle of attendees and the therapist said John should encourage Marillion to enter rehab. When John told us this, we all laughed (possibly too self-consciously), while Ian dryly quipped that he thought everyone was just having a good time.

While John was in rehab Fish and Tammy used the time off to go on postponed honeymoon in the Caribbean.

With an eye on the next album, we agreed that writing in residential studios was getting too expensive as we were taking longer and longer to get the work done and approaching the whole thing like we were living as extras in an episode of *Downton Abbey*. Pete offered the garage in his new house on the outskirts of Aylesbury as a potential rehearsal and writing space for the band. He was fairly isolated, so our noise (beautifully detailed prog rock with nuance and a lightness of touch, but you know what I mean) wouldn't disturb his new neighbours.

Around that time, I received a call from Midge Ure. He wanted to know if I was interested in being part of the Midge Ure All Stars. We were to be the backing back for a succession of singers over a 45 minute set. The occasion was Nelson Mandela's 70th birthday and it was being celebrated at Wembley Stadium on 11th June 1988. Also known as Free Nelson Mandela Concert, it was to be broadcast in 67 countries and watched by 600 million people. I didn't know that beforehand and I was still completely terrified, but how could I say no to such an offer?

The band consisted of Midge on guitar, me playing keyboards and Paul Carrack playing electric piano. Curt Smith from Tears for Fears pulled out of playing the bass as he was even more terrified than I was. Midge brought in Mick Karn from Japan as his replacement. Curt still agreed to sing *Everybody Wants To Rule The World*. We had two great drummers as well: Phil Collins and Mark Brzezicki from Big Country. In addition to Curt, the guest singers were The Bee Gees, Joan Armatrading, Paul Young (the hat-laying one, not the Sad Café, Mike and the Mechanics one), Bryan Adams, Tony Hadley and our very own Fish.

We had three days' rehearsal booked the week before and the plan was to bring in each of the singers in turn on the last day to go through their songs. At the rehearsals everyone was relaxed and enjoying themselves. Despite some pressure from Midge, Phil Collins refused to sing a song, saying he only wanted play drums and enjoy himself. Paul Carrack reluctantly agreed to sing his huge hit *How Long* from his days with the band Ace.

The only real difficulty came when Joan Armatrading stopped the band halfway running through *Love And Affection*. "Only one keyboard player!" she barked. We froze as she made Paul stop playing and asked me to play both parts that he and I had earlier agreed to split between us. Remember that hand independence thing? It was very much at the forefront of my mind at that point. Here I was, being put to the sword by Joan Armatrading. I felt less of a victim when she stopped the legendary sax player David Sanborn too because she didn't like something she was hearing.

Apart from Joan's perpetually raised eyebrow, it went very well. The Bee Gees were real pros and charming too, as were Paul Young and Tony Hadley.

It felt like a real whirlwind and just a week later, Marillion played our biggest ever headline show to over 90,000 people on an airfield in East Berlin. It was also to be our penultimate gig with Fish.

Back at Pete's garage, the writing was progressing at a deathly pace. We were getting the music together, but it was usually just the four of us. Fish did turn up some days, but he was invariably late and didn't usually stay very long. And those few scant hours were rarely fun. Fish would pass comment on some of the things we were working on. I'm not saying all of it was peak Marillion, but he didn't seem to like any of it. We weren't exactly falling over ourselves with praise for his lyrics either.

Had we been in a better place personally, then I'm sure we could have worked together to make a good, if not great, band album. (After all, most of the music from these sessions became *Seasons End* and the lyrics helped fuel Fish's first solo album.) But even if were in denial about it, we were in the endgame for this incarnation of the band, so nothing seemed to fit.

Instead of spending some time apart from each other, we agreed to Fish's suggestion that we all head for the wilds of Scotland to Dalnaglar Castle. On the edge of the Cairngorms National Park, it was 30 miles from the nearest town, Perth, which itself was not exactly a buzzing metropolis.

As if to match our collective mood, even in the middle of summer it was cold and damp. It was a castle built for repelling invaders, not welcoming musicians trying to cling to their careers. With its dusty dark, wood-lined rooms and threadbare rugs, there was little to do except attempt to work on the next album, which nobody was in the mood for. Things deteriorated further when the brother of one of our crew turned up unexpectedly. I found out much later that he had been dragged up to Scotland to make a coke delivery. From that day on we saw less of Fish. I imagine he spent some of his time in one of the castle towers getting off his face and hatching plots like the castle's forefathers must have once done.

One of the ways I held onto my sanity and tried to keep (mostly) out of trouble while away from home was to have a computer with me. I have whiled away the hours in hotel rooms all over the world playing computer games. My first computer was a ZX Spectrum, on which I can remember playing a text only game called *The Hobbit* in my room at The Manor Studios while we recorded *Fugazi*. (I was in a band named after a Tolkien book after all.) I went on to a Commodore 64 by the time we arrived at Barwell Court.

I spent more time than I care to admit in the Hervis Hotel in Berlin playing *Ultima IV: Quest Of The Avatar* (phew, rock 'n' roll), but while we were in that city I was also introduced to the possibilities of how computers could be used for making music. A chap there showed me the Pro16, Steinberg's embryonic MIDI recording software. My interest in computers and music was converging. Little did I know it then, but the seeds of my future were being sewn.

By the time we had got to Scotland I was the proud owner of an Atari 1040ST. Expecting downtime in Scotland, I was grateful I had packed it. Or at least I thought I had packed it. To my significant disappointment, when I opened my suitcase, I discovered it wasn't there.

After a few months at home, it was obvious to me that all was not well. I had become acutely conscious that following just a few days there, I looked forward to leaving again.

On one occasion I was so unhappy that I jumped in the car, sped away from home and lost control at the first roundabout I came to. I skidded down a grassy bank and came to rest wedged sideways on a high-sided single track lane. I just waved at the startled passers-by who were craning to see if I had broken my neck or if my car was about to burst into flames. I'm not sure they were expecting my cheery insouciance, or for me to survive come to that.

Aptly enough, we were in Scotland when we played our last ever gig with Fish. Even though it was for a good cause (to raise awareness of environmental issues), the warning signs were all there that it had the potential to be completely shambolic. In typical Fish style, he had phoned each of us in turn and said that the others, as well as John, were all up for doing it. I remember thinking, 'If everyone else wants to do it, who am I to say no?' On the day we were all standing in a muddy field in the pouring rain from a leaden sky asking why we had agreed to this. Then it dawned on us; we had fallen for it again. You would think we would have learned.

I'm still not sure why Fish was so keen on us playing Fife Aid. I think it had something to do with his new best friend, a chap called Robbie the Pict, a hardcore Scottish nationalist. Robbie was also responsible for finding the castle in Dalnaglar. Either way, we blamed Fish for the whole thing, which didn't help band harmony. One night Fish went out with Robbie and didn't return until the next afternoon. They were both in a terrible state having been beaten up by some bouncers at a club. Another dark talisman, another portent of doom, as if we needed one.

We returned from Scotland feeling demoralised, but we still felt we had enough music to make it worthwhile recording some demos. We went to a studio in Wallingford, Oxfordshire, the aptly named Tone Deaf, to put down what we had so far. Those demos were later released as bonus tracks on the 1999 reissue of *Clutching At Straws*, so you can judge for yourselves how well it was going.

After two albums with Chris Kimsey, we felt it was time for a change. One name that came up was someone we all respected: Bob Ezrin. He came to visit one afternoon and was not impressed by what he heard at all. He said the music just went backwards and forwards, and perhaps fearing we were too dim to understand what that meant, he began jumping back and forth from foot to foot like a performing chicken dancing on a hidden hot plate in a carnival sideshow. He might have worked with everyone from Alice Cooper to Peter Gabriel and Pink Floyd, but it was hard to appreciate all that musical history when he wouldn't stay still. He finally came to a halt to tell us there were no songs and we should go away and finish writing the album before approaching him again. He might have been right, but we never went back because less than two weeks later, Fish was no longer our singer.

John Arnison was moving from his office in Richmond to a new office in the Hit & Run building in the West End. Hit & Run was the management company headed by Genesis manager Tony Smith (not Tony Stratton-Smith who had sadly died a year earlier). Hit & Run had bought out Charisma Publishing, so they were now our publisher too. John was renting office space from them, but the arrangement would soon become significantly more than that.

One day when I was visiting John just before the move, he asked me if I would take all of Mark Wilkinson's original paintings home with me for safe keeping. They had been hanging on his office walls and he didn't want them to get damaged in transit. Besides, they belonged to the band, so we should decide what to do with them.

When EMI commissioned Mark to paint a Marillion cover, they paid him for the right to use the image, not for the painting itself. Mark wanted to keep the paintings, but we came to an agreement with him that Marillion would buy the paintings from him. We made it clear that this was a condition of us using his work. We paid a nominal sum for each painting, which was nothing like what they'd subsequently be worth, but they were only worth more because they were Marillion covers.

Subsequently, Fish had offered to pay the band what we had paid Mark for them, which seemed fair enough.

We all met up at Fish's house on 8th September 1988. It was the sixth anniversary of signing to EMI, but as a band we were very far removed from clinking celebratory glasses and wishing each other well. One of the items on the agenda that day was a book of Mark Wilkinson's paintings that he was planning to publish with Fish's involvement. Collectively, we had all worked hard to get here and didn't think that Fish and Mark should be using the Marillion name without at least consulting us first. It's indicative of where our heads were at then. In happier times we would have toasted the success of their project and left them to get on with it. But we were a band made up of two camps then and everything felt like attrition.

I brought up the subject of the paintings and suggested to Fish that maybe he would agree to let everyone in the band have one piece of artwork each. We had already all agreed that Steve should have the *Market Square Heroes* cover art in recognition of his founding member status. I suggested that Fish should say which ones he was particularly attached to, say the album covers, and the three of us could choose one of the minor pieces for ourselves. The *He Knows You Know* cover was an ideal candidate for me as it was my original idea. But Fish was in no mood for compromise and flatly refused, saying he wanted them all.

And that's how history is made: incremental agitation, picking over the little things without realising that each thing is the sum of its parts, and those parts were now fragmented forever. Somehow, between us, we had poisoned the well we drank from. The meeting broke up with ugly accusations and raised voices on both sides.

The following day I received a letter addressed to the four of us from Fish. I was pretty sure what it would say, but still wary of tearing the seal and seeing those final words for myself.

PG Wodehouse, William Faulkner's collection of letters to his mother and father, Edith Wharton, Graham Greene, the legendary correspondence between Nancy Mitford and Evelyn Waugh or between Anaïs Nin and Henry Miller: each correspondent staked their claim on literary history with the letters they wrote and sent. Those missives attained the lofty heights of creativity with something as mundane as the day's news or the latest stories from a foreign shore. They still echo through the ages, words drifting down to the modern day from far away and long ago, still managing to ignite something in the soul, glorious snapshots of days gone by. This was not one of those letters.

I won't bore you with the letter verbatim (especially as my lawyer has told me not to). But imagine the last and final argument you had with a partner when all the other bad feelings and buried hurt comes bubbling back to the surface, that one time you get to tell them what you think of them and make it count. Think about that and then multiply it by a hundred. Then maybe write it down, seal it in an envelope and send it. It's arguable that the five of us were all equally guilty. We had got everything we wanted and somehow it was never enough and too much all at the same time.

I was singled out in the letter quite early on, and not for winsome praise. Quite the opposite, in fact. Strange to think now of those early days when Fish and I were so tight, partners in crime, brothers in arms. Here, in this letter, was talk of Fish versus the rest of band, Machiavellian subplots, lines drawn grandly in the sand. Hurt and stories of subterfuge creeping through the pages in Fish's scrawly hand.

He wasn't wrong about taking sides though. We had long become entrenched, inured to the other. We had even stopped socialising together; we had decided on different paths and taken them. The letter might have highlighted the argument over Mark Wilkinson's artwork, but that blow-up had only helped reveal the crumbling infrastructure underpinning our band. There was niggling on both sides and scores to be settled.

We had raised a collective eyebrow at the cost of Fish's stage gear and, even while admitting the sheer pettiness of it all, our singer couldn't help but signal the slight he felt that we all couldn't get behind his new trews and stage blazer. Think about it. Here we were, flying high, arena rock stars, attaining goals other musicians can only dream of and it was coming down to the cost of a new pair of flame encrusted flares. Though, as Fish's letter made clear, there was something closer to the dark heart of all this. We weren't even able to make music like we once did, he said. Bob Ezrin might have been incapable of delivering bad news while stationary, but Bob might have had a point.

As the letter continued, Fish lay the blame for the blunting of our artistic integrity on our desire to only make moolah over music, which was a bit rich coming from the singer who had coerced our manager into agreeing to increase his percentage of songwriting to the detriment of ours. Though Fish would argue his was a more deserving case than ours. Besides, as he insisted, he wasn't in it for the money.

He finished up his plaintive pages of passive/aggressive prose with one final shot across our bow. The message was clear: I'll make music with or without you and this monstrous band. Fish was also in the throes of moving home to Scotland; he was soon to be out of sight and mind.

He asked or demanded (depending on your point of view) for change. But for change to come, it has to come from both parties. At this point we were a million miles apart. I don't know if a break from each other would have helped, some time to contextualise it all, but we were done with the other; tired, fractured and spent. It was how we as a band felt and, judging by Fish's letter, it was how he felt too. It was about the only thing we had left in common.

Still, I did wonder if I had gone too far in my confrontation with Fish. When angry I'm sometimes guilty of saying too much. Fish had singled me out in his letter, and I wasn't sure if the rest of the band would throw me (and John) under the bus and try to make it up with Fish. We had never discussed what would happen if Fish tried to get rid of one of us. I needn't have worried; the band and management dynamic was already shifting like sand beneath our feet.

The four of us and John made a number of calls over the weekend and unanimously agreed that we should accept Fish's resignation. We didn't have a plan or any idea what we would do next, but we had reached the end of the road with Fish. Fish was once again trying to exert control over the band, and if we acquiesced one more time, then he would fire John and gradually turn us into his backing band or force us out one by one.

The fact that he was again pushing for 50% of the publishing showed where his heart and motivation truly lay. He wrongly assumed that once again we would back down and want to work things out. When John called him on the Monday, Fish had said as much.

He wondered if he might have been a bit hasty in writing that letter. John quickly made it clear that there was no going back. John knew his chances of remaining our manager were better with Fish out of the picture, so he made no effort to help mend the rift between us.

We replied to Fish's letter.

12/9/88

Dear Fish (Derek William Dick)

We the undersigned hereby acknowledge receipt of your letter dated 9/9/88 and after due consideration have come to the conclusion that we do not wish to make any changes to the current operating procedures of the group 'Marillion'.

We therefore have no alternative but to accept your letter of resignation.

Yours sincerely

Pete, Mark, Ian, & Steve

As strange as it may seem, the overwhelming feeling amongst the four of us was relief. It was like finally being free of a corrosive marriage or gulping air after having your head held under water for too long. No more having to deal with Fish on a daily basis, dreading the phone calls and trying to decipher what he was really saying. Those hidden agendas he always seemed to harbour. It's never easy wondering what your singer might be getting up to next.

I'm sure our fans were shocked, surprised and terribly disappointed. Why would we split up at the height of our success? It was the success that made us all believe that we could carry on without the other. Fish may have assumed that our fans would continue to come and see him perform, buy his albums, and quickly forget us. When people thought of Marillion, they pictured Fish. Only our hardcore fans could even name the rest of us.

We were similarly brazen. We thought we could find another singer to replace Fish. He sang the songs, but the music came from us. His words resonated with some people, but most of our global fans didn't even speak English. QED: Fish needed us more than we needed him.

Hubris and enough money on both sides will do that to a band; it made our split seem not only possible but survivable.

Simon Hanhart and I celebrating Pete's nuptials on 6th October 1984.

Making a point with Freya in 1984.

Kiss the bride. Pete and Fiona tie the knot in 1984.

The keyboards could be more to the fore. Contemplative keyboard player at Hansa Studios, Berlin in 1985.

Why so serious? Marillion taking in the latest Misplaced Childhood *mix at Hansa Studios in 1985.*

Quiet on the set. Hansa Studios at its sublime best in 1985.

We are the road crew. Hanging out with Steve Robinson (guitar tech) Smick Hardgrave (drum tech), Privet (sound) and Robert 'Chops' Flury (lights) in Tokyo, Japan in December 1985.

The Midas touch. Going for gold in Cologne, Germany in 1986.

Blue Steel IV. It's a look that's adaptable live or in the studio. On tour in 1986.

Bubbling under. Pete and I enjoying Rod Smallwood's jacuzzi in 1986.

Tony Hancock's let himself go. Fish suited and booted in 1986.

"You hum it, I'll play it."
Going live with Fish in 1986.

"What do you mean, 'Turn it off and turn it on again'?" Mid-set repairs supporting Queen in June 1986

For some reason I seem startled to see a camera. At Sarm Studios in 1986.

Fish meeting his public on the Incommunicado video shoot in 1987.

Kai checking the latest Clutching At Straws *stereo mix in 1987.*

I can play ANY kind of keyboard! In the studio in 1987.

"It means nothing to me..." Backstage with Midge Ure at Wembley Stadium for Nelson Mandela's 70th birthday show on 11th June 1988.

"What's the worst that could happen? I mean it's not like I'm going to set a barn on fire or anything..." Hot air balloon antics at Hook End Manor in 1989.

Like we'd stepped out of the pages of Italian Vogue, h and I at the Piazza del Duomo, Milan, Italy in 1990.

Keeping body and soul together, as Mark Wilkinson depicted me on the cover of Fish's Vigil... *album in 1989.*

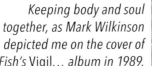

One of your five a day... Marillion go Mexican and mad on mushrooms in 1990.

*Rockin' Rio
in 1990.*

Keeps your whites bright. Paul Lewis and h enjoy Rio's coastline in 1990.

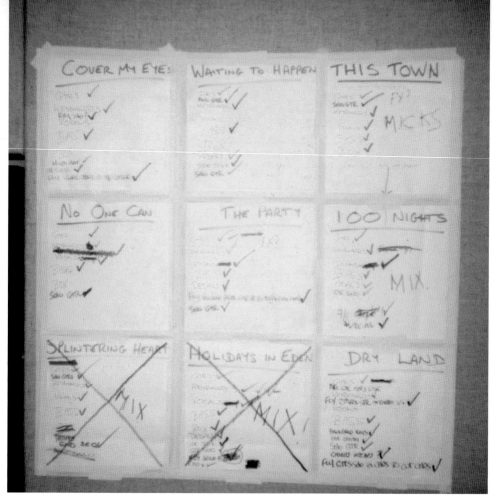

The Rakes' Progress. Holidays In Eden *recording session whiteboard, 1990.*

*In the pink.
h flying
high in 1992.*

The sign of the cross. Live in 1992.

Gothic Horror, or it was for EMI. Marouatte, our home away from home for the Brave sessions.

Putting a Brave face on things. In the studio with Dave Meegan in 1994.

"Now tell me, what interests you about the role in Marillion?" Home working in Oxford in 1999.

Fly me to the moon. With Neil Armstrong at Bogarts in Cincinnati on 3rd October 2004.

The man who… got to play live with Travis at T in the Park on 10th July 2005.

The boys in the band.
Backstage with Travis
at T in the Park.

Made in Europe: soundcheck time on the Deep Purple tour with Don Airey in 2010.

Hitting the wall hard at the Brighton Marathon on 18th April 2010.

Not quite a band of brothers. Marillion fighting more than writing in Portugal in March 2010.

John Arnison heaved a sigh of relief, but it wasn't without some pain. He had just negotiated a new publishing deal with Hit & Run. We would get to share £1 million between us if we could sign the deal before we announced the split. That didn't sit well with us. We asked John to negotiate a new, less lucrative deal that didn't involve Fish.

There was still enough goodwill between Fish and the band for us to agree to make a joint announcement about the split. We also agreed that there should be another double live album to mark the end of this era, although the main reason was to bring in some much needed money while we decided what to do next. We made the obligatory audio repairs at Westside Studios with Nick Davis engineering and mixing. Fish agreed to do his bit but insisted that none of the band were present while he did so.

The Thieving Magpie was released in November and Steve and I made the front cover of *Kerrang!* with the headline 'So long and thanks for all the (lyrics) Fish'.

We got down to the pressing business of finding a new singer. Quite often, when a famous band is looking for a new member, they can be quite coy about the process and try to keep it hidden. We had no such hesitancy and placed adverts that read 'Marillion Require Vocalist', but we could have saved ourselves the cash. Our new singer came highly recommended and by word of mouth. Enter one Ronald Stephen Hoggarth or Steve Hogarth or, if you want to distil it down entirely, just h.

CHAPTER 13

A Man For All Seasons

The Hungarian composer Béla Bartók once observed that competitions are for horses, not artists. Easy for Bartók to say, as he sat back among an array of plumped cushions in his Budapest pile. Bartók hadn't just lost his singer, nor was he embroiled in a very public battle to deliver new music before an angry Scotsman got his record out first. No, Bartók was probably putting the finishing touches to *Divertimento For String Orchestra* and chuckling to himself at his sublime brilliance.

Screw Bartók. We *were* in competition with Fish, and this was a race we had to win.

Currently the only thing uniting both Fish and Marillion was the belief that whoever could get their music across the finish line first had the better chance of gaining attention from our collective fans, pages in the music press, attracting cash from EMI and, dependent on delivering a good record, the most sales. No pressure, then.

And Fish had a head start. Admittedly, he was as surprised to find himself at this metaphorical starting line as we were, but his general unhappiness at not having more control of the music in Marillion meant he had already started casting about for other people to work with. There was the 1986 single *Shortcut To Somewhere* with Tony Banks (of Genesis), which was horribly hamstrung by being tied to the movie *Quicksilver*, a film Kevin Bacon would later describe as the lowest point in his career. And Kevin has had a few bottom feeders to choose from.

There was also the five days working with Clannad that Fish had been quick to describe in his resignation note as more satisfying than working for a year with Marillion. Though that sounded like one way traffic as Clannad quietly drew a veil over their collaboration.

Fish had also spent some time writing with Mickey Simmonds. When we closed the door on Fish, he had quickly invited Simmonds to co-write his first solo record. He had the lyrics mostly done and I imagine that Simmonds was probably ready with at least some of the music.

What about us? Remember that advertising offensive? It certainly got the word out and we were inundated with tapes. They would arrive at our PO Box in London and Ian would pick them up from John's office a few times a week, drive up to Pete's house where we would all meet up to listen to the most promising ones. I can still remember the clattering of cassette tapes being dumped on the table and sifting through them like a kid rummaging through a lucky dip.

There were hundreds of applicants but only a handful were good enough for us to merit calling them back. As Jesus said, 'Many are called, but few are chosen'. Though in our case, few were chosen and even fewer called.

During the mixing of *The Thieving Magpie,* we invited a few of the young (and not so young) hopefuls down for an audition. One poor chap turned up on crutches with a broken foot. I was in the main studio explaining how the audition was going to run when Ian appeared through the control room window doing his best pirate impersonation. For complete clarity, and to make sure I was getting the point, he held up a sign with 'Pieces of Eight' written on it. When he finally fell out of sight, tumbling over sideways, I couldn't keep a straight face any longer. I felt for our one-legged friend, who had no idea why I was chuckling before he had even reached for the microphone.

We had the expected Fish impersonators and prog band singers looking to move up a level or two. Alan Reed from Pallas and Stuart Nicholson from Galahad both put in good performances, but neither was quite what we were after. We invited two of Cliff Richard's backing singers to have a go, but there were forever destined to 'ooh' and 'ahh' behind the man Elton John nicknamed Sylvia, not lead from the front for Marillion. We did have a frontrunner for a while: Carl Sentance, who was singing with Black Sabbath's Geezer Butler at the time. Carl was a very nice chap with an excellent voice, but the elusive magic was missing.

And that magic was what we were after. Someone you believed in. We wanted technical ability, but we also wanted to be moved.

We also needed someone who could write lyrics too (and the moon on a stick at that point, clearly). Fish was a hard act to follow. To improve our chances of ticking all the boxes, we started looking for a lyricist at the same time. Who better to write lyrics for Marillion after Fish's departure than his lyrical hero, Peter Hammill? Putting aside our annoyance at his urging Fish to go solo years previously, Steve and I met Peter at his home to ask him in person if he would be our lyricist. He graciously declined, citing his friendship with Fish as the reason, although I suspect the real reason is that he wanted to keep any decent lyrics he might write for himself.

EMI Publishing put forward John Helmer as a possible lyricist. Coming from the post-punk outfit The Piranhas, he seemed an unlikely fit. Nevertheless, Steve met up with John to discuss potential song ideas. Steve suggested a lyric about Berlin, a city which had been pivotal in the Marillion story. Although John had never been there, he came back with a lyric to give us an idea of what he might be capable of.

While Steve and John were stalking the imagined *Straßen* of Berlin, Ian and I went to see Vivian Stanshall at his flat in London. Apart from his role in the Bonzo Dog Doo-Dah Band, Stanshall wrote plays and lyrics for a number of people including Steve Winwood. To say Vivian was eccentric would be understating it somewhat, but he was a real old fashioned gentleman and we delighted in his company, spending a pleasant few hours chatting about life in his incredibly unkempt flat. But, as much as we liked Vivian, we decided his lyrics wouldn't be right for Marillion.

Like a lot of hopefuls passing through our doors, Steve Hogarth was at something of a crossroads in his life. Though, unlike those hopefuls, Steve, or h as we would soon call him to avoid confusion with Steve Rothery, had very little interest in even crossing Marillion's threshold. He had already been in a few bands, had landed not one but two major record deals and yet was still a long way from the proverbial land of milk and honey.

His most recent band, How We Live, had recently split up and he was hanging around his publisher's office looking for something to do. They suggested auditioning for the singer's role in Marillion. That wasn't the sort of thing he had in mind, not at all. He was an artist who had something to say, and the idea of standing in as a replacement for an overbearing Scot in a band that sounded and looked remarkably out of step with contemporary cultural norms was not a good fit. The publisher persisted and h reluctantly agreed they could send us a tape.

Just before Christmas, Ian arrived at Pete's very excited about a new tape we had received. Admittedly, Ian doesn't do excitement (pirate he excels at; excitement, not so much), but he was almost cracking a smile. One song on the tape particularly stood out: *Games In Germany*. It was full of heart, a little reminiscent of Peter Gabriel in parts, but he wasn't simply aping the former Genesis singer. We had spent years trying to shed the Genesis mantle, so we were especially wary of leaning that way. The lyrics were decent too, but it was his voice that really got our attention. Our enthusiasm was quickly blunted when he turned down our offer to audition and had to be talked around by Darryl Way, Ian's old bandmate and coincidentally a drinking buddy of Hogarth's.

In early 1989 a reluctant Steve Hogarth arrived chez Trewavas, so reluctant that he was a full 24 hours late. He made what sounded like an excuse for not showing up the day before; his car had been stolen. Knowing him as I do now, I think it's more likely that he forgot where he had parked it. He looked as though he had dressed in the dark, his face unshaven. Imagine a feral cat in a trench coat and you're close. He clearly wasn't trying to impress us; he was checking us out, or at least that's how it felt. He was less nervous and more curious than any of the other singers we had met so far.

We explained to him that we had some music (the verse and chorus of *The King Of Sunset Town*) and some lyrics written by John Helmer. This was not yet about the 1989 Tiananmen Square protests. h would rewrite the lyrics after joining the band, but they did open with the line 'A ragged man came shuffling through…'

We asked h to sing the words over our music. He asked what the melody was. We told him to make it up; he raised an eyebrow but said nothing. By the time he got to the refrain, 'Watch a big wheel turning round…', we knew we had our singer.

Not that h felt the same way.

After running through a few more ideas, we all retired to Pete's kitchen for a chat. I said something like, "Unless you turn out to be a mad axe murderer, you've got the job."

"I'm a mad axe victim!" h laughed, revealing a scar on his hand that looked like he had been at the sharp end of a shark attack. He had been injured with a broken pint glass by his former, and very drunken, bass player who was trying to kill the drummer in his band. This all happened at sea on a cruise ship, so his badly gashed hand was sewn up by a sailor who could probably navigate the shipping forecast but was less handy (sorry) with a medical kit.

h made us wait seven whole days – God managed to create the heavens and earth in less time than that – before agreeing to join us for a few weeks' trial to see if we could write and work together.

We decided on yet another residential rehearsal space so we could really get to know each other. We opted for a place in Sussex, close to Brighton. But instead of a barn, acres of land and a nice country house that Blur might have sung about, this was a repurposed mushroom farm. Consisting of a long, single storey building, it was hardly salubrious, but it was home for a few weeks in the spring of 1989.

After the long downward slide that was our final year with Fish, those first few weeks at the mushroom farm with h saw Marillion reborn. We were mere miles from where we had worked with Fish 12 months before, but this was worlds apart. The music hadn't changed particularly, but our creative impulses were renewed. It was like a shot through our collective neural pathway. We were newly industrious, creative and mustard keen. It felt like we were starting the band over again.

Creativity is a funny thing. When you make a piece of art, whether it be music, writing, painting or whatever, there's a moment where you have to reveal yourself to truly get to the heart of what you're trying to say or convey. Which means opening yourself up to potential criticism or hurt if it's rejected by your creative peers. And by creative peers I mean Marillion.

It's easy to tread on each other's toes when you're overfamiliar with one another. With someone new in the room there's a collective urge to make it work, so egos are shelved for the greater good. No cruel comments, more attempts to accommodate the feelings of others. That doesn't always last (especially after a few months in the back of a tour bus), but we were now in a place where we had reset ourselves and it felt both positive and harmonious, characteristics that had been sorely lacking for a long time in Marillion.

Now we were working at full tilt. With the additions of h's ear for melody and vocal versatility to the music we had already written we were, as they say, off to the races. The first four songs came together in a creative flurry: *Berlin*, *The King Of Sunset Town*, *Seasons End* and *The Uninvited Guest*. Not a bad start, I think you'll agree. All four were Helmer lyrics.

We also had *Easter*, a song that h had already written before joining us, the guitar solo growing organically out of the song as we played. The final section was also written in the room. This was the perfect juxtaposition of h and Marillion and promised a bright future for the band's second act.

Music for *The Space* had been written in our broken down castle in the wilds of Scotland, but the song had no lyric yet. h realised that he was able to fit words that he had originally written for his band How We Live to the music. They came from two different songs that were never released: *Wrap Me In The Flag* and *So Far Away*. When his old band mate Colin Woore heard *The Space,* he claimed we had stolen his music. Which is categorically untrue; we had never even heard those songs.

But when h admitted that my chords under the lyric 'Everybody in the whole of the world feels the same inside' were similar to Colin's work, we agreed we had a problem. After a bit of haggling, we subsequently agreed to credit Colin and pay him 15% of the publishing royalties, which still irks me as I know in my heart that they're my chords.

Hooks In You began life as a promising guitar riff from Steve. h loved it as soon as he heard it. It sounded as fresh and life affirming as we were feeling at the time. We didn't have a lyric apart from one of John's that had the line 'when the fear gets its hooks in you'. h took that line as his starting point and wrote a completely new lyric around it. Thankfully, John was not at all precious about how we used the words he supplied.

Seasons End was only compromised by one weak link in the songwriting chain. *Holloway Girl* was written around the scratchy bass intro that Pete started playing around with one day. h liked the sound of it and wanted to develop it into a song. We quickly came up with some verse (h) and chorus chords (me) and the music was done. It's about as underwhelming as a lyric too. h was a good writer in those days, with *Easter* already under his belt, but he was still some way off a song like *The Invisible Man*.

For the cover we invited Bill Smith to pitch some ideas to us. Completely different in scope and tone to Mark Wilkinson, he sent us some photographic ideas to look at. He and his assistant, Carl Glover, began a working relationship with us on that album that, in the case of Carl, continues to this day. Mark tried to convince us that he could produce album covers for both Fish and Marillion, but we felt that he would somehow always prioritise Fish.

Besides, we were not overjoyed with Mark's cover for *The Thieving Magpie,* something Ian likened to a *Mad* magazine cover, which seems unnecessarily cruel to *Mad* magazine in retrospect. After it was released, Ian asked me why I hadn't complained that Mark had made me look like I had just stepped off a UFO. It was a fair point. I did look like I might be about to invade earth with my alien horde and keyboard, but, as usual, Mark had delivered the finished sleeve with no time to spare for changes (or to make me look less like Ming the Merciless). If we had continued to work with Mark, perhaps he would have resisted Fish's petty and rather childish idea to add John Arnison and myself to his first solo album sleeve huddled around some burning tyres dressed as tramps. We were blacked out after the first print run when I complained to EMI about it.

We were being buoyed along by creative *bonhomie*, a band of brothers again, riding a wave that wouldn't come crashing to the shore until we had completed the *Seasons End* sessions.

When the bump in the road came, and it was only a slight one, it was Fish shaped. A solicitor turned up at the recording studio with a policeman to serve us with an injunction. The solicitor brought the policeman as muscle, as he feared we might blow up when we saw the paperwork. Quite the contrary – and this will give you a snapshot of our happy mindset at that time – instead we invited them to join us poolside. The policeman even posed with us for photographs.

That said, we were still in a race with our former singer. While we had been busy getting *Seasons End* ready, Fish had been less industrious with his album. When he heard that we were already recording at Hook End Manor, he tried to throw a spanner in the works. The solicitor was said spanner.

Fish's only route to stopping us recording was the equipment that was still jointly owned by the five of us. He figured that if he slapped an injunction on us to prevent us using that equipment, we would be forced to stop recording until we had reached an agreement about what his share was worth and paid him for it. It sounded like the sort of idea a legal mind might conjure up. So, we stopped using the equipment for a few days, but h carried on recording vocals while our solicitors dealt with Fish's puerile injunction.

It was hard to get too aggrieved about anything working in such a wonderful place as Hook End. It's a fabulous 16th century Elizabethan manor house and was once the home of Alvin Lee, before Pink Floyd's David Gilmour settled there ten years after (see what I did there?). Gilmour converted the barn into a studio but sold up in 1986 (his wife thought it was haunted) to successful producers Alan Winstanley and Clive Langer. They christened the barn Outside Studios (to complement the name of their London mothership Westside Studios) and upgraded it to the standard you would expect to find in a typical London studio at the time; Solid State Logic mixing console, Studer A800 24 track tape machine, Eventide Harmonizers, Lexicon 224 digital reverb and loads of expensive valve mics.

Thrilled by that list of equipment? No, me neither. There was a time when I used to love reading the lists of keyboards used by the prog greats on their album sleeves. We even tried to emulate our heroes by doing the same on the first few Marillion albums. No wonder the ladies came flocking the way they did.

These days pretty much everything I play is created in ones and zeros in the silicon chips of computers. It's hard to get excited in the same way about software, even if the results are startling. That said, if you held a Moog to my head and made me choose just one, it would be Omnisphere by Spectrasonics.

Come back, I'm not finished.

Safe to say then that we had a wonderful time recording *Seasons End*. Nick Davis was our engineer and co-producer. There were no politics, fighting, drugs, or secret meetings.

h was having the time of his life too; it was a great energy to be around. More than once, he remarked that he must have died and gone to heaven. It was a good time to be in Marillion.

However, for every high, a niggling low. I didn't say anything, but when h joined us, I was more than a little nervous about him being a keyboard player too. He was used to being the only keyboard player in the band, as was I. I half expected him to at least insist on playing the music he wrote, like the piano part in *Easter*.

I couldn't have been more wrong, nor h more gracious. He encouraged me to record the piano for *Easter*, even though I knew he would play it better than I could. I'm not saying that because he's a better player than me, but because when you compose a piece of music, it's partly driven by the way the notes fall under your fingers. Everyone has their own style of playing and that comes out in what they write and how they play. Playing someone else's music can never sound exactly the way they originally played it.

We found time to have some fun too. My idea of fun was to make use of the studio workshop while not recording. Ian had introduced the band to the sublime pastime of making hot air balloons from a cross of balsa wood covered in birthday candles suspended under a dry cleaning bag that was sealed at one end. They would float sedately into the night sky until the candles burned down to the wood, causing the whole thing to collapse, extinguish the flames and fall harmlessly back to earth.

Not content with these charming orbs of fire lighting up the evening, I determined to go one better. With supplies from a local camping shop, I proceeded to make a giant balloon from space blankets powered by a camping gas stove hanging from one of Ian's bass drum hoops. I drilled out the nozzle in the stove to increase the pitiful flame size. While testing it out in the workshop, a six foot flame shot out, setting off the fire alarm. The fire brigade duly arrived but seemed disappointed there was no actual fire. They left after the obligatory photos with the band, but not before telling us what to do in the event of a barn fire: "Let it burn. You can't put out a barn fire!"

On my second flight (we managed to retrieve the balloon the first time by chasing it over half of Oxfordshire in the band van), the balloon went missing, disappearing into the blue black of the night. At breakfast the next morning, the local paper bore the headline, 'Manor House burned to the ground' across the front page. My stomach dropped through the floor, but after reading the article I realised that it wasn't my balloon that caused the fire. Phew!

Privet looked up from his coffee. "You're madder than Mad Jack McMad, the winner of last year's Mr Madman competition," he opined and with that Mad Jack was born.

And yet more good news: John was still sober and getting on with booking our first tour with h. He also managed to salvage the publishing deal with Hit & Run. The original deal we agreed in 1982 was for five albums. It was common when a deal was nearing the end of its life, as ours was with only one album to go, that they would try to sign you up for another five albums. We had to take a big cut from the £1 million advance that was on the table before Fish left, but I was still going to bank 50 grand, which was the largest cheque I had ever seen. Charisma, or Hit & Run as they were now called, were in the unique position of being able to offer us a royalty uplift on our first four albums too, which meant we would be paid 70% of the income from here on in.

For my £50k advance I was expected to write a 17% share of the songs on *Seasons End*. This arbitrary figure was a rough average of what my contribution added up to on the previous few albums. When we explained to h about the system we had in place from the Fish days – 50% split equally between the five of us and the remaining 50% split equally between words and music – he was happy to come on board. In order for this system to work when we used John Helmer's lyrics, he would need to agree to a 25% share for his lyrics, which he happily did. Such equanimity couldn't have been further from the Machiavellian twists and turns of our former incarnation.

Lord knows I needed the money. Susie and I had managed to mire ourselves in debt doing up our money pit, sorry, house in Wendover. By mid-1987 we had a £40,000 overdraft and I had a big tax bill to pay. Our house had virtually doubled in value since we had bought it a year and a half before, so we decided to sell it and buy something cheaper to pay off our overdraft. Which we managed to do just before the financial crash of October 1987. A lucky escape.

Our new home was a detached four bed place in Haddenham, Buckinghamshire, a land of SUVs and aspiration. The publishing advance would put us on slightly firmer financial ground, but, like two giddy drunks who have just cleared the tables in Vegas, we continued to live beyond our means, spending hard as my earnings softened, the band's biggest hits now behind us.

Meanwhile, Fish was preparing to go to war. Is there anything so dangerous as a Scotsman scorned? He cut an unhappy figure, perhaps because we were seemingly riding high and had managed to move on without a backward glance to our former singer. He wanted his day in court to argue that the 35% cut he had been receiving since *Fugazi* was only while he was part of the band. Now he wanted an impressive 50% and he wanted it backdated to 1983. Were he to win, it would be expensive for us, but Fish had no chance of success according to our lawyer and he advised that we should fight it.

One evening, towards the end of recording *Seasons End*, I was in the local pub chatting with the landlord (we were on first name terms by then) and he suggested that we could play a gig in the back room. It was a bit small, but I was a bit drunk, so agreed it was a great idea.

Now you may say I was mad agreeing to such an idea and let me tell you that's exactly what the rest of the band said, and perhaps not as kindly as you might have phrased it. (Mad Jack was my new nickname after all.) They came around though. We knew we would have to debut with h somewhere, so why not in a low key backwater like The Crooked Billet in a tiny village called Stoke Row?

Calling ourselves the Low Fat Yogurts, we put the word out locally so that a few people might turn up on the night. The landlord, seeing an opportunity to sell a few extra pints and then some, told everybody he knew, and the word spread like wildfire. And you only have to look at footage of California going up in smoke to know how dangerous that can be. On 8th June we played our first gig with h in the small back room of a pub.

There was no stage, so the audience of 50 or so were packed in right up to an imaginary line that felt like the front of the stage. Everyone was standing, and as Pete and h are both shorter than average, they would only have been visible to the front row. The hundred or so that couldn't squeeze into the room (to make it even more of a fire hazard) were outside trying to look on through the open windows. We only played for about 40 minutes but debuted *The King Of Sunset Town*, *Hooks In You*, *The Uninvited Guest* and *Easter*. We also played a few crowd pleasers like *Kayleigh*, *Lavender* and *Warm Wet Circles*. It went pretty well.

Our next gig was something of a step up from The Crooked Billet. In October we travelled to Besançon, France to play to 4,000 people at the start of a tour that would finish up at Hammersmith Odeon just before Christmas. It seemed that we had survived Fish's departure and life went on almost as before. We had dropped a level on the touring circuit, back to 3-4,000 capacity theatres, but they were selling out and, just as importantly, we were having fun as a band again. To add to our euphoria, wherever we went, the audience reaction was incredible too. Nobody was calling for Fish, though the odd throaty request for *Grendel* could still be heard; the (sold out) rooms were filled with love and respect.

When we got to Glasgow, we heard that Fish was planning to sneak in and check out the competition. We didn't want him there. h was already feeling the pressure of playing to a potentially hostile Glaswegian audience without the thought of Fish looming around by the bar, rallying the troops. Besides, things were getting very ugly with the lawyers, so we weren't in the mood to be convivial. h needn't have worried; the Glasgow audience were one of the best of the tour.

We even managed to fit in two quick shows in New York and Los Angeles in November. As we had a few days spare, h and I flew out early to Canada to do some promotion for the album.

After our promotion for the day was over in Toronto, we went with the record company guy to a bar to watch one of his acts, where a girl came up to me and asked what I was drinking. Being Canadian she should have been familiar with my drink as it was a Bloody Caesar, like a Bloody Mary but with Clamato (clam and tomato) instead of tomato juice. It's not quite the hellscape in a glass that it sounds.

I might have mentioned this before, probably as I collided through my love life like a dodgem car careering around an oval track, but I wasn't looking to meet anybody new, promise. Or at least I didn't think I was. But there was something about this girl, Susan, that intrigued me. Before I knew it, we were deep in conversation, and when it was time to go, I didn't really want to leave. She gave me her phone number and I called her a few days later from LA.

I couldn't get Susan off my mind and over the next few weeks I called her from various hotels on the road. When I told her that we were going to be playing in Rio in late January 1990 she said she had always wanted to see the city and booked herself a flight.

We played as part of the second Hollywood Rocks Festival in the football stadiums of São Paulo and Rio de Janeiro, two shows one week apart. This was our first time in South America, but we were already considered a huge band there. With none of the baggage associated with Fish leaving, h was a star and featured on the front page of the *O Globo* newspaper with a circulation in the millions. We were second on the bill to Bon Jovi, with Bob Dylan, Eurythmics and Tears For Fears all playing during the weekend too. We were treated like stars in Rio and Susan was there with me for the whole week.

To Susan, our relationship was more like a summer romance. She had plans to go back to university and study to become a lawyer. Moving to the UK was never an option for her. That was as out of reach for her as moving to Canada was for me. Our brief fling was over before the reds and browns of autumn appeared.

After the giddy heights of plush hotel rooms and holding hands in Rio, I was now living in a small flat above a shop in the village of Thame, just down the road from Susie and the kids. I hadn't fully thought this through and was now living the life of a sad divorcee in some forgotten sitcom. I would have sat at the window and stared down at the streets of Thame wondering what the hell I had done, if the window wasn't facing a brick wall at the back of the building.

I had to get out of there and so decided to move to London. If I was going to be single for the first time in my adult life, I was going to enjoy myself. So, what better place than the country's capital? I rented a flat overlooking the Thames in Putney. It was in a nice Victorian mansion block but not cheap, so I offered the spare room to our lighting designer, Alan Parker, who was looking for a place to live too.

Alan and I got on extremely well in our boys' flat where we played loud music at all hours and I did things like placing my huge Hammond C3 organ and Leslie speaker cabinet in my bedroom because there was nobody to object. The neighbours must have been thrilled.

Putney was a happy interlude, even if I did miss the kids terribly, and before I knew it, it was time to return to the studio to try and recreate the magic that was *Seasons End*.

We might have been back at Stanbridge Farm, but, even though the environment was the same, the mood was markedly different. h was finding out what writing with Marillion was like and he didn't like it one bit. His take on songwriting was 99% perspiration, 1% inspiration. The rest of us liked to take our time and see what emerged. More like a slow flowing river eroding the soil to reveal a fleck of gold here or there. h was more the babbling brook. Besides, as a band, we were starting with very little, and it was slow going. Even when we did hit upon something that sounded promising we were reluctant to work at it for too long in case we wore it away to nothing.

This exasperated h as he wanted to take any promising idea and fashion it into a finished song. It wasn't the way we worked. So, what happens when an unstoppable force meets an immovable object? It makes your new singer ill, apparently. h's stress levels were off the charts, so we agreed that he should go home for a few weeks. This worked wonders for all of us. We managed to write some music and h came back with *The Party* mostly written.

We all decided to take the edge off and relax and invited John Helmer to dinner. We thought a Mexican theme would be fun, but not just the food. We hired Mexican bandit costumes and grew some stubble. We also bought some makeup and rubber scars to complete the picture. Just to make things more interesting, we picked and ate some magic mushrooms, which were conveniently growing on the lawn outside. In a moment of profound insight, with pupils as big as the Moon, h leaned to me and said earnestly,

"I think it's a great idea having a Mexican evening. I also think it's a great idea taking magic mushrooms but not at the same time. Can you take that scar off your face? It's freaking me out."

As well as the internal tug of war about writing practices, there was the external pressure from EMI to write some hits. *Seasons End* was a perfectly good transitional album from the old to the new, but it was lacking a hit like *Kayleigh*. Sales of *Clutching At Straws* were in excess of one million and *Misplaced Childhood* had already sailed past the two million mark. By contrast, *Seasons End* had only managed to ship a mere 600,000 copies, so EMI were already fretting about our future plans.

Fish's angst over *Seasons End* landing before his album was unfounded, at least in Germany. We were told that, on hearing how good *Seasons End* was, the boss at the label said, "If Marillion can do this without Fish, just imagine how good Fish's album will be." They set their marketing budgets accordingly and, proving how powerful a major label getting behind an album can be, Fish outsold us in Germany. But only in Germany. In virtually every other country his sales lagged behind ours. He was in a far worse financial position too, thanks to his taste for litigation.

He hired the most expensive solicitors he could find in Sheridans. Admittedly, Howard Rubin was an excellent solicitor, who easily outmanoeuvred John Ireland, our appointed representative from Lee & Thompson. What we didn't know, and which would come back to haunt us, was that they had some shared history. Ireland had represented Roger Waters in his scrap with his former Pink Floyd bandmates, who were represented by Rubin. Waters lost the case and Ireland saw our fight with Fish over publishing as a chance to settle the score.

It wasn't until we were in front of a silk charging us a cool £3,000 a day that reality hit us. If the case was decided purely on what the split between words and music should be, then Fish would almost certainly win with his 50/50 argument.

Our case would have to turn on the fact that we had an agreement with Fish under which his share was 35%. Just because he left the band didn't give him the right to overturn that agreement. Unfortunately, there was nothing in writing between us. Just his word against ours and the fact that we had been sharing the income that way until Fish left Marillion.

We were also looking at a solicitor's bill of over £50,000 and it would probably cost us double that to fight the case in court. We were also made aware that Fish had already spent over £100,000 with Sheridans, and if we lost then we would be picking up his tab too.

Good sense, and the desire not to lose our homes, prevailed and we agreed to settle. Fish got his 50%, but not the backdated payment he wanted. We moved on and were happier for it. It felt good not to be in dispute with Fish anymore. I expected to never see or speak to him again, and that suited me just fine.

A footnote: In case you're wondering what happened to the Mark Wilkinson artwork, the spark that set this particular flame and burned the original Marillion to the ground, I took all the paintings around to Fish's house and unceremoniously dumped them on his doorstep. He was as unthinking in how he displayed them, tacking them on the walls of his high ceilinged, brightly sunlit studio in Haddington. The direct beams of the sun were ruinous, bleaching the colours and lines from the paintings, until it was hard to tell what they were any more.

All that creative lustre now muted and pale, it made me think of those original sessions and shows, Fish and I plotting a future for the band that came incredibly good, like bright fireworks lighting up the night sky. What a trail we blazed.

But now it was just embers, as dark and forgotten as the fading jester in that gilded frame, one more flickering reminder of what we had once built and then chosen to tear down again.

CHAPTER 14

Pain & Heaven

History tells us that by the time we were making *Holidays In Eden* our commercial peak had passed.

It's easy to tell when you're in the ascendant as a band. You sell more records, you get your first tour bus after years in the back of a van, venues get bigger, you're closing not opening the shows anymore, your singer starts asking for a clothing budget...

We only had to look over our shoulders now to see our sales dipping under the million mark. But the difference as you rise and fall is that once you've reached and obtained the golden ring, a part of your psyche insists that you can do it all again. Repeat the magic, unearth another *Kayleigh*. There's still the ambition to drive you on, because otherwise what is there, diminishing returns revolving ever further into the darkness? What's the saying, it's the hope that kills you?

They say you can never go back, but that didn't stop us returning to Hook End Manor to record *Holidays In Eden*. But before we got there, we needed a producer. If *Seasons End* had taught us anything, it was that we needed producing and not just an engineer to record the magic. It's rare to find an engineer who can produce too. That prized skill set led us back to Chris Kimsey.

During the writing time at Stanbridge we had a number of calls with Chris, trying to pin him down to a definitive start date for the album. He was mixing The Rolling Stones' live *Flashpoint* album and it was slow going. Eventually, exasperated, I called him up and said, "Chris, either shit or get off the pot!" He paused momentarily: "I'll get off the pot," he said and was gone.

So, we unloaded our gear into Hook End with Chris Neil as our producer. Some of you might be hard pushed to recognise Chris with his clothes on. He made a crust for years as an actor, usually scrambling half naked out of bathroom windows in such gems as *Adventures Of A Plumber's Mate* and *Adventures Of A Private Eye*.

Which is not to say that he spent most of his professional life struggling to keep his trousers up or on. He could don a tunic too, as when he took the lead in the theatrical production of *Jesus Christ Superstar*. Ultimately though, theatre's loss was music's gain as Chris finally settled for a life of churning out hits for everyone from Sheena Easton to Dollar and Shakin' Stevens.

In all honesty, Chris was someone we normally wouldn't have touched with a plunger or a wooden cross. However, he came highly recommended by Nick Davis, who had worked with him on Mike + The Mechanics.

Nick Gatfield, our new A&R man at EMI, loved the idea that we were considering working with Chris because of the (very slim) possibility that we might repeat the success of Mike Rutherford, the Genesis bassist, who took his Mechanics into the mainstream.

Chris did a good job of selling himself too. He said we shouldn't worry about being turned into a pop band because his son was a huge Marillion fan who would never forgive him if he ruined his favourite band.

Say what you like about Chris, but say it quickly. He doesn't stand still very long (probably all those years of having to jump out of windows at a moment's notice while trying to pull his trousers up). *Holidays In Eden* was and remains our shortest ever album recording session at just ten weeks plus mixing.

With a clear brief from EMI to deliver three hit singles, Chris was laser focused on hooks. As we only had one contender for the charts in *No One Can*, he persuaded us to record a cover of *Dry Land*, a song h had written with his former bandmate Colin Woore.

During the routining sessions (learning and finalising the arrangements) at Nomis, Chris also picked up on a Rothers guitar riff which was not even close to being a finished song. As we were short on time, h tried singing his lyrics from the verse of another old song of his called *Simon's Car* over it and eureka! Chris was delighted. The chorus from *Simon's Car* didn't fit, but h had a great melody consisting of nine notes. Rather heroically, he managed to stretch the words 'pain and heaven' across the melody and we suddenly had a song which might fit the template as the third contender for the EMI hit machine.

In some ways Chris pushed us well out of our comfort zone. Which can be a good thing as long as you don't suddenly find yourself recreating Bowie's Tin Machine or thinking what your record really needs is more jazz fusion or bongos.

We resisted the bongos, but Chris did invite drummer Roland 'Roly' Kerridge down to the studio with an electronic drum kit for *No One Can* and *Cover My Eyes*. He sampled Ian's drums and Ian recorded his parts triggering pads with his sticks. Roly then adjusted or quantised Ian's playing, tweaking away until it was precisely in time.

I'm not in any way suggesting that Ian's a sloppy player (he's about a foot taller than me and I'm not an idiot); this sort of adjustment is common practice these days as most contemporary music is produced on computers. Personally, I think music without a human 'feel' loses more than it gains. We were a long way from the days of *Script* with Mick's lumpy drumming, but it felt like Chris's approach was a (perfectly measured) step too far.

I greatly enjoyed working with Chris on a personal level, though I was less happy with the time I was given to record my parts. Chris liked to work fast. There was no room for chin stroking or experimentation. It was a case of get a sound that would do the job and record it. The only time I felt he was willing to really explore some sonic possibilities was when we were working on the first part of *Splintering Heart*.

When we recorded demos and played a few gigs to try out the material for *Holidays In Eden* at the back end of 1990 in the small studio upstairs at Moles Club in Bath, *Splintering Heart* was a much more guitar led song with its incessant grinding riff. This wasn't to Chris's taste and he wanted something that sounded less grunge guitar and more synth pop.

Steve R has always loved tech and has spent, and still spends, an inordinate amount of his money on stuff with flashing lights, screens and digital bells and whistles. It's as if the personal computer was created with him in mind. The constant upgrading, the latest models, the pointless software; Steve couldn't wait to throw his cash at it.

Steve's latest gadget at that time was an Apple II SE computer. It was one of those all-in-one boxes with the small monochrome screen integrated into the same grey box as the computer. It had a floppy drive slot in the front below the screen, completing the pareidolic illusion of a friendly face.

However, it was anything but friendly. Steve and I spent hours scratching our heads trying to get the bloody thing to sync up with the tape machine. Smick, our constant companion and crew boss, even bought us both matching lab coats and I completed the look by sticking a CD to my forehead in imitation of a doctor's head mirror. We were nothing if not professional.

Eventually, after lots of pointing and swearing, we managed to record the backing for the first part of the song. Strange, how just getting one part down can feel like the greatest victory. I think we might have high fived each other in giddy jubilation.

I like the pulsating and machine-like sequence that builds into '...but not as much as this', when the whole band comes crashing in to great effect. This also works well as an intro to the live shows where h can start the show alone on stage with the backing tape until the band brings the song to life at the halfway point.

Ultimately, *Holidays In Eden* was, not unlike the hoariest football analogy, an album of two halves. The pop approach of our singles – quantised drums, less complex instrumentation – and, so as not to scare the horses and some of our older fans, the longer episodic pieces like *This Town* through *The Rake's Progress* and into *100 Nights*, which was written during the summer of 1988 at Dalnaglar Castle.

In an effort to set sail and chart more commercial waters, we made three expensive promo videos for the singles, although the budget didn't stretch far enough to send all five of us to Iceland for the filming of *Dry Land*. h got to spend a few days flying around in a helicopter and standing on glaciers looking heroically off into the middle distance, floppy fringe dancing in the breeze, while the rest of us spent a day on a craggy cliffside in Yorkshire, fringes not even a quarter as floppy.

We had high hopes for a hit when the album was released in June '91. The album performed as expected, coming at in number seven, scaling the giddy heights of the charts just as *Script* and *Fugazi* did; the singles not so much. They sold to the hardcore fans and made a decent chart showing in the first week but failed to cross over to a new audience in the way *Kayleigh* once did.

Told you it was the hope that kills you... Who wouldn't think that songs like *Cover My Eyes* and *No One Can* could chart in a way that made someone in Manchester Square sit up and take notice? Chris Neil had played his part, as had we, willingly walking into the commercial maw of the music business and hoping for the best.

You're usually rolling the dice when you release a record. Which sometimes doesn't mean that those dice might be loaded. The house doesn't always win.

Things with *Cover My Eyes* went pretty much to plan. We even scored a top 20 hit in the Netherlands. It was nothing we could retire on, but it felt like a win. It also felt like the start of something that might propel our album ever upwards. Every journey starts with a single step, which is what I might have mumbled to myself as I eyed the Dutch market and charts. So, we would soften the market up with the body punch that was *Cover My Eyes*. The audience would surely be reeling by the time we landed the haymaker that was *No One Can*.

EMI put their best radio pluggers on the job and spent serious cash on promotion and it was all looking great, as it often is at the beginning. In the early 1990s chart positions were still decided by a relatively small number of shops. It was meant to be a secret which shops were on the chart return list, but this wasn't a particularly hard nut to crack. Consequently, shops that weren't on the list were treated with about as much kindness as Cinderella's stepmother showed her, while the shops that fed into the charts machine were showered in gold and ermine. And by gold and ermine I mean free copies of singles, albums and other goodies, as well as payment for prominent display spots in the shop.

If that wasn't enough, the labels had teams of people spending their Saturdays (the biggest day by far for record and CD sales) travelling up and down the country buying multiple copies of singles from chart return shops in an effort to skew the numbers in their artist's favour.

I have little doubt, and less proof, that EMI played the record shop game when it came to Marillion. Not least when it came to *No One Can*.

The first week of release the Marillion faithful did what we knew they would do and rushed out to buy a song they already owned on the album, propelling it to a respectable number 36. We knew from experience that we now needed some radio play to expand the audience beyond the fanbase. Halfway through the week, the mid-week chart position – an unofficial prediction based on records sold so far – said we were likely to move up a couple of places.

That's when the EMI hit making machine made a sound like someone had dropped a piano on it. h and I practically pleaded with the head of promotion not to call off the dogs, as he confidently predicted we would definitely continue our march up the charts. Sadly, he had stopped listening. Previous experience had shown us that Marillion fans didn't shop for records on Saturdays any more than on other days. Conversely, the teens who did squander their cash on a Saturday would spend their money on records that would push us down the chart in spite of the mid-week prediction.

The head of promotion at EMI smiled in the way a headmaster might just before he expels you, and said he would jump out of his fifth floor office window if we went down in the charts. If we went down, then so would he, so to speak. With the kind of wisdom you would expect from a budgie, he then proceeded to redirect EMI's promotional efforts towards the latest Vanilla Ice single. That stiffed too, but we never did get to see his bloody, fallen body surrounded by police tape in Manchester Square.

Come the weekend, we dropped a few places to number 39. That was the signal for radio stations up and down the country to remove *No One Can* from their playlists. Realising their error just a little too late, EMI went back to pushing *No One Can* back up the charts. Showing how important a record company's heft can be, we moved up to number 33, more than reversing the loss of the previous week, but we were done. Radio stations don't put you back on their playlist just after they've dropped you. Not even if you've started scaling the charts again.

Had we gone up three places instead of down during that second week, who knows how far we might have climbed? Another hit single might have changed the path Marillion were on. We may have worked with Chris Neil again. We certainly wouldn't have made the album that was to follow *Holidays In Eden*, the album some hailed as 'dark and impenetrable': *Brave*.

EMI, like a dog going after a rabbit into a thicket, blundered on with *Dry Land*, as if everything was going to plan. It would only ever have broken through if *No One Can* had made a sizeable dent on the record buying public's psyche. *Dry Land*'s light went out faster than a shooting star. We heaved a collective sigh and resigned ourselves to that familiar feeling of disappointment that seemed to linger after the long build of writing and recording an album. It's the hope that kills you...

Meanwhile, at the other end of the charts, attempting to work Bryan Adams and his monster hit *Everything I Do...* loose from the number one spot was Right Said Fred with the trashy *I'm Too Sexy*. They were managed by Hit & Run, who were now our management company too.

While we were at Stanbridge attempting to write *Holidays In Eden*, John had turned up with Tony Smith, Genesis's manager and Hit & Run boss.

Smith, almost as wide as he was tall with a beard that made you think of an anvil, was an imposing figure. He had driven from London in his V8 Aston Martin to sell Hit & Run to us. John had been invited to join the company as part of their management team. We had no idea of the terms of the deal (when did we ever when it came to John?), but it appeared that Marillion and John were part of the same package that was being bolted on to the Hit & Run operation. John tried to convince us that he was offered the role on his own merits and would be taking it even if we chose not to join him.

Smith, in a voice you would imagine could get him cast as God in a film, dangled the carrot of a record deal with Atlantic Records in the USA in front of us. We were currently signed to IRS Records, a small independent label owned by former Police manager Miles Copeland. Smith also said the opening slot on the next Genesis tour might even be a possibility. Success in America would be virtually guaranteed. The only small catch was John's commission. All Hit & Run artists paid 20% management commission. It wouldn't do for Phil Collins to find out we were paying a lower rate than him. Not wishing to trouble the Genesis singer's sleep, we reluctantly agreed to increase John's commission from 17% to 20% and became part of the Hit & Run stable of artists.

For now, John was required to help out managing some of the smaller artists on Hit & Run, which took him away from us, but as well as his increased management commission he now had the security of a regular salary in return for his time. John was no longer tied to us financially, which started to reflect in his attitude towards us generally. As you'll see.

And I know what you're thinking: 'Mark, I don't recall that record deal with Atlantic or those heady nights with Marillion opening for Genesis.' And you would be right not to, as neither of them ever happened. Tony Smith: talking loud, saying very little.

Talking of heady nights, and I was, I finally took the plunge. I was a single man at the height of his powers on the road in a rock 'n' roll band (I'm certain that many rock 'n' roll bands have played in 13/8 time, if only accidentally). I'm sure you've read or seen the adaptation of Mötley Crüe's *The Dirt*. Their screed to life on the road and all its lurid excesses. Our tours around Europe and North and South America were nothing like it, unless you count the fact that we too had a tour bus and backstage catering. We didn't even have a singer who wore makeup any more.

In reality, most one night stands carry the faintest whiff of desperation, for both parties. Which isn't to say that I didn't try to shake that feeling of low level sadness in among a tangle of limbs and sheets in a few hotel rooms across the States. Meaningless sex can offer an oasis in an arid on the road existence that can be both lonely and mind-numbing. Though, whether they admit or not, most girls who are willing to sleep with you are doing so with the hope that it will lead to something deeper and more meaningful. In my case, knowing this led to feelings of shame and guilt. No, I can't imagine Vince Neil confessing to something like that either.

There are exceptions of course; times when a proverbial roll in the hay is exactly what you both want and nothing more. A lot of people have woken up the morning after a skinful next to someone they hardly recognise. Even me. Though the second time it happened (please tell me you haven't forgotten my confused awakening in college), I wasn't the drunk staggering happily around the bedroom.

On waking and seeing me beside her in my bed, my special new friend regarded me with a quizzical look and asked if she had been laid. I nodded slowly, my skin suddenly prickly. What if her lack of memory of our night together might make her cry wolf? Hand on heart, she was conscious and in possession of her faculties and was certainly willing and more than able the night before. She laughed (let's say with delight, not at the flickering memory of my prowess the night before) and so did I, with relief. Then, we ordered breakfast as a new day began.

Rather than flying, we chose to stay on the tour bus for the long journey west to California because the bus driver had said we could stop off and see the Grand Canyon along the way. For those not familiar with this natural wonder of the world, it's the abyss which Evel Knievel once tried to cross in a miniature rocket. He described a pretty cool arc in the clear blue sky before they found him halfway across the valley floor, pride and rocket dented, though not too much the worse for wear. Evel and his rocket had long gone by the time we got there, but the grandiose view was still spectacular and not the only one we would enjoy that day.

As we made our way to Los Angeles, a red sports car suddenly weaved through the sparse traffic, the sun gleaming on its tailfin. Inside sat a girl, her lipstick the same sheen of red as her car, naked from the waist up. She clearly knew her way around a gear stick and how to make an engine hum. (There's simply no other part of the book where I'm going to be able to use this kind of language, so sit back and enjoy it – which is something I was imagining she might say as she glided past.) Red, as I was now mentally referring to her, deftly sped and slowed to pass us again and again.

Like horny meerkats, we were upright and glued to the window, the monotony of the journey just a distant memory, our heads switching back and forth in unison. Eventually we pulled into a truck stop with her right behind us. Disarmingly courteous, she asked if anybody wanted to drive with her for part of the journey. It seemed like a nice upgrade from the bus, and I wasn't the only taker, but fate was on my side and I won the toss of a coin. We bought some beers and I sat with her chatting for an hour or so.

Eventually I said I should re-join the guys on the bus and she and the bus pulled over so that I could. My final memory of her is the sports car driving by the bus 15 minutes later. By now she was completely naked. She smiled, gave a small wave and mouthed the words "You could have been here with me" and disappeared (much like my ardour) among the traffic, a diminishing red dot revving into the distance.

Back in the UK, Susie, Freya and Kai continued to live in the family home in Haddenham that I had moved out of two years before. It was killing me financially to run two homes, but I didn't have the heart to ask them to downgrade to something cheaper. It was, I guess, a mixture of guilt and fear that my actions would demonstrate to Freya and Kai that my leaving was having a deleterious effect on their quality of life. It wasn't a very rational viewpoint, as they were so young and probably wouldn't have come to that conclusion, but I wasn't feeling rational at that point. More ashamed maybe.

Whenever I went to see Freya and Kai, Susie always made me feel welcome and made it clear that if I were to change my mind, then I would be very welcome to come back. Imagine how overjoyed the kids would be. We could play happy families again.

Never go back, right? I went back. Just as quickly as I had moved out, I made the decision to move back in with Susie. God knows what the neighbours must have thought. Her family were very welcoming and tactful enough not to mention my two year absence (as if I had gone away on some burglary charge, paid my debt to society and it was all behind me now). My family, less so. They didn't really like Susie and always felt she had looked down on them. But for the greater good, and my happiness, they fell in line.

And things worked for a while. But when I say we were playing happy families, it did sometimes feel like a role and none of our differences or the damage to our relationship had ever really gone away. And so it went, back and forth and back and forth, until anything good between us had eroded away to nothing.

In January 1992 Steve R had the brilliant idea of getting our own studio. He had been looking locally and found a nearby farm with four new light industrial units for rent. Two were already occupied by an upmarket kitchen manufacturer, but number 3 was empty and reasonably priced. We took it and proceeded to make it into a sort of studio cum storage unit. As it was just an empty shell, we enlisted Privet and Smick to build some scaffolding to create a mezzanine floor where we could store all of our equipment. We saved cash instantly; for years we had kept a lock-up in the basement of Nomis Studios in London, which was not only inconvenient but also expensive.

Enlivened by our decision, we built a small control room and bought a cheap mixing desk. It was small and it was basic, but it was ours. For the first time we had our own place, which we christened the Racket Club.

One of the first songs we wrote at the Racket Club was *I Will Walk On Water*, based around a riff I wrote on the Hammond organ. We weren't completely convinced by the song but decided it could be put to good use as a bonus track on a compilation of singles which EMI were planning to release. They also attempted to wrestle yet another hit single from us, so we offered them a cover of the Rare Bird song *Sympathy*. This, along with *I Will Walk On Water*, was recorded with Chris Kimsey at Metropolis Studios in London. This was the last time we would work with Chris. Going back, whether at the studio or home, just wasn't working any more.

Pete suggested calling the album *Six Of One And Half A Dozen Of The Other*, as it was made up of six Fish songs and half a dozen Hogarth songs interleaved across the album, with the two bonus tracks on the end. *Sympathy* followed the now familiar Marillion pattern of entering the charts in the first week (number 17) and then raced to the bottom and out of sight. EMI, who wouldn't know they had already burnt their fingers even if their hand was on fire, took another punt on making *No One Can* a hit and propelled it all the way up the chart to number 26.

You'll excuse the pun, but that part of our career had clearly gone pop, so what to do next?

The Racket Club helped take care of that and was about to change the way we worked forever. As we all lived 30 minutes or less from our new studio, we could afford to spend a few hours together writing and if nothing came of it, then we could go home and cut the grass or watch TV. It made a big difference to how we felt about the way we worked together. Now we no longer felt the pressure of paying hundreds of pounds a day to write to order and worrying if nothing resulted from it.

Sometimes h and I would meet up in the evenings for a few hours and take a different approach to how we worked. Those late hours of relative solitude and no real end goal helped us come up with the opening 'bridge' section of *Brave*.

We also worked out the opening bars of *The Great Escape*, but Steve R was circumspect about it at best. Rather than just drop it, h took my chords and used them as a starting point for another song: *The Hollow Man*.

John Helmer had sent through a few lyrics for our consideration: *Hard As Love*, *Runaway* and *Paper Lies*. We wrote some music for both *Hard As Love* and *Runaway*, but it was the latter that pointed us towards a possible theme for the album.

A few years earlier h had scribbled something in his notebook about a news story of a girl found wandering on the Severn Bridge. He started inventing a backstory for the girl, an idea that he was keen to flesh out into a concept album. I'm not sure what he thought our reaction might be, but we couldn't have been happier. Forget the record company restraints of our last few albums, this would give us the freedom to explore unconventional song structures. The creative shackles were off.

For the first time since h joined the band, we felt like we had a common goal to work towards and the method to get us there. h had become more relaxed with the idea of jamming to eke the ideas out. One 10 minute long jam was a contender for the new album almost immediately. It didn't have a typical song structure and grew from a pulsing bass and endlessly rising keyboard chord pattern. We called it *The Sex Groove Thing* and used it to link *Mad* to *Hard As Love* via some other short sections that couldn't categorically be described as songs either. It later became *The Slide*.

Brave ended up being a sum of its parts. Even if all the individual components didn't quite hang together as a storyline, when locked together the result was emotive and compelling. The album felt like a real call to arms, a Marillion landmark.

Lyrically, two songs didn't really fit the concept, *Paper Lies* and *The Hollow Man*. John Helmer's *Paper Lies* lyric took a swing at the British tabloid press. *The Hollow Man* was something of an insight into how h was beginning to feel about his new status as a 'rock star'.

Regardless of the fact they didn't fit, we kept them on the record anyway. We felt the album was mostly low key and *Paper Lies* gave it a much needed boost. *The Hollow Man* I'm still less sure about, but I suspect it was not least because h was so pleased with how it turned out, and it was very much an h song.

Meanwhile, we had a new A&R man at EMI. Mustard keen, sporting a beanie hat and in thrall to the indie guitar bands of the Madchester scene, please meet one Nick Mander.

It turned out he was an iron fist in a woolly hat. After *Holidays In Eden*'s relatively minor sales of 450,000 copies, Mander told his boss at EMI that he would be able to tame Marillion's excesses and get us to deliver a modern sounding album, under budget and on time, and he had just the producer in mind for the job. Mander might as well have been on meds.

When people see what they want to see, it's called motivated perception. This is how Dave Meegan came to be our producer in 1994.

We knew Dave from a decade earlier when he was the young, industrious and dedicated assistant engineer on our *Fugazi* album. Nick Tauber was so impressed with Dave when we met him at Sarm Studios that he persuaded them to let Dave come with us as we moved from studio to studio across London during the final weeks of the *Fugazi* sessions. We were so taken with his almost endless endeavour that our workload put Dave in hospital from exhaustion for a few days.

Since working with us in 1983 Dave had engineered for Rush, U2 and Yes. While we were yet to make up our mind about Mander, Dave's CV spoke for itself. We agreed to give him a go in the producer's chair. Mander was very taken by Dave's work with The Pet Shop Boys, The Blow Monkeys, Public Image Ltd and Erasure and was convinced that Dave was the man to whip us into shape.

Let's hope that Mander wasn't a betting man as he would be living under a bridge by now.

We went along with the EMI directive that we needed to produce a less costly album. A big slice of our recording budget usually went to the producer. Chris Kimsey and Chris Neil didn't come cheap. They both received an advance of £50-60k against their royalties. They also earned more in royalties than any member of the band, around 3 to 3.5%, so they were likely to recoup pretty quickly too. In the case of Dave Meegan, he was relatively inexperienced as a producer (meaning cheaper) and engineered everything himself, so there was a double saving from the off.

Recording in an expensive London studio was out of the question and the Racket Club wasn't nearly well enough equipped to make an album. Besides, and you couldn't make this up, the kitchen people next door made so much noise that we were thinking we would have to move out. The owners came up with a solution: the kitchen people wanted to expand into our unit (possibly to bash even more pots and pans), but the owners were currently building some much bigger units and we could have one of those for the same price as our current home.

It wouldn't be ready in time to make *Brave*, but we had an alternative. Miles Copeland suggested that we could borrow his château in the Dordogne in France to record in.

And so, with a truck full of musical instruments and recording equipment, we set off for the south west of France. Run by former Wishbone Ash drummer Steve Upton, Château de Marouatte was gradually being renovated. Sparsely furnished and with the works far from finished, it still made for a grand façade, its gothic finery set starkly against the lush French countryside.

We had two months to record *Brave*. Think about it, that's *Holidays In Eden* and some time for exploring rural France tagged on the end; easy. Though that's not how things worked out. It became clear very quickly that 60 scant days in Marouatte might not be enough time to capture the expansive, elusive album we wanted to make. By the time we were pulling out of the château's grand gardens and heading home, we were only just getting started.

CHAPTER 15

Fortune Favours The Brave

If you're an avid follower of the popular Broadway and West End hit musical *Avenue Q*, the one populated by shaggy looking puppets and set in New York City, then you'll know that the internet is for porn. Admittedly, if you're a teenage boy, then this won't be news to you either. And I'm paraphrasing, but it was those fur ball monsters who made a musical smash out of the rousing *The Internet Is For Porn* with such refrains as 'Grab your dick and double click'. I can't recommend it enough.

Now, I'm not sure that's what Sir Tim Berners-Lee had in mind when he changed the world in 1993 with his invention of the World Wide Web. Berners-Lee is an undoubted genius, the people behind *Avenue Q* arguably less so, and I'm not even sure where Marillion are on that list, or if we even made the cut. But we beat Berners-Lee to the Web by some 11 years.

In February 1982 we first published *The Web*, which consisted of a photocopied sheet of A4. We named it after our song, though some of you might have been perceptive enough to work that one out for yourselves.

Small acorns and all that, but this flimsy single sheet would help the Marillion name (some say 'brand') flower and grow, until it began to work its way around the world, much like its namesake.

From time to time we (and various other Marillion fan clubs around the world) would hold get-togethers for like-minded fans, and one, two or sometimes all of us would show up to say hello and 'grip 'n' grin'.

In May 1992, in recognition of our tenth year with EMI, we played a small fan club gig at the Borderline club in London. As was often the case back then, the gig was recorded straight to stereo from the mixing desk. The quality was pretty good but not considered suitable for an 'official' release.

Marillion have always been heavily bootlegged by dedicated fans, who collect as many live recordings of the band as they can (hey, everyone needs a hobby). Remarkably, there are recordings in existence (of varying quality) of about 80% of all the gigs we have ever played (even some that we would prefer to forget). Unlike the Grateful Dead, we didn't encourage people to record our shows, or pen them off in bootlegging areas, which the hirsute San Francisco band used to do sometimes, though, much like Jerry Garcia and his ragbag bunch, we do have songs whose duration runs into double figures. Our line in the sand was that we didn't mind people collecting and swapping our music, as long as no cash changed hands.

Unless that cash was going into our hands. We decided to bootleg ourselves, flogging off a few thousand copies of the Borderline show to the fans, mainly through *The Web* and at some of our gigs. This was forbidden under the terms of our recording contract. Everything we had recorded since September 1982, both live and in the studio, was owned by EMI and only they had the right to produce and sell copies of such recordings. We didn't think EMI would have the appetite to take one of their own artists to court over copyright infringement. But just to be sure John spoke to them first and they agreed, unofficially, that it was alright to sell them as long as we didn't take the piss by selling more than a few thousand copies.

This was the first, all important step towards independence. Racket Records was born.

Let's mix metaphors: every journey starts with a single step and hindsight's 20/20. Which might explain why mankind is not above pulling together the random bygone strands of our lives and knitting them together in a cohesive narrative that we sometimes kid ourselves were surely an act of fate. It's an illusion, but something that we still cling to the way a drowning man holds on to a passing piece of wood as his ship goes down. Saying that, some decisions have a way of turning your life around in a profound and impactful way that changes things for ever.

As it was with our decision to breach our recording contract and make and release our own CDs directly to fans: a whole new world suddenly opened up to us. We could see that there was good money to be made being the artist, record company and retailer all rolled into one. In fact, we liked it so much that later in the year we repeated the trick with another live recording, this time from Caracas in Venezuela. This was Racket CD number two.

There was no internet shopping in those days. (Amazon was a couple of years from inception, so, if you think about it, we beat both Berners-Lee and Jeff Bezos to the punch, but do we get hailed as true pioneers? Not a word!) So we mainly sold the CDs at gigs and in 1993 there were no gigs for us because we were busy recording *Brave* for most of the year.

I say recording, but when we returned from France after a very enjoyable couple of months eating good food and drinking fine wine, we weren't exactly weighed down by a wealth of newly recorded material. Don't get me wrong, we worked hard while we were there, especially Dave Meegan (and all that wine wasn't going to drink itself), but we hadn't really finished writing the album by the time we rolled up to the château. Combine this with the fact that Dave was very fastidious in his approach to recording, and scheduling-wise we were on the back foot before we had even fully begun. Dave also believed in letting the music grow organically and seeing what might emerge. As incredibly enjoyable and creative as this might have been, we were wasting valuable time.

About a month into our time at Marouatte we sat down with Dave to express our concerns at our progress, or rather lack of it. Dave, in his soft Irish brogue, asked, "Are we making a work of art here?" We all agreed we were. "Then it will take as long as it takes," he countered, and that was the end of the discussion for all of us.

Back in London, Nick Mander was feeling less relaxed. He'd already flipped out because we spent 300 francs (about £30) on a coffee machine, mistakenly thinking that the invoice was for £300. What's more, he was starting to realise that pairing us with Dave wasn't the tactical masterstroke he had first thought it might be. Not if he wanted the next Marillion album out before Christmas.

With only the drums and some of the bass guitar parts recorded, we set forth to Parr Street Studios in Liverpool. Owned by Hit & Run and managed by Paul Lewis and his wife Annie, it seemed a logical choice. Paul had decided to give up touring the year before and was now working full time at Parr Street. We've had some amazingly talented and loyal crew along the way, with many of them staying with us for years or even decades. Privet, a talented engineer, was in demand everywhere, and finding it harder to keep time free for us when we might need him. He would eventually stop working for us altogether, as the tours he was offered were bigger and more lucrative than ours. Who could blame him? Not us; we wished him well.

We were at Parr Street for five long months for the *Brave* sessions, a world away from a record like *Holidays In Eden*. Working with Dave Meegan was the polar opposite to working with Chris Neil. Dave wanted to explore every possible avenue in the journey from creative spark to finished song. Along the way there were plenty of opportunities to try whatever we felt like doing. There were also numerous happy accidents that Dave meticulously kept records of, some written and some in his head. He seemed to have an encyclopaedic knowledge of every morsel committed to tape and where to find it.

Dave worked extremely hard for the whole seven months we spent recording *Brave*. There is an incredible amount of musical nuance in that album. This was also at a time when everything was recorded on analogue tape. This meant that copying and pasting parts you liked or cutting sections together from multiple takes was at best very difficult or impossible without losing some quality.

Like Dave before him on the *Fugazi* sessions, Mike Hunter was our assistant engineer at Parr Street. Mike was always there to help to set up the studio first thing and, more importantly, make the tea. It's the studio tradition that the assistant engineer makes tea, as much and as often as the producer and band demand. Rock 'n' roll, right?

There's an apocryphal tale about producer Mark Ellis, often told to assistant engineers to make sure they've always got a teapot to hand. When Ellis was an assistant, he was permanently ready with a mug of tea, earning him the nickname 'Flood'. He had a fellow assistant nicknamed 'Drought', who approached a teabag the way a bomb disposal expert creeps up on a suspect device. These days Flood is famous, but who remembers Drought?

Years later when Mike came to work with us, he swore he would never make another cup of tea for anyone, and he's been as good as his word ever since.

Making *Brave* was such a fulfilling creative experience for us all thanks to Dave's willingness to experiment and explore. We would often record parts with little preparation. In fact, once Dave felt like you knew what you were doing, he would demand you stopped. He relished the uncertainty of us not being too familiar with the material. Dave lived for spontaneity. It was a thrill, but on the downside, it made for hours and hours of listening and careful editing and compiling.

The weeks turned into months, summer turned to autumn, and the prospect of a 1993 release quietly slipped away. Only Dave and Mike were required to be in the studio all day. The rest of us had lots of free time as we took it in turns to record. Ian was living in Florida at that point, and we hadn't seen him since France. Judging by the occasional phone call and fax, he was getting as exasperated as Nick Mander with the amount of time we were taking to finish the album.

For the emotional climax to the *Brave* story (*The Great Escape* through *Falling From The Moon*) we invited h's old friend Darryl Way to arrange the orchestral accompaniment. He did a fantastic job in weaving the themes into an arrangement for strings, flute and French horn, although our already blown budget wouldn't stretch to paying for an orchestra to play the parts. (By that point I'm not sure we could have afforded new strings for Steve R's guitar.)

Instead, we invited a few members of the Liverpool Philharmonic to the studio and recorded them multiple times, with the addition of samples to fake an orchestra. As a nice touch, Ian invited his dad, Raymond, a lovely chap with the same understated sense of humour as Ian, to play violin too.

In the midst of all this, a fan called Min Benson got in touch to ask if I was interested in learning about the Marillion mailing list. She arrived at the studio with a pile of computer print outs. Not A4, but reams of perforated sheets joined together with rows of holes down each side. This was *The Freaks Digest*. Not a name you would pay to have printed on a T-shirt, but it was about to become an invaluable resource for the band.

Named after our song *Freaks*, this was a collection of emails shared between hundreds of (mostly American) Marillion fans via a mailing list. Before the World Wide Web really got going mailing lists were a way for like-minded people to keep in touch. Any emails sent to the list were automatically distributed to everyone else on the list. Of course, I signed up – who wouldn't? It was the prehistoric equivalent of Googling yourself (and you thought *The Voyeur* was a Fish song). It was fascinating to eavesdrop on the discourse between Marillion fans around the world. Not all of it was interesting, or complimentary come to that, and I kept my presence on the list secret for a few years. Charmingly, I was what was known as a 'lurker'.

Having missed the chance to release *Brave* before the charts became too busy with the usual flurry of Christmas fare, we were now looking at releasing the album the following February. Not the best news, but at least it freed us up for a short while. During the previous US tour for *Holidays In Eden*, when not cruising the highways in flash red sports cars, we hired an American guitar technician called John Wesley Dearth or just Wes to his friends. Wes turned out to be an excellent guitarist and singer in his own right. We became good friends and when the tour finished, we stayed in touch.

After the protracted sessions for *Brave* and run-ins with an A&R man who was trying to remould Marillion, it will come as no surprise when I tell you that I was beginning to wonder about the future and a life without my band. I mean, what could I do apart from play keyboards? There was always the possibility of a solo career, but I also fancied myself as a record producer. I knew my way around a studio and most of the producers we had worked with didn't engineer their own sessions.

I asked Wes if he would like me to produce his first album. He hired me on the spot and I headed for Morrisound Studios in Florida. What I didn't know was that Wes had already agreed that Jim Morris, brother of the studio owner, Tom, could produce the album. What's more, the brothers were being very generous with the rates they charged Wes for studio time so there was a strong incentive to keep Jim happy. I was starting to realise that perhaps producing wasn't just what you did as you sat behind the studio glass.

Nevertheless, I enjoyed the month or so working with Wes, even if it didn't turn out to be the production debut I had hoped for. I also ended up playing most of the keyboards on the album which wasn't what I wanted or expected when I signed on to produce. On a happier note, as Ian was comparatively local, I invited him down to play drums on the song *None So Beautiful*.

Under The Red And White Sky was released on Racket Records in time for the *Brave* tour, for which Wes was both our support act and guitar tech. He sold thousands of copies of his album to our audience over the course of those shows, proof indeed that this was a business model that might work for Marillion.

We were extraordinarily happy with how *Brave* turned out. It felt like the seismic statement of a band who were capable of realising their creative id and capturing it on tape. We had the chops, the artistry, and the story with a producer/engineer who understood and cared as much as we did about what we were making.

We had the fans that were prepared to make the considerable investment of time and effort to understand and appreciate it too. In all honesty, we didn't take all of our fans with us. For some it was just too dark, too depressing. Others missed the rock and pop that had helped shape our earlier careers. Unsurprisingly, our sales fell further still, *Brave* only shifting 300,000 copies in the first year.

As you might imagine, EMI were less than delighted by this turn of events. We couldn't even assuage their doubts with a strong lead single. *Brave* didn't have one.

Consequently, we thought it would be a waste of money to spend over £100,000 on three promo videos for singles that would trouble the charts only fleetingly, if at all. This sort of video budget was normal in the 1990s, which irked us because it was more than we were supposed to spend making the music and half of it went on our balance sheet. I say 'supposed to' because with *Brave* we completely blew the budget out of the water and spent well over £200,000 on the recording.

We have MTV and Duran Duran to blame for bloated video expenditure. When MTV burst onto our screens in the early 1980s, it became an essential component of the release to produce a video to go with your single. As a promotional expense, this fell on the record company to pick up the tab, and so bands didn't worry about how much they were spending, hiring movie producers and yachts in exotic locations like Duran Duran did with their 1982 hit *Rio*, wearing suits that cost more than my first house. Adapting to the changing times and always looking for new and creative ways to pass as much of the cost of doing business as possible to the artists, EMI started to make 50% of the video production costs recoupable from the artists' royalties in time for our 1982 contract. Thanks, EMI.

We reasoned that if we were paying half the cost, then we should have some say in how the money was spent. So, we approached EMI with the idea of making a movie based on the *Brave* story rather than the usual three promo clips. I can't say they were in love with the idea (or with us come to that), but they gave us the go-ahead.

Finding a director willing to attempt to make a 70 minute movie built on the story of *Brave* for £120,000 was not easy. We found our man in Richard Stanley who had two cult horror movies to his name: *Hardware* and *Dust Devil*. Stanley was remarkable; remarkable in that he managed to make *Brave* the movie even less accessible than our album.

The filming took place over a few weeks in early 1994, already too late for the album's February release date. The British Board of Film Classification delayed it further still because they objected to some of the more disturbing scenes on the grounds that this was a music video and might be viewed by minors. (Footage depicting a realistic looking wrist cutting suicide attempt will raise the hackles of a film censor, it seems.) This delayed the release yet again, but in the end, it probably didn't matter too much because the film was hardly likely to worry the mainstream.

Stanley later disowned the film, claiming that it was re-edited without his involvement. This is untrue as the only edits were the cuts made by the BBFC. I may have been Mad Jack, but Richard Stanley made me seem the picture of propriety. He gave off his own villainous, untrustworthy vibe and in 2014 he was accused of sexual, emotional, physical and financial abuse by screenwriter Scarlett Amaris. Stanley's directing career hit the buffers a few years after *Brave* (though you can't pin that on us) when he was publicly fired from the set of the disastrous *Island Of Dr Moreau* just one week into filming.

In a turn of events that will come as no surprise to those of you who have read this far, during the filming of *Brave* I met a young Italian girl called Emanuela, who I later discovered had made her way to the UK with the sole aim of getting a job with EMI in order to meet me. The closest she had come to that thus far was the offer of unpaid work as a runner on the Marillion film shoot. She jumped at the chance and got close enough to get my attention.

By this stage in my life, I was not hopeful that Susie and I had a future together and I decided to leave her again, this time for good. It was even more traumatic than the first time, at least for the children. Freya and Kai were older now (11 and 9) and much more aware of what was going on. I felt terrible about hurting them, but I didn't want to be with Susie, not even for the sake of the children.

As you might expect, this harmed my relationship with them even more. The damage I caused to my relationship with Kai and especially Freya is my biggest regret in life and it haunts me still.

The aftershock from *Brave* was both bad and good. On the downside, it lacked commercial clout and EMI were closer to giving up on us than ever. Our balance sheet had never looked so bad. On the upside, we had solidified the allegiance of the fans we somehow hadn't managed to shake off yet. They were more committed to Marillion than ever, knowing that we weren't going the way of some other prog bands in pursuit of a hit record.

We toured extensively with *Brave*, playing over 70 shows across Europe but barely made a penny. Touring the USA was out of the question as we were no longer signed to a major label there. I insisted that I wanted to see a full breakdown of the tour accounts and for the first time John supplied them. They weren't a pretty sight. The management commission was healthy but little else was. From an artistic point of view, we had an excellent tour, playing the whole of the album in one set. This had a similar effect as the album had on our fans: some adored it, while others walked away baffled and longing for more simple times when they could bounce happily up and down to *Garden Party*.

Taking *Brave* on the road was a technical challenge too, like building the pyramids was challenging. There was so much going on within the grooves of that album, and it was something we very much wanted to capture live without resorting to backing tapes.

Which was where I came in. I spent the first six weeks set aside for rehearsals grappling with samplers and computers. Ever since the early 1980s I had always pushed my equipment to do more than it was designed to. The particular issue with *Brave* was lack of memory combined with the sheer number of samples and what to do with them. When there were a few samples that needed to be played at various points in a song it was a simple matter of assigning them to a key at the dusty end of the keyboard (either very top or bottom) and just hitting the required key in time. As the number of samples increased to 20, 30 or more per song, deciding where to put them and then remembering where they were became trickier than The Times crossword and about as much fun.

To offset my desire to hit my keyboards with a hammer and toss them out of the tour bus window, I came up with the idea of offloading some samples onto Pete. Pete had a set of pedals, usually reserved for playing bass notes, which I loaded up with samples for him to trigger too. Pete did a brilliant job of playing the bass, singing backing vocals and triggering samples all at the same time, while still managing to run around the stage like a man who is being chased by a wasp.

My assistant in all this was Mike Hunter. We got on well during the *Brave* sessions and I invited him to come on tour as my keyboard technician. He thought it would make a change from studio work and, as an added bonus, he would get to see the world too. Poor, sweet, innocent Mike. He almost had a nervous breakdown from the stress. Things were always going wrong during the gigs. I suppose I had become used to it, but for Mike it was all a bit too much. Ditto h, as he was the guy at the front of the stage trying to sell *Brave* to the audience as his confidence slowly eroded, convinced that the music to which he was performing might suddenly stop playing.

Believe it or not, the reliability of my equipment had been steadily improving since *Seasons End* when I had the stellar idea of inviting my fake cousin Colin (I say 'fake' because he is the brother of my mother's sister's husband), an inexperienced software programmer, to write me some software to control my keyboard patch changes during the show. Unsurprisingly, this turned out to be a disaster as the software was constantly crashing. I was forced to switch to some new hardware from Germany half-way through the tour. I continued to use this piece of kit up to and including the *Brave* tour.

However, the lowest point equipment-wise for me happened at the Bonn Biskuithalle on 17th March 1994. We were being broadcast live on German radio and through an act of abject stupidity (plugging a cable into the wrong socket) I fried the Kurzweil K2000 sampler during the soundcheck. With no hope of obtaining a replacement (it was souped up and modified) I had to limp through the show with a much reduced palette of sounds and zero samples. It was like going from watching a top end colour HD TV to an old black and white Grundig.

It was possibly the longest two hours of my life. The band never knew it was an unforced error. Well, not until now.

Thankfully, as the *Brave* tour went on things improved with my equipment's stability, but it never did quite reach 100% bulletproof status. This was a source of friction between h and me for many years. I finally sorted it out in 2014 when I switched from using Windows PCs to Apple computers and a new piece of software called Mainstage that was finally able to do what I needed it to, soothing our singer's nerves as a result.

The *Brave* tour finished at the amazing Auditorio Nacional in Mexico City in September 1994. This 10,000 capacity venue was purpose built for live music and laid out like a Roman amphitheatre. The sound was great and even the sub-optimal hired-in instruments couldn't prevent us from having a great gig.

With the tour over and not much money in the coffers there was only one course of action: get back in the studio and make another album quickly. We put it to EMI that we wanted to spend our recording budget on studio equipment. They were unsure but agreed we could because it meant the budget wouldn't balloon out of control as if we were making a record in a remote French château. The new Racket Club was complete and big enough for us to record in too.

The recording equipment which we bought was new technology. Instead of the old 24 track machines with two inch tape, these were digital recorders using Hi8 video tapes. Each machine could only record eight tracks at a time, so we had three of them linked together to give a total of 24 tracks. They were adequate, but not as robust or reliable as the much more expensive professional equipment we were used to. But we made it work because we had to.

Dave Meegan was back on board, with Mike Hunter as his assistant. Almost without noticing we had shifted in the way we wrote and arranged songs. In the early days a song would start with a musical idea in someone's head. They would play it to the band and if we liked it enough then we would work on it, turning it into a song. Then, and only then, would a rough recording be made of it onto cassette.

With *Brave*, having our own studio and the means to record every writing session onto tape or mini disc, we started to build a collection of jams and half-formed ideas that would otherwise have been forgotten. Many of these ideas were terrible, both in their composition and the quality of the recording, but a few showed promise. Over time, some of them made it on to the *Brave* album, but there were still plenty of pieces that didn't yet have a home, musically or lyrically.

When we came to write *Afraid Of Sunlight*, we brought Dave Meegan in almost from the beginning, partly because we had a studio, but also because we valued his opinion when it came to choosing what to focus on. Carrying on from where he left off with *Brave*, Dave helped us to arrange the ideas into songs. His contribution was invaluable with something like *Out Of This World*, because he insisted that we attempt to segue from the guitar solo in 4/4 time to the 'only love can turn you round...' section in 3/4 time. Admittedly, it took a few attempts before we could realise his idea, but it remains one of my favourite transitions on the album. There are plenty of other examples of Dave's creativity stamped all over that record. I confess that not all of them were welcomed by me at the time. I was disappointed with the finished album, deflated almost, but years later I've re-evaluated my opinion of it and think it belongs in our top five releases.

Remarkably (I'm surprised someone at EMI didn't faint when they heard the news), we wrote, recorded and mixed *Sunlight* in under six months. We also felt that we had managed to get the balance right between radio friendly tracks like *Beautiful* and *Cannibal Surf Babe* and the more immersive material like *King* and *Afraid Of Sunlight* itself. *Beautiful* also turned out to be an unlikely hit in Brazil after it was used as a theme in a popular TV soap. I had the ever helpful *Freaks* mailing list to thank for that news.

Not that this mattered to EMI. Our relationship with the label was lower than our record sales. They had held a meeting and Marillion were no longer an EMI artist – we had been dropped.

CHAPTER 16

Down, Not Out

Just for the record, I don't want you thinking that I see myself as some armour clad hero atop my trusty steed, flinty eyed with a thousand yard stare from the travails of battle. Though I'm pretty sure I could rock some brigandines and a pair of gauntlets, but not on stage; that would play merry hell with my playing. The reason I draw on this clanking metaphor is something called the monomyth, or, more commonly, the hero's journey.

It's the archetype of a countless films, TV shows, books and stories. Simply put, the hero goes on an adventure, is victorious in a decisive crisis and comes home changed or transformed. Along the way there is a smattering of existential angst, peril and a moment when the future looks bleak and the hero surely doomed to fail.

Without wishing to sound too alarming, these next few chapters see our hero down at heel, trudging ever onwards, fate hanging over him like the sword of Damocles. The horizon a mesh of dark clouds, waiting only for the sun to break through and shine again.

Onwards then...

Harold Wilson said that a week is a long time in politics. Harold Wilson didn't know he was born; he should have tried living in the real world for a while. Your average Joe or Jane will spend five years in the same job. In relative terms, most bands have the lifespan of an amoeba. Remarkable then that Marillion had managed to stay afloat for 14 long years as staples of EMI Records. In that time, we had recorded eight studio albums, two live albums and a bunch of singles totalling well over five million sales. Yet here we were being dropped, discarded and shown the door while owing EMI in excess of half a million pounds. We seemed to be well and truly sunk.

Not that you would necessarily conclude that judging by the brave (the irony!) face we were putting on things. We said that parting company with EMI was long overdue (which it really was) and that a smaller independent label who genuinely cared about us would be better in the long run (they didn't, and it wasn't). Big fish, small pond, etc. Though Fish had been swimming in ever decreasing circles long before we began playing to more selective audiences. He had decamped from EMI even before we had been pushed, subsequently releasing a couple of albums through Polydor before taking the DIY ethic to its natural conclusion and setting up his own label around the time that we released *Brave*.

We had come to depend on the advances from EMI to pay our wages. While fun (and profitable for John Arnison), the touring brought in relatively little money considering the miles and hours we put in.

The one sliver of light in this Stygian doom was the Racket Club and our studio set-up. Most bands when dumped by their label can easily lose their moorings, look inward and turn on each other. It's easy for things to turn ugly.

John negotiated us a new three album deal with Castle Communications, a mid-sized record company who mainly dealt in re-issuing music catalogues at mid-price. Catalogue that the major labels didn't know what to do with or simply couldn't be bothered to deal with. This was low margin stuff but not without profit, but they were also keen to have current artists on their roster as well as selling CDs by bands who were either dead critically or commercially or literally six feet underground.

We were no longer in the sightline of the (then) six major labels, but they would experience their own life and death struggles by the end of the decade. Streaming would finally shock them out of their complacency and deal three of them a death blow that would rattle any hero's teeth. Not that the majors were inundated with many heroes; one or two villains, maybe…

Years later they would look back on the burnt out wreckage of their expense account lunches and limo hire and dream of having artists that could shift a few hundred thousand units, but that scenario was still some years away. It was 1996 and we were idling, and it still felt darkest before dawn.

Selling 200,000 or so CDs to a loyal fanbase but currently without a deal, we were the perfect target for Castle. We were more than happy to sign, although the advance was only £100,000. This was a far from trifling figure, but less than half the money we were used to. In order to buy us time to write the next album without running out of cash, John also negotiated a deal for Castle to release a double live album. The only snag was that EMI owned all the recordings made while under contract to them, including the live ones.

In another example of their largesse, EMI agreed we could have access to the tapes only if they could release the live album in the UK, our biggest market, and if we paid them £100,000. Castle agreed to pay them the money on our behalf and it was added to our debt with our new album. Knowing no bounds to their generosity, EMI also stipulated that the £100,000 we paid them was not to be subtracted from our outstanding balance, so that left us owing over £700,000 to just two record companies.

On reflection, *Made Again* should have been called *F**ked Again*.

But we were learning, albeit slowly. We agreed to license the three albums to Castle rather than assign them for life of copyright (70 years after the last one of us perishes). It was a ten year licence, but it would come around soon enough and then we would be free to do with those albums as we wished. On such small foundations are empires built, and by empires I mean self-sustaining prog rock bands with an ardent fanbase.

Pretend to be surprised when I tell you that my personal life was in a worse state than my professional life. Living in a small flat in Watford with my fiancée Emanuela (yes, I was planning to get married again because marriage was clearly a model that was working for me), I was having a reverse mid-life crisis of sorts. I say reverse because most people's idea of a mid-life crisis usually involves quitting the rat race and doing something irresponsible like buying a Harley-Davidson and getting a new tattoo. By contrast, I was wondering if it was time to give up the life of rock 'n' roll and get a proper job.

But I wasn't planning on becoming a bank teller just yet. Instead, I tried my hand again at producing, this time with a band from High Wycombe called Jump. The singer John Dexter Jones reminded me a lot of Fish when I first saw them playing (though without the huge, bare feet and greasepaint). They were opening for a screening of the *Brave* film in Milton Keynes. I liked them and their music instantly and felt I could do a good job of producing them.

They agreed and we spent a few happy weeks working on their album *The Myth Of Independence* at the Racket Club in mid-1995. In all honesty, they could have made just as good an album without my sitting through the glass noddingly thoughtfully. I didn't bring much, if anything, to the table. Perhaps producing wasn't for me? I don't lead from the front; I'm more of a team player. But almost every album, if it's to have any kind of impact, needs someone to help conceive and convey the message, to cheerlead it and bring it home.

Next, like a man looking at a long stretch alone inside and eager to find ways to fill the time, I decided to write a solo album. Channelling my Inner Rick Wakeman (who doesn't fancy themselves in a cape?), I plucked the idea of Dante's *Inferno* as a theme out of the air. Rick had made such a strong series of records using King Arthur and the wives of Henry VIII as his starting points, so I decided that the bold, thematic approach was for me. Not sure what might rhyme with 'inferno', I even asked John Helmer to write me some lyrics, which he did.

Truth be told, I never got past writing the first part, which was less than ten minutes long. I was starting to discover that I wasn't very good at flying solo either. I lack the confidence to press ahead without encouragement, and I often get bored and distracted with whatever it is I'm working on. I spent the next 25 years deflecting questions asking when my solo album was coming out, wishing I had never mentioned it in the first place, until I could finally reveal the *Marathon* record with something of a flourish in autumn 2020.

It was long overdue. Steve R and h were both more successful than I in coming up with solo albums (not difficult when I couldn't even magic something up in over two decades). Ian had managed a collaboration with his saxophonist friend Ben Castle (son of Roy, the famous record breaker), while Pete had joined prog supergroup Transatlantic.

Besides, I had more pressing matters to deal with than Dante and his bloody inferno. I woke up one Sunday in early January 1997, the curtains still closed, keeping out the weak winter sun. As I lay there, slumbering fiancée at my side, I was thinking that I was getting married that summer and I wasn't sure I wanted to. Our relationship was starting to show signs of stress. We had fallen out in spectacular fashion at Christmas while we were in Italy and I had flown home alone.

There were other little signs that maybe we weren't on the same life path. I was getting married to please Emanuela and not because I wanted to. It had nothing to do with the fact that she wanted to get married in a Catholic church in Italy and I had never been confirmed. This meant I had to go through the charade of attending religious classes (it filled the time, I suppose) and become 'confirmed' before the priest would consider marrying us in God's house. And it wasn't because she had revealed to me that she had made her mind up aged 15 that she was going to marry me. On reflection, that should have seen me slipping away under the cover of night, never to be seen again. She was 26 now and I was merely unsettled by her misguided teenage ambitions. Which might give you some idea of where my head was at then.

Much worse, for me at least, was that this all just felt like history repeating itself. Had I learned nothing? There's no fool like a fool in love. Or who thinks he's in love. And then knows with absolute certainty that he's not.

I blurted out that I had changed my mind about getting married and she ended the relationship there and then. Which sounds more seismic than it was in reality. We parted on pretty good terms under the circumstances. I even helped her move into her new flat. I left sunny Watford for good and headed for Aylesbury. I was travelling light. When I had split with Susie a few years before, I left with nothing but my clothes, a bookcase and some books.

With the kind of insight sorely lacking in my life, when Ian had moved to Florida a few years earlier he had bought a small two bedroom house in Aylesbury to have a base when in the UK. He kindly lent me the house until I found something more permanent.

It wasn't just my mental state that was in the bin; financially things were in a parlous state too. John informed us that there was no money in the bank so we wouldn't be getting wages for the next three months. That was a real shock because in all the time we had been managed by John that had never happened before. Not to worry, John was still getting his pay cheque from Hit & Run. To make matters worse, John was then managing the reggae group Aswad. They expected the sort of exclusivity from John that we had enjoyed ('enjoyed' is such a subjective word) up until his joining Hit & Run. Aswad's big hit *Shine* was less than two years old, so they were in demand as well as demanding.

Cutting our cloth accordingly, we let Dave Meegan know that he wouldn't be producing the next album. As much as we would have liked his involvement, we simply couldn't afford to pay him. As a creative compromise we asked him to mix the album and set about writing and recording with our live engineer, Stewart Every, behind the desk.

Even with these seemingly daily setbacks, *This Strange Engine* was an enjoyable album to make and, by Marillion standards, quickly conceived and completed too. Still fresh from his mostly acoustic Wishing Tree solo album, Steve R kept that vibe going and stayed unplugged more than usual during the recording. Which meant, unusually, that I got to play a solo on almost every track. Given the choice, I think most people would rather hear a mellifluous Rothery solo over one of mine any day, and that includes me. Of course, not all songs work as well with a guitar solo. Sometimes a keyboard solo is what's required. And that's the point: we all try to be sensitive to what the song needs ahead of what our egos might want. Of course, we don't always agree on just what a song needs. We're only human.

h, as the lyricist and singer, wants the music to bolster the words and help convey their message. I want the music to stand up in its own right, while helping bring the lyrics to life, and engage the listener. Ian is very aware of the energy levels and how they might work in a live setting. As you would hope, Steve and Pete also have their own ideas of what makes for a good song too. As listening to music is a very subjective experience, much of the above is open to discussion, the occasionally raised voice and, less seldomly, the slamming of doors. Not that we were like The Police, who could come to blows over a flattened fifth, but music is emotive, and emotions can be charged, but we'll return to that.

Then there's the matter of taste, or lack of it. Like many of my stage outfits, musical styles and sounds go in and out of fashion. The typical Minimoog sounds and solos that I grew up listening to and playing in early Marillion sounded dated and a bit naff to some ears by the mid-1990s. There are some things which we can all agree on, but music isn't always one of them. With Marillion we try to find a common ground and that's both a strength and weakness of the way we work. If a song gets past the five of us, then it's probably good enough to go out into the world. But getting past all of us is rare and so we consign a lot of promising music to the dustbin, which means it can take months or even years to write an album.

This doesn't mean the process is without its rewards. Look at the title track of *TSE*, clocking in at over 15 minutes and the highlight of the album, loved by band and fans alike. It's a musical journey driven by a deeply personal lyric, which only emboldens the song. And there's room for both guitar and keyboard solos and a shuddering, climatic ending that never fails to bring the house down. The keyboard solo came about because there was an instrumental section driven by a loud guitar riff which prevented Steve from soloing. h wanted to keep it like that, but I played a solo over the whole section. h may have looked at me the way he sometimes did when we played *Brave* live and my equipment conked out, but I felt strongly enough about it to insist the solo stayed.

So, creatively things were going fine, but financially we were in a hole. We needed to bring some of our inventive thinking to bear and bend a rule or two. Since releasing the first few unofficial bootlegs on Racket we had also put out Wes's album and an instrumental record called *The River* created by Mike Hunter to play in the venues prior to the *Brave* shows. I know what you're thinking, but it was very unlike the Bruce Springsteen album of the same name; it didn't mention a broken down truck or marriage once.

Because of the way we had written *Brave* there was an audio record of the writing and arranging committed to DAT tape. I spent a few weeks sifting through it in order to put together a double CD, which we called *The Making Of Brave*. We clearly weren't using our creativity the day we came up with that title. This was Racket release number six.

To add to our woes, *This Strange Engine*, while very well-received by the fans both on CD and live, sold only half as many copies again as *Afraid Of Sunlight*, so we barely recouped the £100k advance.

We were starting to realise that the lower royalty rate we often complained about from EMI was more than offset by their better distribution and greater marketing budget. Too late we realised that Castle were not interested in trying to expand our audience. They simply wanted to exploit our existing fanbase in the easy to reach markets until the sales dwindled to a point where they ceased to make a profit. They would then move on to the next mid-sized artist. They were like the predatory boyfriend and us bands the shrinking wallflowers waiting to get asked to dance and then unceremoniously dumped. On reflection, I might be taking this all a bit too personally.

Talking of predatory and being dumped, back at EMI they were thinking up new ways to exploit our catalogue. With the usual creative genius we've come to associate with major corporations, EMI had scheduled a 'Best of...' album for March 1997.

And then fate intervened. Had it not been for the fact that it caught the attention of a new EMI employee called Lucy Jordache, it would have been something akin to *Six Of One...* released a few years earlier.

Lucy was a Marillion fan and asked to be involved in putting the new release together. She asked us and Fish to write some sleeve notes. Taking a leaf from Fish's book (and showing some of the managerial nous she would later become known for), Lucy told each camp that the other had already agreed to do it. She curated a carefully chosen selection of music from both eras split between two discs entitled *Best Of Both Worlds*. It sold well to the fanbase and succeeded in reducing our unrecouped balance to around £200,000.

In the early days of the CD, many record companies started to re-issue their old recordings on this shiny new format with the express aim of selling the same records all over again to the same audience with the promise of noise free digital versions. The reality, as many audiophiles soon found out, was that the record companies often used second generation masters as the source material, meaning that the CD versions weren't quite the digital audio higher ground the fans might have first imagined when they slipped the CDs into their machines. It was almost like the labels didn't care about the fans at all.

We felt that not only could our early albums be improved with some digital wizardry and remastered properly, but they could also continue to reduce our unrecouped balance.

Plus we now had someone on the inside. Lucy Jordache still cared about Marillion, arguably the only person at EMI who did. So, we worked with her to not only remaster our eight albums but also expand them with a bonus disc of mostly previously unreleased material.

By this time John Arnison was almost fully disengaged from our affairs apart from the basics like paying the bills (when we had the money to pay them). There was an opportunity to renegotiate our contract with EMI for more favourable terms in return for all the work and material we had been putting in to make the new versions attractive to our fans. Not that John noticed. We were out of sight and clearly out of mind.

The *This Strange Engine* tour covered Europe through May and June 1997 and we played mostly large clubs holding between one and two thousand people, usually situated in the less salubrious parts of town. Some were better than others. We were at that point where we could fit band and crew on a single 12 berth tour bus, which avoided the need for hotels most nights. The luxury of a hotel bed was reserved for days off. That said, many of those hotel beds were far from luxurious.

Even with these cutbacks it was hard to make money touring. The USA and Canada were out because we were no longer had a deal with a major worldwide label. In fact, *TSE* wasn't even scheduled for release in the USA.

By January 1997 I was a regular contributor to the *Freaks* mailing list, answering questions and thanking people for their support. I was asked if we would be touring the USA with *TSE* and I explained that it wouldn't be possible without tour support. A few days later this was posted to the list.

Date: Mon, 27 Jan 1997 16:03 -0500 (EST)
From: PELLETJ@cliffy.polaroid.com

To: freaks@ax.com

Subject: EMi reply, USA touring Message-ID:

Here's a radical idea. What if all the US freaks donated to a "Marillion Tour the USA" fund. I'd gladly throw $50 in the hat if that guaranteed a chance to see them in several US locations. (And I would hope that preferential seating would be made available to contributors, in case they venture beyond the clubs to some smaller theaters.) What do you think? There's several hundred US Marillion fanatics on this list alone, right? I know it wouldn't cover all the costs but it might help...

All for now,

Jeff Pelletier pelletj@polaroid.com

Jeff was a relatively new fan and as innocent as a child; this wasn't how things worked and his suggestion was naïve at best. But sometimes, without you even asking, the universe decides to give something back, and who knows what shape that gift might take? I certainly didn't expect it to manifest itself as a long haired Midwesterner with a Marillion patch on his backpack (which, in my mind's eye, was Jeff).

The response from the Freaks wasn't to guffaw in Jeff's face, but quietly pitch in. Before long another Jeff (Jeff Woods) offered to set up an escrow bank account. He was a software developer and had the facility to take credit card payments, so it was a simple matter for him to collect the contributions. Did we trust him? We hardly knew him, but we had come across him a few years before in London. He wrote to us asking if he could propose to his girlfriend during a gig in front of our audience. Seeing a chance for some theatre no matter if she broke his heart or not, we readily agreed. Michelle said yes and they're still married. Perhaps I should have proposed on stage? There seems to be some longevity in it.

I had given a nod of approval when Jeff Woods assured me that he would return all the donations should they fail to raise enough money to help fund a US tour, but I didn't take it too seriously. I imagined they would raise a few thousand dollars and then the initiative would fizzle out.

Less than six weeks later they had reached a staggering $18,000 and I still hadn't mentioned it to the rest of the band. Still fuelled by fan power, the marillion.com domain had been registered by US fan Brian Vogelsang in December 1996 and was run by Dutch fan Jeroen Schipper from early 1997 as Marillion Online, a website devoted to Marillion and Fish. Like most people we were yet to realise just how important the internet would become and saw Marillion Online as a fan thing, run by fans for fans.

I finally told the band and John about the tour fund. The reaction was mixed at best. John was dead against the idea. He saw fans as a nuisance to be tolerated at best, rather than the source of all of our income and the reason we had a career as a band in the first place. He also pointed out that we might look bad or even amateurish going cap in hand to the fans for cash. The rest of the band were unsure (as was I to be honest) but thought it could work if they raised enough money and we really wanted to tour the USA again. We still hadn't giving up on making it there, even if John had.

John secured us a US distribution deal for *TSE* with a small label called Red Ant. They hated the idea of the tour fund too, as they thought it made them look bad. (Why everyone was so precious about free money and saving face remains a mystery still.) We suggested that they match the tour fund money from their own pockets and then we would be somewhere close to meeting the shortfall as the tour fund was now around the $30,000 mark. They agreed to stump up the money and some dates were scheduled.

Then, what we have come to call the 'unseen hand' struck, and the tour was suddenly in jeopardy. Red Ant, the label who had baulked at a fan handout, had filed for bankruptcy. The Freaks greeted the news with the kind of gusto Fish used to reserve for a hotel bar. They determined to raise enough cash themselves so that the tour could still happen. Jeff Woods got more involved and made plans to promote a number of the shows himself. We agreed with him that the fund would pay for the flights and equipment shipping. This would leave the gig income to support us while there, although, however hard we tried, some of the gigs just wouldn't make enough money to square the circle.

We needed some way to cast the net wider and raise more money. I suggested that we record one of the shows and make a special edition CD which we would ship free of charge to anybody who contributed $25 or more to the fund. This incentivised people outside the USA and Canada to get involved, although some already had, including one chap from the UK called Paul Baines who chipped in a remarkable £850 just because he wanted to see it succeed. Rochester in New York state was the chosen gig and we gave away around 1,000 copies of *MARILLIONROCHESTER* to the fans who qualified. These CDs were later changing hands for as much as £250 on eBay. Who knew that investing in Marillion could make you money?

The tour fund eventually reached over $61,000 and we made the news. This wasn't something we had even considered, but the huge amount of coverage the tour fund received boosted our profile and helped us sell even more tickets. We had our best attended US tour for years.

Close to nervous and physical collapse, Mike Hunter had hung up his touring spurs after the *Brave* tour. I had never managed to find a permanent replacement for Mike, so I was on the lookout for a new tech and decided to deploy the *Freaks* list. The band were sceptical of my recruiting methods but saw it as just another example of Mad Jack doing his thing and let me get on with it.

I wanted someone who was both computer and keyboard savvy. I had never worked with a tech who knew more about keyboards and computers than I did. This usually meant that in the event of an onstage emergency (of which there were many) I was tasked with fixing the problem as well as continuing to play. This reached a comical (if you weren't part of the comedy) peak where I literally opened up a keyboard, screwdriver in hand, to repair a stuck key in the middle of a gig. We even had a song, *The Bell In The Sea*, arranged for bass and lead vocal which Pete and h could perform at a moment's notice should something go wrong with the guitar, or as was more usually the case, the keyboards.

Erik Nielsen, a 23 year old from Cleveland, Ohio, applied for the job along with a few others. I called him up and we chatted for 15 minutes and he told me about himself. I asked him to meet me in San Juan Capistrano for the first gig of the tour.

Erik had a respectable job managing a database in a local hospital. He also played keyboards and was a big music fan who was as excited as I about the latest developments online. When I met his parents a few weeks into the tour they barely managed to conceal the disdain they felt towards me for pulling their son away from a promising career and into a life of debauched rock 'n' roll.

When I arrived at the Coach House around lunch time with the plan to show Erik how to set up and plug in the keyboard rig, I was pleasantly surprised to find he had made a pretty good fist of setting everything up unaided. I liked his confidence and initiative and we hit it off straight away. He gave me a new nickname, Astroman, on account of the fact I wore a pair of silver trousers and tie-dye top on stage for that tour. (Throughout my career I have often gone on stage looking as if I had dressed in the dark.) As my sidekick I christened him Bucket Boy (we would have made a terrible crime fighting duo) because he had bought a big plastic bucket to keep my stage beer on ice, ensuring I always had a cold beer whenever I wanted one throughout the gig. I told you he was smart.

Ensuring he would never be nominated for any sort of humanitarian award, John held the crew in similar high regard as he did the fans. Smick once overheard John calling them 'scumbag crew' and in revenge had 20 T-shirts printed with the legend 'scumbag crew' emblazoned across the back and which they all wore on the day John visited the tour. John was made to feel about as welcome as I was in any one of my previous marital homes.

And while I'm on the subject of marital homes, in October I finally left the Watermead Estate in Aylesbury for the city of Oxford. Angie, my girlfriend (a new girlfriend, please try to look astounded) of six months, whom I had met at an h solo gig in London back in February, suggested that I might move in with her. I was starting to think that the old joke about drummers was actually about keyboard players. You know the one:

"What do you call a drummer without a girlfriend?"

"Homeless."

Within a year we would buy our first house together, also in Oxford, as a sign of our commitment to each other. Things were looking up, at least on a personal level.

Professionally, less so. Marillion was starting to feel like a bit of a treadmill. Write, record, tour, rinse and repeat, with no end in sight. We called a meeting with John to discuss the band's future. You will be surprised to hear that he was devoid of ideas or a plan to get us out of the gradual decline we found ourselves in. His lacklustre response was to tell us that we should all find something else to do for six months of the year (it was working well for him) as Marillion was no longer a full-time job.

We responded by relieving him of one of his jobs and fired him on the spot. He barely flinched; he knew the writing was on the wall and didn't even put up a fight. Hit & Run's loss was our gain.

Besides, we still had our quest to contend with.

CHAPTER 17

Candlelit Dinners

The more keen eyed among you won't have failed to notice the elephant in the room in my story so far. Looming above this tale like a musical behemoth almost from day one, two words: Iron Maiden. If it wasn't for our former record label wanting to make our logo more metal to reflect Maiden's stature and success or being confronted with their grinning/sweating/screaming faces every time we entered the EMI offices (on pictures and posters tacked to the walls; they weren't working on reception), Maiden, like the poor, were always with us.

Later still, Fish would even become friends and neighbours with Maiden singer Bruce Dickinson. It was like we were a parochial town in middle England, and we had somehow been twinned with a larger, more glamorous Polish port city like Gdańsk. And here we were again…

Talking of small towns, if the music industry was an urban hub, it would probably be Swindon in terms of scale, population and sense of ambition. I like to imagine that news travels fast around the highways and byways of that Wiltshire town and, similarly, it wasn't long before news reached Maiden manager Rod Smallwood of John's departure. Rod called us up with an offer of help.

We had known Rod a long time and had nothing but respect for him and his management skills, so naturally we accepted. Sanctuary was by this time a large and growing operation with one eye on world domination, much like the band who had spawned the song of the same name.

Sanctuary was a travel agent, record company, publisher and artist management business all under one impressive roof in London's Olympia. We had an informal arrangement without a written contract and, in return for charging us 20%, Sanctuary took over arranging and booking our tours. They had their own crew boss, Johnnie Allan, who ran the whole show while we were on the road. He was deferential, obsequious even, towards the band but the crew liked him the way Prince William likes his brother, which is to say not at all. I could see why. Subscribing to the Arnison school of thought about road crews, scum was something like high praise from Allan. This wasn't what we were used to as a band. We found both his faces highly objectionable, but as we were the new kids on the block we didn't say anything to him or indeed complain to Rod.

As an operation, Sanctuary was tuned to extracting profit wherever they could find it. For example, as the travel agent who booked hotels and flights, they attempted to make a profit at every stage of the booking process, meaning that their bands footed the bill for everything. A band like Iron Maiden generated so much revenue touring that there was still plenty of profit left for them after all the expenses were tallied up. For us it was even harder to turn a profit than it had been with John. At least John, with a bit of arm twisting, was willing to forgo some of his management commission if we weren't making any money.

Don't get me wrong – I believe Rod is honest, honourable and genuinely wanted to help Marillion, but his company had grown into a hungry monster (like *Sesame Street*'s Cookie Monster, but much less lovely) that had to be fed and we (and the other artists on his roster) were the cookies.

The original plan was to employ Erik Nielsen for the US tour, but when it was over I invited him to join us in Europe too. This was problematic (perhaps 'illegal' is the word I'm searching for?) because he didn't have a work visa, so he travelled as a tourist. Eventually his options ran out and he had to return to Cleveland.

Erik was as interested in the online world (not like *Avenue Q* were interested in the online world) as I was and had some knowledge of website coding. It seemed like the logical step to ask him to take a stab at designing a Marillion website. I had constructed a very crude site myself, but it looked like it had been designed by a colour blind child with one hand tied behind his back.

Undeterred by earlier setbacks, I had also made a start on digitising our database of fans. With the help of Rick Armstrong (son of Neil), who worked for Filemaker, a database developer owned by Apple, I started to transfer the contact details of the few thousand fans from paper cards onto a computer. I lamented the fact that we had neglected this valuable resource for so long (including destroying the cards of the thousands who had cancelled or allowed their membership of *The Web* to lapse instead of holding them on file).

I also enlisted some of the band to help. Picture, if you will, h, Steve, Pete and me, laptops in hand, typing names and addresses into the database for hours at a time between writing sessions. Ian was exempt from this tedious chore because we were too afraid to ask for his help. I kid because he had rather heroically volunteered to take on the task of managing the band's finances.

We couldn't have chosen a safer (or larger) pair of financial hands. Not only is Ian tight as a drummer but he's even tighter with the band's cash. He has carried out this almost thankless task for a quarter of a century (that's a Silver Jubilee if you're a monarch) without ever landing us in debt or failing to pay a bill on time, while keeping the wages coming every month, rain or shine.

It was becoming increasingly difficult for Erik to work remotely from the US using only a dial-up connection, so in February 1998, with the band's agreement, I invited him to come to the UK and base himself at the Racket Club. As he had nowhere to live, Angie and I said he could stay in our spare room until he found something more permanent. He ended up living with us for a year.

We knew the various Marillion fan clubs around the world also kept databases, but they jealously guarded them (not unlike how Cerberus guarded the gates of Hades, if Cerberus was the kind of dog you could play fetch with) from each other and indeed from us. Erik and I hatched a plan to gently persuade them to part with the data. We proposed that Marillion send a free Christmas CD to every fan club member. This would appeal to the worldwide fan clubs because it would help recruit new members, while costing them nothing. But as we were paying for the manufacturing and shipping, they would have to supply us with the names and addresses of all their current members.

With little time to rest after the *TSE* tour we were back at the Racket Club working on the next album. Our writing process had evolved gradually since *Brave* to the point that we were very comfortable jamming with no advance plan and just seeing what happened. It was my job to hit the record button if anything sounded good. In practice, this meant that I often missed great moments, only hitting record after the moment had passed, never to be repeated. It annoyed me that I had to be the one to stop playing the keys and press record as this could really break my flow if I was onto something good. Just to add to the general merriment, I would occasionally be chastised for not recording something I didn't like but someone else in the band did. As you might imagine, some of those sessions just *flew* by.

We tried taking it in turns overseeing the DAT machine, but we were about as in sync and slick as the cast of *Dad's Army*. Even though I regularly missed the odd musical gem, the rest of the band were even worse than me. If they weren't forgetting to hit record, then they were failing to press stop when the moment had passed. I can't begin to tell you the hours of musical dross or us talking bollocks we've amassed on tape over the years.

From these rather average recordings we would compile tapes of the most promising ideas. We even went so far as to compile the comps into the aptly named 'supercomps': the absolute best ideas we had to work with.

Because we relied on the album advance money, we were forced to work more quickly than we might have liked. So, we arranged these latest ideas into the songs that would become the *Radiation* album.

Personally, I think the album suffered because we rushed the writing and arranging stage. While not exactly bad, I think the songs lack the musical depth that people had come to expect from Marillion. While expansive, even *A Few Words For The Dead* is still musically short on ideas. There's a good pay-off, when you finally get to it, but it's probably not strong enough to hang a whole 10 minute song on. Lyrically, it's much better, so at least there's something there to keep the listener holding on.

The sound quality was also a step down from our previous albums. The Racket Club wasn't equipped the way most professional studios are equipped. Stewart Every did his best with the recording and mixing, but he wasn't in the same league as a Dave Meegan. We still gave Stewart a co-production credit, but he was as much a producer as I was, which is to say not at all.

Erik stuck his head around the door one day when we were working on *The Answering Machine* and suggested we speed it up and add some electric guitar rather than go down the folky, Jethro Tull-like path we were following. The result was certainly more in your face, but I'm not sure it's any better than what we had in mind. However, in the spirit of trying something new we went for Erik's heavier approach.

We had disagreements over the opening of the album, and by disagreements I mean arguments. Retaining the spirit of wanting to try something different and as "a statement of intent", h argued that the first thing the listener should hear would be something to shake up their perception of what Marillion were. It certainly did that, but was it music? To me, opening an album with 40 seconds of discordant cacophony that had very little to do with the music that followed was like castigating the audience who turn up to watch you play a half empty venue because you're peeved with all the people who stayed at home.

The very people whose perceptions h wanted to change were unlikely to ever listen to one of our albums, except by accident. The loyal fans, while expecting and hoping that we would continue to surprise them, didn't want us to shake them off completely. They wanted us to evolve but still sound like Marillion and not jump on the latest, say, trance bandwagon.

For the 2013 remix of *Radiation* by Mike Hunter the controversial opening was omitted, improving the sound and the opening song in one go.

Speaking of trance (not a sentence either of us were expecting), we were approached by a couple of remix engineers, Mark Daghorn and Marc Mitchell, about remixing *Estonia* from *This Strange Engine*. This appealed to our general demeanour of wanting to expand our musical horizons and resulted in them remixing almost the entire album. We released it as our seventh Racket CD in January 1998. As you might imagine, it was hated as much as it was loved by the Marillion fanbase. It sold a few thousand copies regardless and we trudged on to the next thing in our quest to reinvent ourselves and avoid sinking into obscurity. If this all smacks of desperation that's because we *were* desperate. We might have been travelling on our own hero's journey, but we still felt very far from heroic. Redemption was still some way off.

In June 1998 we moved to Oswestry to mix *Radiation*. Phil Beaumont, an old friend of the band, had recently opened The Forge studio there. Around the corner was a large restaurant called The Walls where we planned to dine every night for the entire two weeks of mixing. As we weren't exactly flush, someone (and it wasn't me this time, I was practically sober-ish) suggested to Geoff, the owner, that we would play a short acoustic set in the restaurant at the end of our stay in exchange for his feeding us every night. Geoff readily agreed and immediately set about maximising the return on his culinary investment by spreading the news far and wide that Marillion were playing in his restaurant. Within a few days he was taking bookings for 'A candlelit dinner with Marillion' from as far away as the USA and Japan. Finally, we had made the dinner and drinks circuit.

What started out as a low key 30 minute set turned into a major undertaking. We ended up playing two nights so as not to disappoint too many people, though the demand for tickets still far outstripped supply. We divided our time at The Forge between listening to mixes and arranging unplugged versions of some of our songs and a cover version of Radiohead's *Fake Plastic Trees*.

The unplugged gigs were special for the people who were there, and that includes us. We recorded both nights on multitrack tape with the idea that we might release them for posterity further down the line. Not that the recording wasn't without its problems. The restaurant piano wasn't the finest example of a pianoforte I had laid my hands on and it was less than a metre away from Ian's drum kit, which made anything which the microphones on the piano picked up unusable as soon as Ian started hitting his kit.

I re-recorded my piano parts, keeping as closely as I could to the original, not least because if I didn't, then the 'shadow' of the original would be audible having been picked up by the other mics in the room. I decided that any loss in authenticity would be worth the trade off as it improved the sound quality immeasurably.

With the Marillion shop up and running from our website, *Unplugged At The Walls* was by far our best seller in the growing catalogue of Racket releases. I'm not talking gold discs, but 5,000 or so sales would net us a decent amount of money and help keep the wolf from the door for a little while longer.

We only played a total of 24 gigs in 1998 and two of those were in a restaurant, which, on reflection, was better than working in one. Though how far off was that scenario?

Our audience was dwindling, and we were unable to turn a profit in all but our most popular countries: Germany, the Netherlands and the UK. We managed to reach a few other cities by being creative. Instead of taking a truck all the way to southern Europe or Scandinavia for one or two shows, we scaled our equipment right back and flew with it as excess baggage. I can only imagine the short shrift Ryanair might have afforded us had we attempted to clamber aboard one of their aircraft. This innovative approach to touring raised the odd, alarmed eyebrow at check-in and sometimes resulted in huge excess baggage charges. But with the kind of careful planning usually reserved for escaping a prisoner of war camp, we managed to spread the equipment across the band and crew to avoid getting ruinously hammered by charges.

One such encounter was captured on the docu-soap *Airline*, as we were about to board an EasyJet flight where we agreed to play the song *80 Days* for the check-in staff in return for them turning a blind eye to our excess luggage. It all felt a long way from the days of upper class travel on Virgin. Like a plane waiting to land, we were coming down. The evidence was everywhere: from economy flights on budget airlines to the graffiti scrawled dressing rooms with foul smelling toilets we previously thought we had left behind. We consoled ourselves that we were still a full-time band and making a living, if barely. But how much longer could we sustain this?

On the way home from a fly-in, fly-out gig in Gothenburg, Erik was detained at the airport. He didn't have a visa to enter the UK and had already outstayed his welcome. We were shocked, but he was put on a flight to New York and disappeared into the evening sky and out across the Atlantic.

It would be months before he would be able to return. Sanctuary might have been costly, but they proved to be priceless in helping Erik return to the UK. Nevertheless, it would continue to be a problem until he eventually married his girlfriend, Rachael, a UK citizen. Love conquers all, not least immigration problems.

I'm not sure what we'd done to upset them, but as the 1999 new year rolled around, the fates were still aligned against us. Pete's fondness for a drink had resulted in him getting banned from driving a year or two previously. Ever the optimist, he took it as an opportunity to get fit and regularly cycled the 12 miles or so to the Racket Club. One foggy January evening, while cycling home from the studio, he was hit by a car throwing him and his bike into a ditch, shattering his leg and shoulder and putting him in intensive care for a few days. We all went to see him in hospital on his 40th birthday. Happy birthday, Pete.

He was eventually released from hospital with some extra metalwork in his leg and began the long road to recovery. I suspect all those weeks of lying on his back gave him time to reappraise his life and he made the decision to quit drinking for good. Over the years I have been hugely impressed with Pete's total commitment to stick with that decision. We live and work in an environment where drinking is not just tolerated but encouraged. Everyone we meet wants us to share a drink with them. They even offer to buy the drinks. Our dressing rooms are full of wine, beer and spirits. Despite that and without complaint, Pete has never touched a drop in all the years since his accident and I believe he's happier for it.

Somehow during the writing of *Radiation*, when we had remembered to turn the tape on and off, we had also managed to knock out *Interior Lulu* and *Tumble Down The Years*. Neither song was yet quite to our liking, so they were put on the shelf for another time. Which came around more quickly than we might have liked; yet again we were under pressure to deliver another album and pick up the advance from Castle.

By this time, we were thoroughly fed up with working with a bunch of wide boys that passed for the upper managerial strata of the Castle organisation and were looking forward to delivering our third and final album of the deal and disappearing as quickly as Erik had once immigration had felt his collar.

We hadn't thought too much about where we were going next, but I was starting to think that some sort of independence away from the traditional record company model might be the way forward.

It's hard to imagine now but I thought we needed to advertise the fact that we had a website and were open for business. What better way to flag the news than call the album *Marillion.com*? Besides, it wasn't like we could afford roadside billboards to spread the word.

The rest of the band could see that we were already starting to make some money from our online sales. Not enough to live on, but it was a start.

Erik had been educating us about the value of building a database, but we were still a long way off knowing who most of our fans, some might say customers, were. We had heard about other bands putting mail-back inserts into their CD cases and about retailers (especially the independent ones) removing them before putting the CDs on display. There was a high street backlash brewing against online retail and mail-back cards were seen as one of the ways the labels might be trying to bypass the shops.

I conceived a simple way to prevent the retailers removing the cards: make it part of the CD booklet. We got Carl Glover to incorporate a simple request for name and address into the last page of the booklet, which people could simply send to us in return for a free CD with various live tracks and some enhanced video content. In this way we increased our email database to over 6,000 and our postal database to over 15,000 names and addresses. Not that we were completely sure what we might do with them. Like Adam and Eve, a little knowledge could be a dangerous thing.

The writing and recording of our latest album followed a now familiar pattern. We would jam for a few hours a day and record anything that sounded promising to DAT tape for review and refining later. h wrote all the lyrics for *Radiation* but had several Helmer lyrics to fall back on for *Dot Com* as he was finding it difficult to write another album's worth of lyrics in such quick succession.

For me, *Dot Com* is a better album than *Radiation*, not just in the way it sounds, but the songwriting too. We recruited Steven Wilson to mix most of the album. We also brought back our old friend Nick Davis to work on what we considered to be the most commercial sounding tracks: *Deserve*, *Rich* and *Tumble Down The Years*. The only controversial choice to work on the record was Trevor Vallis, who h recommended to mix *House*. There are usually one or two tracks that fail to move me on practically every Marillion album. I always put that down to the fact that we work as a democracy and you can't please everyone all of the time, least of all me, but *House* was just too long for such a slim piece of music.

Clocking in at over 10 long minutes it mostly consists of two chords going back and forth in a not unpleasant groove. And did I mention the mute trumpet? If only it were truly mute. I've always disliked that sound; it resembles nothing so much as a wasp trapped in a jam jar. But I shouldn't complain too much because the worst sound choice I ever made came in the shape of the synth solo on *Interior Lulu*. I think it must have been a symptom of us all as a band looking to redefine or reinvent ourselves. Becoming stupefied in the face of looming entropy.

Instead of looking outwardly at how we were selling ourselves to the world, we gazed inwards and questioned our creativity. We wondered if we were becoming irrelevant as the new millennium dawned. We never had such doubts before, even when we were being written off as outdated. It had always been like that. We needed to pull together and reaffirm the 'us against the world' approach we had once fostered. We needed to take back control of our destiny again.

Things were also coming to a head with Sanctuary, not least because of the amount of our money that was making its way into their coffers. Since they started to handle our tours, the number of dates we played had halved. This was myopic marketing at best, as getting out and playing to our fans was the one way we could let them know we were a band still worth caring about. It was also the sure-fire way to sell CDs. The Sanctuary touring machine didn't understand small tours unsupported by a major label as there was little to no money in it.

Much like with John Arnison, we were becoming increasingly unhappy with the amount of time Rod could spare us when he could actually make a meeting. Also, he kept referring to our album as *Radiation Leak* (admittedly, that could easily be the title of an Iron Maiden B-side, but still…), which was a small sign that he wasn't really paying attention to what we were doing or to our needs.

More importantly, we were concerned that he was pressuring us to sign a management contract with Sanctuary. This was tied up with a proposal that we could make a lump sum by selling the rights to all our future royalties up front. While this idea had some appeal (we were completely broke, remember), we couldn't help noticing that it would be a neat way for Sanctuary to extract 20% of our future royalty income whether they would continue to manage us or not. We were still not yet in the black with EMI, but we were close. So, we decided to hold off and not sell the farm just yet.

Looking over the management contract I noticed there was no provision for what would happen if we wished to leave Sanctuary. I asked Rod about it and his rather ominous reply was: "Nobody has ever left Sanctuary." It was like we had just stepped into the *Hotel California*; you can check out any time you like, but you can never leave…

Now we were finally free of Castle (imagine that scene at the end of *The Shawshank Redemption* with Tim Robbins standing in the rain washing away the tunnel of shit and you're close), who should we go with next? We had an offer from Eagle Rock, another independent who also owned Velvel, who had released *This Strange Engine* in the USA after the collapse of Red Ant. Eagle Rock were a more artist oriented label, trying to break new acts as well as working with established artists. There was also Snapper Music. Set up by Dougie Dudgeon, who left Castle shortly after signing us in 1996, it appealed because we felt that Dougie at least understood what we were trying to do.

We had a meeting set up with Rod to discuss our next move and he told us he had some exciting news about a new recording contract.

His big reveal was that Sanctuary had bought Castle and he wanted us to re-sign with them under the Sanctuary Records umbrella. We were horrified at the thought, not just because it was Castle by a different name, but also because of the potential conflict of interest that comes with being managed by your record company.

We've made some stupid decisions over the years but even we weren't about to drive down that road. It was another example of Sanctuary's mission to vertically integrate every aspect of their business. If you manage a band, why not supply their crew, be their booking agent, travel agent, record company and publisher? The potential for making a profit from a successful band is multiplied all the way up the food chain. What's not to like? Plenty as far as we were concerned. Who was going into the record company to ream them a new asshole when they'd fucked up the promotion of your latest album?

We left Rod's office still friends, but Sanctuary no longer managed us.

We entered the new millennium without a manager, record company and still in debt to our old label EMI, but we were free.

What was it Janice Joplin sang?

"Freedom's just another word for nothing left to lose…"

And though we didn't yet know it, we were slowly leaving our dark valley behind and heading towards the brightly lit uplands. We just couldn't feel the sun on our faces yet.

Many happy returns. With Jacques Villeneuve backstage on our joint birthdays during the Marillion Weekend in Montreal on 9th April 2011.

Lost in France with Tallulah, Delilah & Jude in 2012.

Fuck everyone, let's run: stretching my legs with Pete and the fans at Port Zélande in 2011.

A great couple of gongs. Double trouble at the Prog Awards with Lucy Jordache on 5th September 2012.

All the President's Men, Marillion make a state visit.

Sometimes I even plug them in. Lining up the keyboards at Real World in 2012.

Friends reunited? With Fish at Haddington in 2013.

Tales from Topographic Oceans, all at sea with Roger Dean on Cruise To The Edge *April 2014.*

Love walked in. The first time I met Karina in her hometown of Belo Horizonte on 8th May 2014.

Kelly's heroes - the men of the house: Alex, Greg, me, Garrett, Mike, Barry and Phil in 2016.

Cruise to the Edge: reaching Key West with Kai on 16th November 2015.

Thunder fly: h about to take flight through the Chilean skies at Arica airport on 9th May 2016.

At Rock am Ring with the king of Queen, Brian May, plus Steve and Pete, in 2016.

A power in the darkness. The indefatigable Tom Robinson visits Racket in 2016.

And then there were three: me and my youngest children in 2016.

Flat out with h, Lucy and Karina backstage at Port Zélande on 25th March 2017.

Freewheeling at Port Zélande in 2017.

Voice in the Crowd: Mob handed with Marillion fans at Port Zélande in 2017.

Not just vapour trails in the sky. All one tonight live at the Royal Albert Hall in London on 13th October 2017.

Even road warriors need to sleep. The Marillion machine powers on through Chicago in 2018.

Hooks in you. Dining with Fish during the Clutching At Straws *album reissue documentary filming on 22nd May 2018.*

Computing technology: I told you I was an early adopter.

Beach bums. h and I go on shore leave from Cruise to the Edge at Belize Harbour on 5th February 2018.

I finally got to duet with the great Arthur Rubinstein in Łódź, Poland on 14th September 2019. Sadly his performance was a little wooden…

High rollers. Jude and I prepare to take to the skies at Thorpe Park, Surrey in 2019.

Head start: Lost in Germany in November 2019 after mixing it up with a truck in Frankfurt.

Happily ever after. Karina and I tying the knot in June 2021.

◀ *Every journey starts with a single step: Marathon wait for Joaquin Phoenix's Joker to arrive.*

Caught between a rock and a happy place. With Karina and the latest additions to my extended family, Pedro and Arthur, in Gibraltar in June 2021.

Blue Steel V. Still at it in 2021…

CHAPTER 18

The Mother Of Invention - Crowdfunding

Welcome to Center Parcs, Port Zélande, Holland. Surrounded by water, with a river running through its heart, it's strangely idyllic for a holiday camp. Ducks, swans and hens amble around the chalets. Walk towards the edge of the site and you're staring out at the North Sea, a flat expanse of greys and blues as the sunshine glimmers off its surface. The ruddy gold of the sandy beach populated by Marillion fans that seem surprised by this display of beauty, as if the resort has suddenly disrobed.

Take the path through the chalets that hug the cove and work inland down towards the onsite supermarket, bars, swimming pool and the giant white marquee Marillion have erected in the car park. The March sun is low in the sky but the promise of summer is in the air. Almost every window and door are open, Marillion fans seated in the sunshine, cradling beers. Every doorway is filled with the sound of a different Marillion song; each person is wearing a perfectly preserved Marillion T-shirt.

Head past the Adventure Factory, which doubles as the second stage, a cavernous merchandise hall, and, on Saturday, hosts the fiendishly tough Marillion Quiz. From the distance the giant white tent which will play home to Marillion's three shows looks like it's fallen out of the sky and landed there. After the weekend is over and the tent has been dismantled, Marillion's crew replace the lampposts and trees they have uprooted to put it in place.

Feels like a dream, doesn't it? Some mad fantasy. It was a new millennium and the idyllic place in the sun described above was a few years off, but it hung there like some glittering prize just waiting to be unwrapped.

What was it Oscar Wilde said?

"An idea that is not dangerous is unworthy of being called an idea at all."

Anybody who has stuck with this story so far might be able to guess what was coming next (unless you picked this up thinking it was a picture book). We had a database of fans. The whole world was waking up to the potential of the internet and the dotcom bubble that would change the world was just drifting into view.

We had no record contract and the US tour fund of 1997 had highlighted the fact that our fans would be willing to spend money up front when it came to the band. Saying that, it still took a few months from parting company with Castle and Sanctuary for the penny to drop. We might share the same barber (and by barber I mean that God cuts both our hair), but I was clearly no Jeff Bezos.

Not that we were sitting around idly. We were beefing up our website with lyrics, news, interviews and anything else we could think of to drive traffic there. As part of our push to become totally independent we even decided to take on a new employee to work alongside Erik. We had no money but one more mouth to feed wasn't going to make much difference.

We had been very impressed with Lucy Jordache's work on the remastered albums series and over the years we had found out how much she cared about Marillion, even under the auspices of EMI. We invited her to come and work for us full time as our Marketing & Communications Manager. Her head turned by the offer of a pay cut and the wilds of Buckinghamshire, she quickly quit London and her corner office at EMI for a portacabin in the car park of the Racket Club. Not just one portacabin, we had two! Affectionately referred to as the kebab vans. What a perfectly tuned beast the micro-sized Marillion machine truly was.

We had already started work on the next album and were still debating if we should sign one of the deals on offer. As Brian Wilson almost sang, God only knows we needed the money.

And then, just like that, it occurred to me. We needed the money, but that was all we needed. We didn't need anything else from a record company that we couldn't do ourselves. No lightbulb flash of inspiration, just a problem and a solution.

Standing around the kitchen with mugs of tea in hand, I said to the boys that we should ask the fans to buy the next album in advance through an online pre-order. The money it would bring in would fund us through the making of the album. I did a quick back of a fag packet calculation and figured that about 6,000 orders would be enough to make it work. History turns on such almost imperceptible moments, though I'm not sure they're always accompanied by a cup of Yorkshire Gold.

I got a few looks that suggested I had pulled a live raccoon from a sack and deposited it on the kitchen floor, but there was general agreement among the band. Lucy and Erik were especially receptive to the idea. Understandably, all the things that might go wrong were raised: What if we didn't make enough money? Would we look bad asking for a handout? Might the fans expect some control over the sort of album we were going to make? And so on. There were plenty of reasons why we shouldn't do it. But there are always plenty of reasons not to do anything. But as I argued (in the most genial way), sometimes you just have to dive off the top board and see how you land, so I pushed for everyone to at least try it.

Ideas go through several stages: from impossible to dangerous to the bleedin' obvious. Crowdfunding (a new word, it wasn't coined until 2006) wasn't impossible since the dawn of the internet, but it wasn't as omnipresent as it is now. It still felt a bit wild west, but I was drawn to the unknown and the untested. Much like I was drawn to speeding red sports cars and the windswept high ledges of European hotels. I like a little bit of danger. How can you truly enjoy life when there isn't a small risk of death? Or at least an interesting scar you can tell your grandkids about.

I have always believed that taking risks is good. If it goes awry, then try something else instead. I'm either right or may just be lucky enough to never have my belief truly tested.

Our first and most pressing need as a band was to find out if the fans loved the idea as much as we did. On 16th June 2000 (Ian's birthday) we sent out an email to the 6,000 email addresses we had collected asking fans if they would be willing to support a pre-order for the next album. So that we didn't have to read all 6,000 replies, we simply asked that they send their reply to yes@marillion.com or no@marillion.com (the mailboxes are now closed in case you had something pithy in mind to send) and we could simply count the replies. Almost everyone answered the call and there were only 200 emails in the "no" mailbox.

Over the next few months, we fleshed out the idea of the pre-order (sounds sexy, I'm here to assure you it's not). We needed to make the album feel like an event, so the pre-order version came with a bonus disc, not available in the shops. We also offered to include the name of anybody who placed their order before the end of the year in the CD booklet. This served the dual purpose of personalising it for our backers and it gave them a reason to not wait too long before ordering. It sounds like small beer these days but was pretty revolutionary at the time, as was deluxe packaging and an array of formats.

Not that I'm claiming the credit for every great idea in the campaign. These would often evolve out of the frequent chats and meetings we had, though my enduring memory of the campaign is that Erik and I were leading the charge.

Although Marillion have been credited as the inventors of online crowdfunding (and not afraid to go on stage dressed in sackcloth with eyes emblazoned on their backs either), and I sometimes get the credit as the band member who came up with the idea, it doesn't take a genius to see how it evolved from Jeff Pelletier's tour fund idea. We just ran with it. Besides, crowdfunding as a concept had been around in one form or another since at least the 19th century. Remember the debentures at the Royal Albert Hall?

Still, we were pioneers after a fashion. Imagine Hillary and Tenzing scaling the frozen white face of Everest, the perishing wind whipping through their beards. Substitute a warehouse full of boxes of CDs and some Excel spreadsheets for one of the most dangerous peaks in the world, and that was us, pretty much. At least that's what I tell myself before I bed down each night.

And, almost as a happy accident, it meant that as a band we had suddenly found our way again. Like stepping out of a dark forest and into the light of day. Like the monomyth I referred to earlier, we had taken a journey and come back changed, but changed for the better. It was us against the world again. We were making the album we wanted to make, confident and sure of ourselves, with our fans behind us both spiritually and financially.

Around this time, I brought up the subject of money and how we distributed it. For many years we had continued to split the publishing income unequally, a hangover from the Fish years. Having not quite shed my communist tendencies, I suggested that we should revert to splitting the publishing equally again. We had been through a near death experience and were closer than ever. It seemed like a good time to put our money where our mouths were. Once we started talking about it, then it seemed an obvious step to split all Marillion income, whatever the source, equally, which is what we agreed to do. This was a sacrifice for h and Rothers and principally benefited Ian and Pete. But it felt good to all be equals again. All for one…

As the money started coming in from the pre-orders, we also realised that we could afford to hire Dave Meegan again. Things were looking up.

Dave joined us at the Racket Club, and we worked together on the arrangements and recording throughout the second half of 2000 and into early 2001. There was some discussion about what sort of album we were going to make. We felt the pressure of knowing that the people were paying up-front and deserved our very best, but we were brimming with confidence that we could deliver.

From the uplifting opener *Between You And Me* to the roiling closer *If My Heart Were A Ball It Would Roll Uphill*, we knew we had something special.

I know you're scratching your head at such an obtuse song title, so I'll tell you the story behind it.

It's the smallest of battles, but since the early days of the band there had been a struggle between the music and the vocals. Which takes precedence? Who should be louder? Naturally, the singer (every singer, it comes with the territory of leading a band) wants the listener to be able to hear every word they utter. What's wrong with that? Nothing, except that if you make the vocals louder, then the instruments go down in the mix. It's simply not possible to have "everything louder than everything else", as Ian Gillan famously requested during Deep Purple's performance of *The Mule* on their 1972 *Made In Japan* live album.

If the vocal is too loud then the band can sound miniscule in comparison, which might work in the pop world, but in prog rock? Never! This endless war for dominance often came to a head during the mixing. It could get unpleasant when two or more members of the band had a disagreement over how a mix should sound. Not in a Gallagher brothers, I'll break your guitar and glasses way, but in a much more English way: the sort of smouldering resentment that can lead to an ulcer in later life.

It's stressful and unpleasant enough that when it was time to mix *This Strange Engine*, I decided to give it a miss altogether. Like a spoilt child I just refused to attend the mixes and let the rest of them and Dave slug it out. It wasn't because I didn't care. Instead, my reasoning was that no matter how upset or angst ridden I have felt about a mix at the time, a year or two down the road when I heard the song again, I wouldn't give it a second thought. From experience I learned that whatever I thought about the mixes at the time would be fleeting and I would end up listening to the songs later like most people and not notice that the guitar was one decibel louder than the piano, thus slightly obscuring my minor third arpeggio as we entered the chorus. Besides, I trusted Dave's mixing expertise.

Got a little off track then, didn't I? Embroiled as I was in memories of the mixing wars. So, why such an ungainly song title? It was h's backup plan in case the final mix meant his vocals were too quiet and that people might miss out on his carefully crafted lyrics. Calling the song *If My Heart Were A Ball It Would Roll Uphill* would leave no doubt as to the exact words he was singing. Thankfully, he held off including the song's entire lyric in the title, so a minor win for the rest of the musicians in the band, and for the audience when he introduced the song each night.

For the album, we tried to cover as many musical bases as possible, from the funk groove of *Quartz* to the heavy rock riff of *Separated Out* to the understated *When I Meet God*. The first song we wrote for *Anoraknophobia* was *This Is The 21st Century*. We were all very excited about how good it sounded but, not unlike many first dates, the initial spark of excitement sometimes sputters out. If Dave Meegan has a weakness as a producer, it's that he sometimes lets a song outstay its welcome. Often, he can't bring himself to take a razor blade to a few unnecessary bars. Which was the case with *This Is The 21st Century*. Lyrically, I would like to imagine h was thinking of me when he wrote that first verse. We are very different, he and I. He believes in magic and I believe in science. It works though, our shared world keeps spinning.

Not that I want you to think that *Anoraknophobia* was beset by problems; it wasn't. Gripes were minor, arguments few. We got on well together and it was a real pleasure to be working with Dave again. Even calling the album *Anoraknophobia* was a statement of intent we could all get behind; it was how we felt about ourselves and our fans. Prog and proud of it. Anoraks all. No more trying to be 'relevant' or hip, whatever that even was. We even had some T-shirts printed, emblazoned with the legend 'Marillion, Uncool as F**k', which the fans loved. Us and them against the world.

Which isn't to say there weren't a few teething problems.

After practically pleading with the bank for a credit card machine, we had it installed in one of the kebab vans. For some reason the bank assumed we couldn't be trusted with such a tempting piece of kit. At first, it was exciting watching the little machine process the payments and experience the money flowing into our bank account. After a while, punching in credit card numbers reminded all of us why we hadn't pursued a career in accountancy. And to think, I once contemplated a bank job. It was mind-numbing stuff, even if we did know that it was helping fill our coffers with every order. We all took it in turns to spread the tedium.

Besides, Worldpay (the payment processing company), like many music critics before them, thought we were a bunch of wrong 'uns. Becoming suspicious of our sudden influx of cash, they started asking questions. They didn't like us taking payment for goods that didn't exist yet. They had a point. On the face of it, it sounded like a scam. Eventually they agreed to release enough money to us so we could pay for the manufacture of the CDs, holding on to the rest until they had been shipped.

We now had over £200,000 in our account and we hadn't signed our lives away. Having experienced the world of the indie record label of the late 1990s, we thought favourably of EMI once again. Lucy set up a meeting with her old boss, Nigel Reeve, and she, h and I went to see him with an offer to license the new Marillion album. No advance, we simply wanted the promise of a decent marketing budget and worldwide distribution, which he accepted. Win-win, or so we thought. We learned that not having an advance to recoup meant the record company didn't have as much incentive to sell the record. Their lacklustre approach to promoting the album meant that we resolved to utilise a much more hands on approach when it came to our next record.

There was also the matter of the album cover. We really liked Carl Glover's work but felt it was time for a new approach. We pitched the title to a few different artists. One, Matt Curtis, came back with the cute guy in an anorak with a coat hanger in his hand. We thought it was perfect and told him so. He then, perplexingly, proceeded to change it. We spent the next few weeks trying to get him to give us the anorak guy (who we christened Barry) we first saw and liked so much. It was as if he was deliberately trying to change the design we had initially approved. Eventually, after much haranguing, we got him back to where he had started, and the cover was given the green light.

A few months after the album was released, we found out why Mr. Curtis was so desperate to change it. Barry was a car thief! Not unlike our artist friend, ironically. In a plot twist you would scoff at if you saw it in a movie, he had stolen the image from an anti-theft poster belonging to Toyota. The coat hanger was the thief's method of entry into the cars. Toyota threatened to sue for copyright infringement. EMI settled with them and went after Curtis for the money. We stayed out of it and got to keep Barry in the end.

While we waited for the album to reach the shops and our subsequent European tour, Lucy booked us a short set of university shows to see if we could reach a new and younger audience. The tour lost money as the ticket price was kept deliberately low in a bid to attract the student audience. We tried to discourage our usual fans from buying up all the tickets, but it was an impossible task. They went after these new, cheaper tickets the way dogs pursue squirrels in the park but with considerably more success.

One good thing to emerge from all this was that Lucy discovered she had a talent for booking tours and, what's more, she enjoyed it. She asked to be excused from her marketing and PR duties to concentrate more on the management side of things. The sky hadn't fallen in after John Arnison's departure but there were some big holes in the day-to-day management that Lucy stepped in to fill. Things were on the up.

On 5th December 2001 Angie gave birth to her first and my second daughter, Tallulah Judy May Eva Elsie Jo Philly Maggie Joy Blackfoot Moxham Kelly. Try saying that after a few drinks.

Barely able to fit on the birth certificate, her dozen names were kind of a tribute to women and ancestors who came before her in both of our families. The road to our first child took longer than we anticipated. So, by the time Tallulah arrived she was a very welcome addition to our lives and Angie wanted her to have all the names we might have considered for any number of offspring.

We had moved out of Oxford city centre earlier in the year to a bigger house surrounded by fields on the outskirts of Marcham, a pleasant village close to Abingdon. We already owned two Cavalier King Charles spaniels and now we had a child together too. We hired a nanny called Storm (she was a force of nature, so suitably monikered) as Angie was working long hours and, as part owner of a rapidly expanding PR company, she didn't take much downtime before returning to work.

I was very much a hands on dad, spending a lot of time with Tallulah while Angie started work early and finished late. This arrangement suited us both as I could go to the Racket Club later in the day and be home in time to take over from Storm. I was enjoying being a father the second time around, maybe even to the extent that Angie felt I was competing with her for Tallulah's attention.

I have an annoying tendency to try to take over if I see somebody doing something I think I can do better, which is most things, singing or drumming aside. I may have also been subconsciously compensating for the terrible job I had made of being a father to Freya and Kai. Tallulah and I were close, developing that special bond that only fathers and daughters have. You know the one, where she wraps me around her little finger, and I don't seem to notice or mind.

For the first time since leaving EMI, the band didn't feel any pressure to get back in the studio and produce another album. We had a bit of time to spend at home or on other projects. I enrolled on an Open University science course. This didn't go down too well at home, but I wanted to do it for myself, if only to prove that I was capable of some academic success after my disastrous school years. I only completed the first year of the course, but I haven't given up hope that maybe one day I'll go back and get a degree.

In September 2001 The Stranglers played a fan convention over two nights at Pontins holiday camp in Somerset. Lucy had been contemplating the idea of Marillion possibly trying something similar, so she asked Andy Rotherham, a longstanding friend of (and occasional guitar tech for) the band and keen Stranglers fan, to go along and check it out. Andy reported back that he believed the model could work for Marillion. The Stranglers' convention was organised by the band's manager, Sil Willcox, who Lucy knew from her EMI days, so she asked him to help to organise a Marillion weekend in return for a percentage of the takings.

The band were sceptical, and we told Lucy so. I was probably the most unsure, mainly because of the chosen venue. The British holiday camp was derided even in its 1960s' heyday and its reputation had not improved with the passage of time. If you haven't experienced one, imagine a series of breeze block buildings leading to a function room staffed with grinning staff pushing forced hilarity and entertainment down your throat. And a swimming pool populated with bobbing band aid plasters. And imagine it all in an endless grey rain. That's Butlin's, or Butlin's in my mind's eye, in case Mr Butlin decides to send in the lawyers.

Pontins is a step down from that. I should add that I had never visited one as my parents couldn't even afford that when we were kids. I joked with Lucy that if we sold more than 1,000 tickets that I would eat a bowl of tripe. We sold all 1,650 tickets, but the tripe remains untouched.

Even Lucy, the most enthusiastic advocate of the weekend idea, couldn't have predicted how successful they would become. Like crowdfunding, which grew into a multi-billion worldwide industry and spawned numerous companies and copycat projects, the Marillion weekend has changed our lives. Every two years we devote four months to preparing for the weekends in multiple countries (five in 2019 and possibly six in 2022).

In 2007 we moved the main weekend to the Netherlands. There is nothing quite like the atmosphere of Center Parcs at Port Zélande; fans come from all over the world to be part of it. It has grown into something much more than three Marillion gigs set over one weekend. It's a party of reunited friends, it's a music festival, it's a family holiday, it's a weekend piss-up depending on your personal preferences. In truth, it's all of these things and more.

221

It's also a lot of hard work, worry and stress before it happens. But the pay-off is that it's equally rewarding and magical too. Plus, it brings in enough money to enable us to spend more time in the studio between albums and tours getting the next record ready. I will always be grateful to our fans for making this possible and Lucy for pushing past my cynicism and dragging us through those holiday camp gates that first time at Pontins Brean Sands in Burnham-on-Sea in April 2002.

The format of the weekends was set from the start with the decision to play *Brave* in its entirety. We really do test our fans. As I said earlier, *Brave*, like lunch, is best consumed in one sitting. When we first performed it live, the audience hadn't even heard the album. I can still recall those quizzical faces looking confusedly upwards at us. Over the intervening years many people had grown to love that album but regretted never seeing it played in its entirety. We thought it would be a good draw to announce that we were playing it again as a special one-off for the weekend.

That set the mould for every subsequent weekend, where we would elect to play one album in its entirety on the Friday night. We also wanted to make the Saturday night something special and have tried several ideas over the years. People say there are no stupid questions. They don't say that about ideas though and there's a reason for that.

Over the years, it's been a pet project of mine to come up with a different theme for the Saturday night. For the debut Marillion Weekend at the aforementioned Pontins in April 2002, my great idea was Marillion bingo. This involved randomly choosing numbered balls from a bucket where we had to play the song that corresponded to the chosen ball. I'll be honest, I hadn't properly thought this through because we had to learn and rehearse about five hours of material to compile a credible list of songs. Knowing how much we hate rehearsing, you can imagine how that went down. As Pete once remarked: "I'd rather be worse than rehearse."

There were a few 'dummy' songs on the list too, not least *Grendel*. We had no intention of playing it and consequently there was no corresponding ball in the bucket. In any event, the songs that came up randomly were mostly songs we usually play live, which made the whole thing appear to be rigged. What's more, three balls with the number for *Grendel* had been secretly added to the bucket by the crew in the hope that it would surface. Thankfully, the prog gods were smiling on us that night and *Grendel* remained languishing in the bucket. We quietly filed Marillion bingo away and moved on to the next thing.

Something else we introduced that first weekend and have repeated ever since was Swap The Band, where we invite members of the audience up to replace one of us for a song. Five members, five songs. There was some scepticism from certain quarters that this was not our brightest idea, so we indulged in a bit of damage limitation by mostly inviting people we knew. Rick Armstrong played guitar on *80 Days*; Jan Henrik Ohme, the singer from Gazpacho, performed *Afraid Of Sunlight*; and Phil Harrison played drums on *Sugar Mice*. I first met Phil in 1997 in San Francisco where he was working for Sony PlayStation. He invited Rothers and me to his office with the promise of some free swag and we instantly struck up a friendship. We've been best friends ever since.

With the financial pressure off thanks to the pre-order and the weekends, two years passed as we worked away on our next album. We were in great shape and had a lot of material to choose from and we brought Dave Meegan back on board again to produce. This was something of a record for us working with the same producer for four albums, an indication of the high regard we all held him in.

This, sadly, would be the last time Dave would produce us. Not long after finishing *Marbles*, Dave quit producing full time. And for once it wasn't working with Marillion that drove a producer off the rails. With a growing family in the Irish tradition (three kids and counting) he wanted something more stable with less time away from home and retrained as an electrician. A big loss to music and a sign of where things were heading generally as the industry shrunk to half its size in the decade following the new millennium.

We had no concrete plan for the sort of record we wanted to make, but almost in spite of ourselves it grew into a double album. Dave didn't like to stifle creativity, so couldn't bring himself to abandon any of the half-formed songs we were working on. This unsurprisingly meant everything took a little longer and Dave, like Boxer from Orwell's *Animal Farm*, began working harder than ever. His single-minded dedication to getting the job done probably had a lot to do with his decision to quit producing altogether. Something had to give.

Like most double albums it could be said that there are a few fillers on the record, but it's hard to argue with the depth of material in songs like *The Invisible Man*, *Ocean Cloud*, *Fantastic Place* and *Neverland*. Songs that are still greeted like old friends at our live shows.

Somehow, and so unlike us I know, we were running out of time with a tour approaching, so in order to get the mix done on time Dave suggested asking Mike Hunter to work on a few tracks. Mike had quit Buckinghamshire for good after the *Brave* tour (or so he thought) as he missed Liverpool and seeing his beloved Everton get beaten most Saturdays.

With Dave working in the control room, Mike set up in the main studio with the task of mixing the four short *Marbles* sections, while Dave got on with the more substantial material like *The Invisible Man* and *Ocean Cloud*. We all enjoyed Mike's mixes, including Dave, so he asked Mike to mix a few more until Mike ended up mixing the majority of the album.

With a double album on offer for the pre-order, we hiked the price up as high as we dared in order to create a war chest for the launch of the album to rival the sort of budget a major label might lavish on a release. They used a simple formula to decide how much to spend: £1 for every copy they expected to sell. With 18,000 pre-orders, we had about £300,000 to spend after clearing costs. We still needed to keep something to live on, but that meant we could give *Marbles* the push it deserved. The first tangible result of this was *You're Gone* charting at number seven, our best showing in the UK singles charts since *Incommunicado*. By 2004, singles sales were in steep decline, so in terms of sales it was a fraction of a 1980s hit, but it still garnered us some attention.

You'll recall my earlier point about there being no stupid questions, but some pretty dumb ideas, so read on. We hired digital marketing company 1000heads to help us reach a new fanbase. Working with them I helped to develop a competition we called Musical Mystery. Congruent with the prevailing thought within the band that nobody who didn't already know our music would touch us with a shitty stick, the idea of the Musical Mystery competition was to introduce Marillion to a new audience by stealth. There was a cash prize of £4,000 for the winner and the campaign cost us a cool £25,000 on top of that.

The quiz was in eight rounds with the final three rounds consisting of sound clips from the yet to be released *Marbles* album, with participants having to guess the band. It certainly helped to bring some new fans on board, but it simply didn't reach enough people. The competition's participants numbered in the low thousands at best.

We concluded that maybe this marketing lark isn't as easy as it looks, and we should stick to the day job, which in our case was getting out and playing to people. Between May and November 2004, we played nearly 70 gigs throughout Europe and North America.

Not only could we start to feel the sun on our faces, now we were almost standing in the light.

CHAPTER 19

Big Mouth Strikes Again

I was caught in a reverie, torn between crushed beetroot and powder blue, when my phone burst into life. For those wondering if I was either trying to recapture my youth with hallucinogenic substances on the nearest golf course again or debating my next stage outfit (who could forget my silver trousers and tie-dye top? God knows I've tried), but it was neither. It was early June 2005 and I was adulting. Standing in a shop in the middle of France looking at tiles. Tiles, incidentally, which appeared to come in all the colours of the rainbow. It was like a giant packet of spilled Skittles, if Skittles came as ceramic squares.

I was trying to decide what would look best on the kitchen floor of the holiday home we had recently bought with Angie's sister's family. I looked down and my phone was still ringing. It was Ian McAndrew, the manager of the band Travis. Apparently, Morrissey had pulled out of the Isle of Wight Festival at the last minute and Travis were stepping in to replace him and needed a keyboard player.

Ian said our mutual friend Phil Harrison had suggested me as a possible replacement for Adam Wakeman, who was the regular session player for Travis. Adam was unavailable; he had gone from Travis's bucolic *The Man Who* album and opted for the less understated *Diary Of A Madman* instead and headed off on tour with Ozzy Osbourne.

I was unsure. I knew and liked their album, but just how much? I asked how long I had to decide. "15 minutes," Ian replied.

I hung up, called Adam and asked how difficult the Travis gig was. He said it was easy and I should do it. He was right. Travis were a guitar band with minimal keyboards. No Keith Emerson-like histrionics here. Still, I was glad we had a warm-up gig in Norwich before the big festivals. It was now the Isle of Wight and T in the Park, a gargantuan Scottish festival. Travis were also invited to play at Live 8, but I had to turn it down because Marillion were booked to play the Bospop festival in the Netherlands on the

225

same day. Live 8 was only a few songs, but Adam happened to be available that day. I'm glad it was him and not me because the keyboards refused to work and they played on without him. Poor Adam.

It was an interesting experience being in a different band for a few weeks, even as the hired hand. That said, Travis made me feel welcome and invited me to fly in their private helicopter to the Isle of Wight. Instead of flying straight back to London after the show, I opted to return by ferry the following day and I'm glad I did. How many people can say that they've been on a ferry with Bryan Ferry, who was also on the bill? (Apart from all the other people who shared the boat home that day.)

One thing I did notice about Travis was that the audience reaction mirrored the band's music and therefore wasn't as intense as the Marillion crowd, so I was glad to return to the fold when it all came to an end. We're so very lucky in that regard.

While I was off moonlighting with Travis, Rothers, Pete and h were experimenting with touring as a three piece under the moniker of Los Trios Marillos. It was an inexpensive way to get back to North America following the revived interest caused by the *Marbles* album and tour.

The full band closed the year with an early Christmas tour of Europe. This ensured that I was back home in plenty of time for the birth of my third daughter Delilah on 20th December.

2006 was a quiet year for Marillion with only two summer festivals to play. Angie and I moved to a new and bigger house in Uffington, which came with a view of the famous white horse carved into the nearby hill. In case you're thinking that Marillion were suddenly in clover, I should say that, while things were certainly better than they had been for several years, it was Angie's business that was booming.

It annoyed her that people automatically assumed we lived in a lavish home because of Marillion's success. Consequently, she wasted little time in telling anyone in earshot that it was mostly her money that paid for the house. Just to be sure she hadn't missed anyone, she even roped me into an interview with the *Daily Mail* for a feature highlighting 'women earning double their husband's wage'. Not that I was emasculated in any way; Angie may have been earning more than me (and would casually drop it into any conversation the way a farmer scatters seeds), but I had a far more enjoyable job and saw a lot more of the children. I call that success.

With two successful album pre-order campaigns behind us and the upturn in our fortunes, we had finally reached a point where we weren't having to scrabble around just to make ends meet. Remarkably, we even had some record royalties coming in from EMI and songwriting royalties from our publisher too. We weren't about to buy racehorses and start lighting our cigars with bank notes, but the combination of these royalties and the income from Racket Records, touring and merchandise, plus the steady hands of Mosley on the purse strings and Lucy at the helm, meant that the good ship Marillion was on a steady course and in calmer waters than it had been for years.

Nobody questioned that we would do another pre-order for the next album, except me. Like a spectre at the feast, I said it didn't feel right if we didn't need the cash. It seemed like borrowing money from a friend when it wasn't needed. I persuaded the band and Lucy that if we didn't need to do it, then we shouldn't.

Reader, I was wrong. Even though the pre-order concept had been my idea, I hadn't fully grasped the notion that for the fans the pre-order was more than just a financial transaction. They enjoyed the special editions with the beautifully crafted books and artwork with their names printed alongside ours, plus they also liked being involved, being a part of the journey Marillion were on.

Eventually we would take orders before the album release, but the absence of a proper pre-order caused disappointment in some quarters when *Somewhere Else* was released in April 2007. It wasn't just the fact that there was no special edition that dismayed people either. Sonically and in terms of songwriting, *Something Else* proved to be something of a challenge too.

After finishing *Marbles*, Mike Hunter had returned to Liverpool, but we had asked him to travel to Minehead with us for the third Marillion Weekend in March 2005, as we needed someone to take charge of the sound recording for what would later become *Marbles By The Sea*. Much like many a seaside romance, one thing led to another and before long he was back working with us at Racket on the next album. He didn't want to leave Liverpool again but was willing to be a weekly commuter, returning home at weekends.

After such an intense writing and recording period with *Marbles*, we decided to engage in a shorter project and record an EP or mini album with Mike producing.

We had a few half-finished songs, but the four we settled on for the EP were *Say The Word*, *Circular Ride*, *Real Tears For Sale* and *Faith*. Mike hadn't yet experienced the way we now worked together, from the jamming through to the finished recording. He also hadn't realised that we don't all agree on what makes a good song, nor are we always open about what we think of the songs we are working on. Behaviour that can be described as disquieting at best.

This wasn't because we had decided to play mind games with Mike. It was just that experience had taught us all that sometimes the embryonic songs we love don't turn out so well and that music which initially left us cold could go on and grow into band favourites. Nothing kills an unfinished composition quicker than one of the band dismissing it in the demo stages. As we're fond of saying, a song might be only one overdub away from being great.

With that in mind, it came a something of a shock for Mike to learn rather late in the recording process that Ian hated *Say The Word*. I can't say I hated it, but I wasn't about to take it home and introduce it to my parents either. We were all a bit lukewarm on *Real Tears For Sale* and *Circular Ride* too, so we agreed to abandon the EP idea and start all over again.

I think Mike felt that his role in *Marbles*, finishing Dave's work, was fairly restrictive. He was brought in to mix and he did a great job, but I remember him saying how easy it was and he could do it standing on his head, something I wish we had tested him on. Regardless, he did a great job. I got the impression that coming in to produce *Somewhere Else* meant he wanted to challenge himself just that little bit more.

Armed with the knowledge that it's hard to reach a consensus within the band, Mike worked with us to pursue every musical idea to its natural conclusion, then leave the decision as to what made the album for us to argue over at some later date. As Mike was now intimately involved in the writing and arranging of our songs we had to learn to work together as a team. This process unfolded over the next three albums, and it wasn't until we got to *Sounds That Can't Be Made* some five years later that we were truly in sync and capable of working in a way that didn't lead to finished songs that made some of us frown.

Throw a rock and you'll probably hit a Marillion fan who will agree with me when I say that *Most Toys* is a song only a mother could love. At under three minutes it still manages to outstay its welcome. I'm still not sure what made the rest of the band and Mike want to record it, but my objections (some verbal and the occasional hand sign) were overruled.

Somewhere Else had a harder edged production than anything we had made previously. Consequently, Mike took something of a battering from fans on the Marillion online forum. Crucially, he made the schoolboy error of reading what people were saying about the album, its production, and, consequently, him. People can be rather forthright from behind their keyboard and Mike's confidence was pretty shaken by the comments, so much so that he started to wonder if he really was the right producer for Marillion. He took some persuading from us that he was.

The woeful *Most Toys* aside, songs like *See It Like A Baby* and *The Wound* didn't exactly thrill us as a band either. There were a few others – *Especially True, Throw Me Out, Older Than Me* – from the writing and recording sessions that hadn't even made the album cut.

To mop up this unused material we created a disc of also-rans, called *The Hard Shoulder*, to accompany the next album, *Happiness Is The Road*. Not so much a double album, think of it as more of a single record plus a bonus disc. Typically, we couldn't agree on which songs deserved to be on the main road and which should be shoved over onto the hard shoulder like a clapped-out Cortina. It's a bit unfair to call *The Man From Planet Marzipan* an also-ran and *Real Tears For Sale* was rescued from the doomed EP session because Lucy kept pestering us to include it.

We had now released three CDs worth of new songs in a scant two years. That was faster than when we were under the financial cosh of the late 1990s. It's unsurprising then that some of it was below par creatively. Though not all; there will always be a place in my heart for the songs *Somewhere Else, This Train Is My Life* and *Happiness Is The Road*.

But we needed balance and a new way of working that meant the weaker material could be addressed and jettisoned before we found ourselves making another *Most Toys*.

I was confident that we knew what we were doing, and it was all eventually resolved before we recorded our next album, but not before the furore that almost broke the band up.

In March 2007 we had played our first Marillion Weekend in Center Parcs, Port Zélande in the Netherlands. This would prove to be so popular that we would return there every two years to sell out audiences until the Covid pandemic forced us to miss a year in 2021.

We toured through April, May and June throughout Europe and I was back home in plenty of time for the birth of my second son Jude on 7th September. He was nearly delivered single-handedly by me in the playroom of our house in Uffington, but the midwives arrived with five minutes to spare. If I'm honest, I was a bit disappointed they arrived in time; Dr Kelly has rather a nice ring to it.

Following the tradition established with Tallulah, both Jude and Delilah were also christened with 12 names. I have to admit that we were struggling for inspiration when it came to Delilah, but we dusted off some obscure relatives' names (the way Harrison Ford dusts off artefacts and human skulls in *Indiana Jones*) along with feminising an uncle's name to make up the numbers.

Although Jude wasn't exactly planned (and when I say not exactly planned, what I'm saying is that he wasn't planned at all), he was a welcome and much loved addition to our growing family. After Jude was born, I unilaterally decided to visit my local GP and get the 'snip'. As I was already the father of five kids and 46 years old, I felt like I had done my bit for the human race (they would have carted me off to jail in China at the rate I was going). Besides, I think it's irresponsible to father a child when you've reached the stage in your life where each time you get up from a chair you make an involuntary sound like air escaping from a tyre. I was knocking on and it was time to knock it off, as it were. The taps were duly turned off.

With another album out in 2008, the band was back on the road in the autumn for just a month. Our touring schedule was being pared back due to a number of factors; not least because we weren't as successful as we once were, there were fewer places to play profitably. Plus, we all had young families now and more of a say in what we chose to do and not do. We didn't want to be on the road all the time.

Also, my going on tour caused upset with Angie and had done almost from the beginning of our relationship. This issue only worsened as time went on. There were frequent arguments in the weeks leading up to a tour, including periodic break-ups in our relationship just before I departed to go on tour or while I was away. When I eventually returned home, things would slowly return to normal until the next time I had to go away again. Two words: domestic bliss. Or do I mean blitz?

In early 2009 I received an unexpected call from David Stopps. We had bumped into each other from time to time over the years, so I knew there were no hard feelings about the way we had once fired him in a manner akin to someone dumping an old sofa on the street. He knew about our crowdfunding success and thought that I might make a valuable contribution to a new organisation being formed to champion artist rights and independence. Almost accidentally, Marillion had become an inspiration to a new generation of artists hoping to avoid the shackles of a major label deal and make it in this brave new world of the internet. He asked me not just to sign up but also to join the board of directors.

It was exciting being part of something that so many successful musicians had already committed to. I would be sitting at a table with Nick Mason (Pink Floyd), Ed O'Brien (Radiohead), Dave Rowntree (Blur), Billy Bragg, Fran Healy (Travis), Robbie Williams, and David's own act, Howard Jones, among others. It was quite the table.

As well as David Stopps, there were a number of heavyweight managers involved too. I felt completely out of my depth trying to navigate the complicated world of copyright, the making available right, equitable remuneration and neighbouring rights. It was like learning to read all over again and we all know how I once struggled with that. Copyright alone was so complicated that even the so-called experts struggled with some aspects of it. The world was changing thanks to the advent of the internet and as usual the creators and artists were getting the thin end of the financial wedge.

The Featured Artists Coalition (FAC) was formed to give artists a unified voice and a seat at the table when this new digital frontier land was getting carved up. As Nick Mason quipped at our first board meeting: "If you don't have a seat at the table, you're probably on the menu."

We had endless discussions about where the music business was headed and one of the issues that concerned everyone was that some record labels were still trying to pretend that as far as recording contracts were concerned, nothing had changed. They continued to account to artists as if they were still making CDs and records, hitting them with all their associated costs: manufacturing, shipping, warehouse storage, breakages, etc.

I was an early adopter of streaming, joining Spotify in February 2009 after it was recommended to me by Jake Shillingford, a singer turned lecturer at the Brighton Institute of Modern Music. Jake had invited me to give a talk to the students about 'Autonomy in the Music Industry' following the success of our crowdfunding model. Almost in spite of ourselves, Marillion had become famous for something other than our music.

We had people beating a path to our door to find out how we did it. Tony Smith invited me to dinner to gauge whether it was something he could use with Genesis. As I told him, there was no big secret. If anything, he should look to our fans. They were the reason for our crowdfunding success. Smith wasn't the only big hitter to come calling. Elton John even upped Tony Smith's dinner, offering Erik Nielsen a job. It seemed like the smart move to take it. Elton had a much bigger operation than we would ever have, with multiple artists on his Rocket label. We wished Erik well, but we couldn't quite shake him: he came back every two years to help Lucy organise the Marillion Weekend at Port Zélande for a while.

Streaming wasn't on most people's minds back then; it was downloads that had everyone's attention. I found the whole subject fascinating (I am the man who used to dismantle keyboards to relax, remember) and before long I was totally on board with (and on the board of) the FAC. Within a year they had made me joint CEO along with Crispin Hunt. Clearly desperate, they also suggested that I should volunteer to stand for a seat on the board of PPL (Phonographic Performance Limited) in the upcoming elections.

In 1934, our old label EMI (clearly as much fun then as they were when we signed with them) took a coffee shop in Bristol to court for playing their records (or 'phonograms' as they were known to the great and the good) in public without permission. Much to EMI's delight, the court ruled that public performance of records requires the permission of the copyright owner. Sensing an opportunity to make a quick buck, EMI and Decca formed PPL to collect and distribute the cash collected from this new performance licence.

Many years later (but possibly also in a coffee shop) some of the more astute artist managers cottoned on to this little wheeze and demanded a share. By then all the labels were in on the PPL action but keen to keep the spoils for themselves. There was an informal arrangement whereby if an artist manager asked for a share, they would be written a cheque and sent on their way.

Without wishing to bore you (don't look at me like that), the edited version of history is that in 1996 everything changed when the EU introduced a directive entitling performers (that's us) to an equitable share of this windfall which the labels had been keeping to themselves for the best part of 70 years. Equitable remuneration doesn't exactly roll off the tongue, especially for someone like me with a latent stammer, but, once I was on the PPL board, it became something of a watchword.

For the record, and because I like saying it out loud, I was the first featured performer to get elected to the PPL board. 'Featured' meaning somebody whose name or band name appeared on an album cover as opposed to a session musician or orchestra player. The learning curve was even steeper than at the FAC, but I embraced my new role. David Stopps was invaluable with his expertise on the nuances of the Rome Convention of 1961 and the Copyright and Related Rights Regulations of 1996. My, how those four hour meetings simply flew by.

I remained on the PPL board for 11 years with the kind of re-election winning streak Red Rum might have baulked at, until I was finally defeated in 2020. I wasn't sad to go. I think I did my bit for performers' rights; it was somebody else's turn.

Conversely, after a few years on the board of the FAC, I was becoming more and more disillusioned with how the organisation was being run. Among other things, there were funding relationships with companies such as Google and Spotify that, considering what we were trying to achieve, didn't sit comfortably with me. Plus, there were internal power struggles within the FAC and between the FAC and the Music Managers Forum that would eventually result in both Crispin and I resigning from our roles in 2014.

Saying that, I do still believe in the FAC. It's a much slicker proposition these days and I fully support their aims and objectives. In the few years that I was there, I learned a lot from the managers and artists I spoke to. Some, like Billy Bragg, had been smart and kept ownership of their copyrights, only licensing them to record companies for a few years as opposed to the entire life of the copyright like we once did. Others, such as Pink Floyd, had successfully renegotiated their contracts to reflect the new digital landscape.

One thing was becoming clearer, namely how difficult it was to come by the exact details of these new digital deals. The bigger artists went to their respective record companies and secured more favourable terms for themselves, but, almost invariably, signed non-disclosure agreements so they couldn't tell anyone how they had done it or what their specific digital terms were. In this way the labels divided and conquered their artists. Handing out as little as possible to the musicians powerful enough to take them on and next to nothing to the rest.

A light went on. I wrote to EMI and told them they didn't have the right to make our music available for streaming because our contract didn't cover it. EMI, being peak EMI, pretty much told me to fuck off.

I couldn't do this alone; I wasn't a lawyer and our recording contracts were long and complex. Also, there was more than one: the original 1982 contract and the 1990 one we all signed after Fish left and h joined. Just to add to the hi-jinks, there were also a bunch of contracts entered into by Marillion Limited, Marillion Overseas Limited and the various individual companies each member of the band owned in the mid-1980s. All of which we had allowed to be struck off the UK's official register of companies in the early '90s, despite the fact that they held all our performers' rights for the Fish era material and, unbeknownst to us, we were months away from being too late to resurrect. This would have meant saying goodbye to all our future royalties from albums like *Misplaced Childhood*; they would have gone directly into Queen Elizabeth's coffers. It was a mess, like dropping a jar of pasta sauce on a shag carpet is a mess, and it was going to take more than me to clean it up.

Then, like a bolt from the blue, EMI went under and my one man crusade (I like to imagine I'd cut quite the figure sat astride a horse) to get a better deal for Marillion was temporarily put on hold.

By chance, Pete mentioned to me that Guy Vickers, a fan of the band who I was vaguely aware of, was a barrister. Interest piqued, I managed to meet Guy after a gig in San Francisco where I casually asked if he could look at a few contracts for me. Luckily enough, he was willing to agree to meet for a drink in Amsterdam a few weeks later.

Apart from a shared interest in contract law – people can't get enough of us at dinner parties (or is it that people can't get away from us fast enough at dinner parties? I forget) – we also discovered a mutual love of 1970s era Yes. We also agreed to disagree on whether the *Drama* album is crap. (It's crap.)

Regardless, a friendship was forged over the next few years as it took at least that long to conclude the work Guy had started on our behalf, which included restoring our companies to the register with weeks to spare and long enough for them to transfer our performers' rights to us as individuals. I will have to draw a discreet veil over how the business deal was precisely concluded, but suffice to say we reached a satisfactory agreement with our catalogue's new owners, Warner Music. This resulted in us working together with Warners on deluxe editions of our first eight albums starting with *Misplaced Childhood* in 2017.

Guy and I also went on to collaborate creatively together a few years later, but more on that later. He's still wrong about *Drama* though.

In March 2010, while writing our sixteenth album (seventeenth if you count 2009's acoustic *Less Is More* album), we decided to decamp to a country house called Casa de Juste in Lousada, Portugal. There was a generous main room that normally functioned as a restaurant from which we cleared the furniture and replaced it with our equipment.

Like schoolchildren fudging their homework, we had already put off the daunting task of knuckling down and writing our next album by spending most of 2009 reworking existing songs into new acoustic arrangements for a range of instruments we barely knew how to play (and by we, I mean me). I had gone with the autoharp and glockenspiel.

I had also had fun buying a real pipe organ on eBay for £200; it was an acoustic keyboard after all. I then pissed the rest of the band off by setting it up in the studio where it blocked out any semblance of natural light and occupied a sizeable chunk of space (you could unwittingly walk into and quite hurt yourself at almost any time). Eventually I gave up trying to tune it and offloaded it on an unsuspecting fellow progger, John Mitchell, for what I paid for it.

I mentioned the daunting task of knuckling down to write again because we didn't feel quite ready to start again. The metaphorical cupboard was bare after the *Somewhere Else* and *Happiness* albums had used up practically everything we had.

We arrived at Casa de Juste without h. Linette, his wife, was unwell and he was naturally reluctant to leave her home alone with their young child. The rest of us just got on with things. My wariness was misplaced; working together again wasn't so bad after all. We were having fun jamming and with the benefit of hindsight I would say that the sort of music we were creating was on the classic end of the prog spectrum. You know, inventive time signatures, odd chord progressions, the sudden urge to wear a cape. Fun to play, hard to like or listen to, even harder to sing, I suspect. But who cared? We were blowing off steam.

In the great Marillion tradition, whenever one of us is not in the room, he instantly becomes the main topic of conversation among the other remaining members. I distinctly remember walking into the studio at Racket once to a sudden hushed silence. It was an odd and awkward moment until it hit me: "You're talking about me, you bastards!" They all burst out laughing. I've no idea what they were saying and I've no wish to know. Sometimes you just don't need to know.

Naturally, h was one of the topics of conversation before he arrived in Portugal, not least a lyric he was working on and had tried a few times in previous writing sessions. The consensus was that none of us were that keen on it and perhaps one of us should say something.

For his part, h had reluctantly dragged himself away from home, conscious of the need to not waste the limited time in Portugal that we were paying for. The first day we tried making some music together he looked at us the way I imagine early English explorers must have looked the first time they encountered hieroglyphics. Surprise, some consternation, but mostly puzzlement. Our prog wig out was falling short of its mark. In no uncertain terms, he told us he didn't like it.

It's moments like these when a man needs to take stock, look at the bigger picture, think of their friend who has had to leave his ailing wife behind and make an unwanted journey. I'm not that man.

"Crap?" I seem to recall saying, "I'll tell you what's crap...", and then, quite possibly, the subject of h's latest lyric might have raised its ugly head.

To say h was furious is to understate it somewhat. He stormed out of the room, and I think he would have flown home that day had we not been booked to play a *Less Is More* show at the Casa de Vila on 27th March. We didn't see a lot of him for the rest of the time in Lousada and, when we did, it was like bumping into an ex-girlfriend and her new beau: awkward. Big mouth strikes again.

We limped on to the end of our allotted time there, and while the sun shone brightly outside, the atmosphere between us remained somewhat frosty.

Months of silence passed, with no hint if or when we might write or work together again. After braving years in the wilderness and finally getting back on track as a band, we had managed to run ourselves off the road one more time.

Chapter 20

The Road To Happiness

They say life comes at you quickly, but what speed then death?

Here's an equation you might not have seen on your GCSE maths paper: If x (being a keyboard player) meets y (in this case a cement mixer truck) at a crossroads, then at what speed is z (an oncoming bus full of commuters) travelling?

Don't ask me for the answer though. I was splayed out on the road, staring at the greys and blacks of the morning sky overhead, my breath coming in hard, painful gasps. Where, I thought, is my phone? And, more importantly, is that bus still bearing down on me?

It's strange the things that run through your head as you stare into the abyss.

It's November 2019 and that's me on the ground, the prone figure scrabbling to get to my feet, adrenaline kicking in and dragging me to the safety of the kerb.

Where was I? Ah yes, Germany on a day off. The band had played a successful show in Frankfurt the night before. One of my great pleasures on tour is running. I really enjoy planning my route beforehand, hoping to take in the sights or climb a particularly challenging hill such as Mont Royal in Montreal. Rivers are another favourite as there are usually paths and parks nearby. It's time to think and listen to music during a turbulent 24 hours of travel, soundchecks and shows.

Which is why on the morning of 24th November I was heading back towards the hotel after running along the River Main. Momentum was with me and I had a light wind at my back. I came to a junction with traffic lights. Not wishing to impede my pace, I ran across the road just as the lights were changing. Everything was fine; I had clocked the approaching bus to my left and was confident that I could make it across the junction before the bus bore down on me.

I can only imagine what was going through the mind of the driver of the cement mixer truck to my right as I bounded into his path with not a care in the world. A moment of *joie de vivre* on my part that was to be fleeting. On the upside, while I had somehow failed to spot his enormous truck trundling towards me, he had been much more aware of his surroundings. With a string of expletives at his lips, he braked hard.

Physics being what it is, he was unable to stop and so hurtled past me, but not fast enough to bypass me completely. I saw him too late and tried to stop. With my arms out in front of me, as if like Superman I could ward off a careening truck with the palms of my hands, I bounced off the side of his vehicle when something hard, angular and unforgiving hit me side on in the chest, throwing me backwards into the air and into the path of the bus.

With no time to feel the pain of the impact or register the dull thud of my head hitting the road, I leapt up, grabbed my phone and ran to the kerb. I sat down abruptly as my brain registered the news that all was not well. The driver of the cement mixer leapt out of his cab and started yelling at me in a language I didn't understand. Not that I understood much in that moment. The world was suddenly a new and terrifying place. When he noticed I wasn't responding, he yelled "English?". I nodded. He stared hard and shouted: "Why? Why?!"

It was a good question.

Once in hospital I learned that I had four broken ribs and would be in no shape to play the following day in Essen where Marillion soldiered on as a quartet without me. I'd like to think that I was sorely missed. Then, against my doctor's advice, I checked myself out of hospital after one night and made it to the second gig in Essen after a further night in a hotel in Frankfurt. Patched up and contemplative, but still, somehow, very much alive.

Strange then to consider that I once thought running might save me. Good for head and heart, it helped my mental state no end after I'd dropped a bomb on the band's writing sessions in Portugal. Sending h scurrying off to the furthest reaches of the band's temporary home before we all flew back to the UK, h walking ten paces behind the rest of us as we trudged out of Heathrow Airport dragging our luggage behind us. The only positive emerging from that accidental self-sabotage was that I suddenly had more time to run along the balmy trails of Portugal.

I was in the final stages of training for my first marathon. Nobody warns you about the huge commitment in running hours that's needed to prepare for such an endeavour. I ran most of the time while the band was in Portugal: 10, 12, 15 miles most days and one

20 mile loop over an undulating landscape beneath a sun filled sky. I completed this last lengthier circuit in three hours and was feeling confident about finishing my impending marathon in under four hours when we raced a few weeks later.

How wrong could I have been?

Race day dawned full of promise. The sky over Brighton, a high, blue dome for the first ever marathon in the city. Marillion biographer Jon Collins and I had entered together and managed to secure our places by offering to raise money for Water Aid. Thanks to the generosity of Marillion fans and my music biz contacts we raised over £3,000. The Water Aid people (perhaps having secretly monitored my running technique and judged it accordingly) asked if I would be willing to race dressed as a toilet.

In truth, this was to raise awareness of the lack of sanitation that over two billion people on this planet have to live with on a daily basis. This is a serious health issue, which I agree needs publicising but not to the degree where I was going to parade around Brighton dressed as a toilet. I can see the headlines now: 'Marillion keyboardist's career goes down the pan' etc. As you know, I've worn some pretty awful outfits over the years but a bowl, seat and cistern is where even I draw the line.

By chance we bumped into Brighton resident and singer Jake Shillingford at the start line. We three agreed to run together, but after five or six miles I was becoming impatient that Jon and Jake were running too slowly, especially after we were passed by a man dressed in a giant foam beer bottle and another running backwards. As much as I was enjoying their company, I decided to run on ahead and pick up the pace. This was very nearly blissful; I was feeling pretty good for the first 15 miles or so and I even sped up around mile 18. But then it hit me, or should I say I hit it. Like a buffalo being dropped on me from a great height, I collided hard with racing's notorious wall.

Having never run more than 20 miles before (they say you shouldn't run more than that in training because of the risk of injury) I had never experienced it first hand. No wonder Pink Floyd dedicated an entire double album to it, it was agony. All joking aside, my body started screaming at me to stop. Every step became an exercise in incremental effort that hurt. I wasn't just tired; I was sore and broken, it felt like both my legs had been gone over by the Kray brothers.

It's said that a marathon is a race of two halves. The first 20 miles and the last six. How true.

Around mile 22 as I was staggering down Brighton sea front, Jake appeared, loping leisurely along. Instead of gliding on past and leaving me to limp on, which is what I entirely deserved, he slowed down and did his best to encourage me onwards to cross the finish line with him. After a while, like some doomed soldier staked out on barbed wire in no man's land, I told him to go on without me and I'd be OK if he left me here to die.

Eventually, I crossed the finish line in 4 hours and 22 minutes and about five kilos lighter. The last six miles took me an hour and 22 minutes. Many people walk faster than that. Jon came in 25 minutes after me looking like he'd been sat on by a bear.

I swore I would never repeat the experience, but a few weeks later I found myself sending in my entry for the 2011 London Marathon. I became fixated by the idea of completing a marathon in under four hours. My time in 2011 was 4:06. I tried again in 2013. This time I managed 4:08. I was getting slower and decided that running marathons wasn't for me.

With no talk of resuming writing for our next album, the band saw little of each other through the summer. We had a few short sets at festivals which required little rehearsal as we naturally played our most popular songs and could pretty much do that in our sleep. The summer of 2010 quickly turned to autumn and still we were yet to regroup to write, but we had a commitment in the diary that there was no escaping. We were booked to open for Deep Purple.

Smoke On The Water? Oil on troubled waters was more like it. It was the tour that slowly healed the rift in our band. In a typically English way, we didn't discuss what had happened in Portugal, but I made a promise to myself to try to be more thoughtful in how and when I addressed things. Blurting out something in retaliation because I felt irked by h's comments was stupid and shallow. How you say something is almost as important as the very thing you're trying to say.

At the time of writing, Marillion is in its fifth decade and the current line-up has been together for over 30 years since h's arrival in 1989. Few bands have maintained such a consistent line-up and only a handful of bands have been together longer: U2, The Rolling Stones, Genesis and our old friends Iron Maiden come to mind. We're often asked our secret for staying together for so long. h's usual reply is "forgiveness". I think he's got a point.

2011 was another Marillion Weekend year in which, as well as playing Port Zélande, we returned to Montreal for the second time. The Saturday night happened to be my birthday and a friend from England called to wish me happy birthday. He mentioned that a friend of his in Montreal wanted to come to the show. As I know as much about Formula 1 motorsport as I do, say, aeronautics (if you board a plane and I'm flying it, might I suggest you disembark double quick?), I barely raised an eyebrow when they told me it was one Jacques Villeneuve.

Rich, our tour manager, insisted that we invite Jacques backstage before the show so that he could meet him. Like millions of devotees around the world, F1 is an obsession for him. We don't normally allow people backstage before the gig. However, that night a young lady had somehow finagled her way into the dressing room while we were entertaining Jacques.

Before politely asking her to leave, we agreed to sign something for her by way of recompense. As we passed the paper around, she spotted Jacques sitting mutely in the corner of the room and almost did a backflip. We, and our signatures, were instantly forgotten. Here was a real star. She moved across the room the way Villeneuve passes other cars coming out of a hairpin and glued herself to him like an unsupervised child left alone with a bottle of UHU.

Chatting with Jacques, he revealed that he used to practise for his races while listening to *Holidays In Eden*. It seems a strange choice of music when you're rattling along at 200mph. I imagine Motörhead, or even our old pals Iron Maiden, would be a better fit. We also discovered that we shared a birthday that day; it was his 40th and my 50th. Happy Birthday, Jacques.

2011 would also be the year when we resumed writing again. Tentatively at first, just meeting up at the Racket Club to prepare for the weekends, which require months of preparation. With three completely different sets to learn (plus Swap The Band) adding up to approximately seven hours' worth of music, it's a feat of memory as well as a musical marathon (and you now know how I feel about marathons), which doesn't get any easier the older we get.

Mike Hunter, who was now working with us full time and who we had come to think of as the sixth member of the band, had asked us to set aside up to an hour a day to jam before starting rehearsing. He didn't have to ask us twice. We enjoyed the jamming much more than the rehearsing and welcomed anything that would delay the start of yet another run through of our songs.

In this way we started to collect the musical pieces that would make up the *Sounds That Can't Be Made* record. With three Marillion weekends (in the Netherlands, UK and Canada) plus a tour of Germany with Saga later in the year, we didn't get the album completely written. But thanks to the income from the weekends, the money worries of the late 1990s were a distant memory.

Together with Mike we had honed the 'jamming for writing' into a method that produced results. The most promising jams were used as a starting point for more structured jamming (have I mentioned the benefits of jamming enough yet?). In this way we were able to develop them further before finalising the arrangements into finished songs. We always have endless discussions at this stage about whether an A minor seventh with an added ninth works better than C sixth. You can only imagine the larks we have in that rehearsal room. Naturally, this kind of repartee drives h and Ian up the wall, but we eventually reach a reasonably happy consensus. I say reasonably because I always think there's room for improvement, but sometimes you simply have to let a song go.

Mike is a genius (and I don't use that word lightly) at turning our disorganised noodling into something resembling carefully crafted music. He is endlessly patient and blessed with the gift of seeing the magic in the music, even when that magic is buried beneath a pile of metaphorical slag. Like raising a miracle survivor from a catastrophic earthquake, he always seems to find the spark of life where the song is hidden, the penetrating light in the gloom. It's quite the trick if you can do it and Mike's been doing it without fail for years.

One day in June I had a message from a fan called Frans Keylard asking if I would be interested in playing piano on a song for a band I had never heard of called DeeExpus. Odd name, I thought. I later learned it was derived from The Andy Ditchfield Experience. Andy, a straight talking northerner with a great sense of humour (I know that makes him sound like the notes from a sitcom script, but it's him to a tee), was the man behind the request.

It was for a song called *Maybe September* which I liked instantly, so I agreed to send Andy something. And then I sat on it for a few months until he called me up to ask where his bloody piano track might be. Admittedly, I was a bit slow to get started, but once I did, I enjoyed contributing to the song very much. Which eventually led to me spending a few months in late 2011 adding keys to most of the album which Andy called *The King*

Of Number 33. I really enjoyed working with DeeExpus and struck up a friendship with Andy and their drummer, Henry Rogers. Hen was barely out of school, but he played drums with skill and precision that belied his tender years.

On something of a roll, I agreed to play some gigs with DeeExpus in the new year, but my future as a keyboard player (or any kind of musician) was suddenly in doubt as February dawned.

It seems that trouble in paradise actually is a thing. In January 2012 Angie and I went on holiday to Thailand. A few days before coming home we went on a boat trip to the Similan Islands, which, if you've ever had the good fortune to visit, you'll know have incredible snorkelling and a host of exotic wildlife populating the seabed. I saw a turtle swimming lazily over the rocks and sand about 20 feet below me and swam down to take a closer look. When I returned to the boat a few minutes later I had a ringing in my ears. As we sped back to the resort I was listening to some music on my earphones, and I noticed I was having trouble hearing properly. I put it down to the water pressure or just residual seawater still in my ears.

Over the next few days my right ear returned to normal, but, disturbingly, I went completely deaf in my left ear. My normal hearing had been replaced by random noises. When we arrived back in the UK, I went to see a hearing specialist. At first he seemed untroubled by my plight, confidently assuring me that it was probably wax. After a few simple tests his demeanour changed completely and he declared it a medical emergency, advising me to get to A&E as soon as possible. I sat in A&E for four hours as people came and went with various injuries from dog bites to burns while my emergency status went unattended. Eventually I was seen by a junior ENT doctor who said there was nothing they could do and that I should go home.

Over the next few days, I tried desperately to find a specialist who would see me while my brain refused to let my ear go quiet, substituting the silence with an array of weird noises to replace my lost hearing. It was as if, bereft of stimulus, the part of my brain that processes hearing was having auditory hallucinations. Finally, I was diagnosed with SSHL or Sudden Sensorineural Hearing Loss, which is a catch all for sudden unexplained hearing loss that has no cure, and nobody really understands what causes it.

Over the next few weeks some hearing started to return to my left ear. But not the hearing I was used to; it was horribly distorted and out of tune. It was like my brain was tuning into the world's worst radio station. I was seriously wondering if I would be able to continue working as a musician at all.

Marillion were booked to spend a few weeks at Peter Gabriel's Real World Studios near Bath. This became a regular fixture in the Marillion calendar, usually reserved for the last stages of album writing/recording and something of a treat for us after months in the less salubrious Racket Club. The kebab vans were retired by then as we had taken over the unit next door and expanded across the yard to another building as our little empire grew. But still, compared to Real World it was still a series of sheds on an industrial estate.

The band were very understanding and did everything they could to help with my situation. I was finding it especially difficult to cope with loud noises and the guitar was especially painful to listen to even with Rothers' sublime talent. Finally, the distortion lessened, the tuning resolved itself over time and I learned to live with my somewhat diminished hearing. I wasn't sure how I would ever cope playing live as it's so difficult to control the intensity of the volume coming off a stage. I reluctantly backed out of the planned gigs with DeeExpus.

For our part, we were at least consistent in our inconsistency, approaching yet another tour with an incomplete album. We were booked to play North America in June and the album still wasn't mixed. In what can only be described as less than ideal circumstances (like rock climbing in flip flops is less than ideal) we toured the USA and Canada, getting together from time to time in hotel rooms to listen to mixes and discuss changes. Strangely enough, in some ways this was less stressful than doing it at home because it was hard to judge what we were listening to on our basic set-up. We were in Mike's hands, but what hands.

When *Sounds…* was finally released in September 2012 it was very well-received by both fans and critics alike. We were back on form and it felt thrilling. There was some upset about the 17 minute *Gaza* from a small number of fans, mostly American, who thought h was being anti-Semitic, which he wasn't. Interestingly, we didn't get those sorts of critical barbs from the Jewish people living in Israel and Gaza who were probably better placed (quite literally) to judge h's handling of the subject in our song. He took great care to try to speak from the perspective of children struggling to live in Gaza and sidestep any political overtones. He even looked into the possibility of visiting Gaza but was warned it would be too dangerous and difficult. He settled for the next best thing, getting in touch with people living on both sides of the conflict and speaking to them via Skype.

We picked up a bunch of awards from the *Prog* magazine readers' poll including best album, best singer and best keyboard player, which was a big surprise for me as I had become used to lagging behind the likes of Rick Wakeman, Jordan Rudess and Keith Emerson (all far better players than me).

Almost without us noticing, the world had changed, as had our place in it. We were respected, admired even, for having invented crowdfunding and leading the way for a new generation of bands. The success of *Prog* magazine and their annual awards demonstrated that there was a place for our music, and that it was still relevant and important to a lot of people, and not just those people who had once paid to see us play in sackcloth and face paint. We were not only pioneers, but leaders in our field too.

Even the mainstream media offered a tentative hand to prog rock. It had returned intact from the wilderness, outliving punk and the new wave and was now just another genre of music to be plundered and sampled like every other genre. Case in point: my 10 year old stepson, Pedro, discovered *Roundabout* by Yes from a video meme just the other day.

What did Andy Warhol, the king of reinvention, say? "Don't read your reviews, weigh them." Sound advice from someone who has had more than his fair share of brickbats.

In 40 years, Marillion have gone from unfashionable throwbacks to unlikely pop stars, to irrelevant has-beens, to innovators, to respected veterans. Where next, national treasures? Let's see if we live long enough first.

In May 2014, while on tour in South America, we played a show in the city of Belo Horizonte in Brazil. A gig like many others, apart from a chance meeting with a young lady called Karina. We spoke briefly after the gig, and she explained that she didn't know Marillion but was there with a girlfriend who was a huge fan. It turned out that, by coincidence, she would be in Buenos Aires less than a week later when we were booked to play. I invited her to the gig and she gave me her phone number.

Things at home were less than rosy (and by less than rosy I mean things were going off like a box of Roman candles in a warehouse fire about every second day). Angie and I had several break-ups over the years, but we always seemed to work it out.

When I met Karina, Angie and I were in the middle of one of our by then familiar break-ups, but it would be almost a year before Karina and I would start a relationship. I was acutely aware of not wishing to repeat history. Angie and I had three children together and I had no desire to split our family up.

We tried a reconciliation for six months until Christmas 2014, but I think it was probably too little, too late. They call 3rd January 'divorce day' and that was the case with us, except we weren't actually married. In early January I reluctantly moved out of the family home for the final time.

Rich, our tour manager, kindly offered to put me up for a few months until I sorted myself out with a place to live.

Following a few years of rented places in and around Oxford, I eventually bought a house in a small village equidistant between where the kids were living and their school. Angie and I were locked in a protracted spat that could best be described as ugly. In June 2017 the kids came to live with me and the amazing Storm came back into our lives to offer help whenever it was needed.

Sounds That Can't Be Made was the fourth album we had funded using the business model we had created. We were old hands at it now, not that it made the process any easier. Rich and Stephanie Bradley from our backroom team were always run off their feet as we came towards release date. There was the sheer logistical horror of getting the albums manufactured, delivered and shipped on time. It wouldn't do for us to miss the release date and have our loyal supporters kept waiting while the album was available on Amazon. Some things were out of our control and manufacturing was always prone to last minute hiccups. So, when Pledge Music came to us with a proposal for taking the whole thing off our hands for 15% of the sales we didn't take long to say yes.

And that was how we planned to release our 2016 album *Fuck Everyone And Run* or *FEAR* as it became known. It was then that we discovered that Pledge were just as prone to the sort of snags and upsets that had dogged our previous releases, with the added danger that we didn't control the finances. The risk we were exposing ourselves to only became apparent to us after Pledge suddenly went under in 2019 owing lots of bands and artists money. Frankly, we dodged a Pledge shaped bullet. Had they crashed with our money, then it would have sunk us too.

FEAR felt like the culmination of many years and albums working with Mike. Many longstanding bands can fizzle out creatively. They stop making new and interesting music or just stop making new music all together, relying on their catalogue to see them through. We had managed to circumnavigate that with our jam sessions and Mike's judicious editing.

On a personal note, and it is my memoir after all, I was (and still am) having a particularly fertile period, coming up with most of the musical ideas that made up the *FEAR* album. Jamming with the band suits my style of creativity. I don't think about what I'm playing but just let it happen. The downside of this would normally be that as I'm not really in the moment, then I might forget what it was that I was playing. As we record everything now (remember the golden years when I would forget to press play and record?), it isn't a problem anymore.

For Rothers another downside is that I'm not as attentive to what he's playing (a self-centred musician, heaven forfend) or will play something that's at odds with what he's doing. Some might say I'm playing in the wrong key. I'm here to tell you that those people are communists and liars! It's clearly experimentation and moments where anything goes!

Besides, this occasional discord can lead to unexpected results that are both fresh and exciting (and useable), and not at all redolent of two cars colliding on a busy motorway exit.

h was by then writing all the lyrics, having used up the last Helmer lyric, *Pour My Love* (written many years previously), on the *Sounds* album. With our finances in better shape than ever we didn't have to rush to get an album out either, so *FEAR* was done when it was done. With these contributing factors in play, I think we produced our best album in years. Almost unheard of for a line-up then in its third decade together.

The *FEAR* tour was not only special for Marillion because we'd created a landmark album, but on a personal note I also had the privilege of having my son Kai tour with us as my keyboard tech. He was nervous about the role, but I reassured him that I'd cover for him if anything went awry. I didn't want the rest of the band to think it was a case of plain old nepotism (even though it was). Neither he nor I should have worried because he did a great job and fitted in with the crew like an old pro. A bit too well if I'm honest. It was an adventure for him and a rare chance for me to spend time with my son that wasn't a lunch date.

In the autumn of 2017, Karina, who I had been in a long distance relationship with since early 2015, was finally able to join me here in the UK with her two young sons, Arthur and Pedro. We didn't live together at first, not least to give our respective children a chance to get used to the idea. Plus, I had been enjoying being a single dad with my three kids, even learning how to cook.

Eventually Karina and I moved in together in early 2019, but our aspirations of becoming a modern day Brady Bunch didn't quite pan out as Tallulah and Delilah decided to go and live with Angie. I respected their decision as I felt they were old enough to decide which parent they wanted to live with. Jude stayed with us for another year before joining his sisters. I'm still grateful that I got to spend so much time with my children at a crucial stage in their lives and, happily, they regularly come and stay with us.

I might have brought it on myself (big mouth strikes again, remember?), but after 25 years of being asked when I would get around to recording a solo album, I finally got to it in 2019. Guy, my barrister friend, was a keyboard player in a weekend band. He had also written several lyrics over the years. At some point in 2016 – the details remain hazy – he had offered to write some lyrics for me, so I shared some music with him.

His words were good, my music less so, so it was put on hold. By the time we got to *FEAR* I literally had hundreds of musical ideas that hadn't made the album cut but were still languishing on our virtual shelves and gathering digital dust. I shared a bunch of them with Guy and he felt inspired to write two brand new lyrics for the ones he had loosely threaded together into rough arrangements. They might have been unfinished, but I could see their potential. *Amelia* and *2051* would become the cornerstones of the album *Mark Kelly's Marathon*. It took the extended downtime of the lockdown in early 2019 for me to find the time to devote to it, but once I got started it didn't take long to finish writing the music and finalise the arrangements.

Henry Rogers, my old (yet disturbingly young) pal from DeeExpus, was always going to be my first choice for a drummer if I ever got around to making this mythical solo album. At the suggestion of my brother Barry, I also invited my nephew Conal to join us, first on guitar and then later switching to bass after I filled the guitar slot with two excellent players, Pete 'Woody' Wood and, on Rothers' recommendation, John Cordy. With history repeating, it was the singer who remained the missing piece, one that would take me over a year to find.

I knew the sort of singer I wanted for Marathon. In fact, while trawling through a bunch of little known bands on Spotify, I chanced upon an artist called Big Blue Ball. I loved the sound of the singer's voice, although admittedly he did sound an awful lot like Peter Gabriel. Unfortunately, after a quick check I discovered it *was* Peter Gabriel. Big Blue Ball being an album project that Gabriel had taken part in with a bunch of other artists from around the globe. Back to the drawing board.

Never knowingly hamstrung by my own stupidity, I recounted this story in an interview for *The Web* magazine, which led to an old friend, Andrew Wildman, messaging me with a recommendation for a singer he knew, one Oliver Smith. My search was over. Ollie had a fantastic voice and his delivery worked perfectly with my music and Guy's lyrics.

I might have promised the world a solo album all those years ago but must admit that I probably wouldn't have finished writing the record if it wasn't for Guy's initial insistence and encouragement. (He goes after songwriting the way he goes after legal documents, which is to say doggedly.) Now that I've made one solo album, I'm already working on the next. Guy's along for the ride again, though I'm not going to set a release date just yet. I mean, who knows what the next ten years might bring?

EPILOGUE

I don't know how you celebrate Christmas, if at all, but if you're anything like me, then you enjoy taking a morning stroll through the crisp Oxfordshire countryside, the breath leaving your mouth in fleeting clouds.

Home for a few snacks, one or two cold drinks, the house suffused with the glorious scent of an oncoming Christmas lunch, gifts strewn beneath the tree, family close at hand.

Then I like to pick up the phone and insult our former singer. Or at least I did the Christmas of 1998.

The turning of the year can do strange things to a man; you reflect upon the past, wonder at the future. And ruminate on what the lanky Scotsman you once dropped acid with is currently up to.

"Happy Christmas, you old bastard!"

These were my first words in ten years to our former singer and one time friend.

I expected Fish to hang up or tell me to fuck off, season of goodwill or not.

"Aww, it's great to hear from you," he replied, laughing.

What was it that L.P. Hartley wrote in *The Go-Between*? 'The past is a foreign country; they do things differently there.'

And talking to Fish truly did feel like another place and not just another time.

Simply put, I don't hold grudges, so I was pleased that Fish had let go of the uglier aspects of our shared past. Forget the Machiavellian manoeuvring, a band divided, our sometimes vexed history. We were both happily in the now.

We agreed to meet up in Oxford a few weeks later when Angie was away, as I suspected that things might get messy. Like a volcano spewing lava is messy. Erik Nielsen was still living with us too, so he came along for the evening. It ended in unsurprising disarray, with me laughing hysterically from a trapdoor that led under the house. I'm still not sure why. While Erik threw up all over the stairs, which accelerated his departure from our house by a few weeks. It was like nothing had ever changed.

As we were now on speaking terms again, Fish was keen to meet all of us (including h) for dinner in London. In advance of that dinner, within Marillion we had conceived a half-formed plan to take Fish up on his previous offer to play on the same stage together in some sort of reunion. We duly convened in a restaurant in the spring of 1999. Nothing came of that plan in the end and most of the evening seemed to be taken up with Fish explaining to h in graphic detail how to glass somebody if he ever got in a bar fight.

In summer 2007, Fish was billed to play at the aptly titled Hobble On The Cobbles, an open air gig in Aylesbury's market square. He asked us to join him on stage to play the single which the place had inspired some 25 years before. I'm glad we did it, if only to lay the ghosts of expectation to rest. And by that I mean the spectres that sometimes haunted our band from a part of our fanbase calling for a reformation with our former singer.

Though, as that day proved, sometimes it's best to leave memories of the past unscarred by the present. In reality, we were playing on unfamiliar equipment and Fish was struggling to hit the high notes. We certainly weren't the finely tuned five piece, taut and finessed from months on the road. In fact, we were five ordinary guys opening ourselves up to a few minutes of happy nostalgia. Us and that day's audience briefly connected across the decades. Since then, Fish and I have kept in touch and sporadically met up, mostly at Marillion or Fish gigs.

But eight years later when Stuart Galbraith sat across from me in that sun filled Soho restaurant (as I baulked at the price of a rocket salad) and asked that we get back together for one last hurrah with Fish, I knew in my heart that it would be a mistake to say yes. Our paths diverged in 1988 and will, no doubt, cross at more points in the future, but they will never truly be joined again, and, on reflection, I think that's for the best.

You can either believe in the words of Socrates – 'The unexamined life is not worth living' – or use Oscar Wilde as your rule of thumb – 'To live is the rarest thing in the world. Most people exist, that is all'. I'm not one for introspection, but I am alive to the thrill. And by that I mean the next exalted undertaking, the next moment that will move me, the next thing that will make me feel alive, another quest...

I attribute that restlessness (along with childhood poverty and failed relationships) to having lived in 30 different places and never longer than ten years in any of them. Like the myth about sharks, you keep moving or you die. Or at least I think a part of me might die if I stood still.

I turned 60 this year, but I still feel it's never too late for another adventure or to change lanes. That said, it is too late to right my wrongs or correct the mistakes I've made; that damage has been done. We don't get to do it over, all we can do is acknowledge the hurt we've caused, realise where we went wrong (so we don't go there again), and seek forgiveness. Sometimes you might even get it.

But I try not to dwell on my past mistakes or bad choices. I'm sure there will be more to contend with in the future. Life isn't a rehearsal. Mine has been more like hastily arranged improvisation at times: entertaining and thrilling, but nerve-racking and scary all the same. I've rarely, if ever, been bored and I'm happy with that.

Despite my lack of forward planning (you've watched me spill from one scenario to the next throughout the entire book), I've ended up in a good place. My career has been long and rewarding. I have a wonderful extended family. Kai is doing well in his career and is a great father to two beautiful daughters. Tallulah is studying at Cambridge University. Delilah and Jude are both doing well and growing up fast despite their parents. Arthur and Pedro have accepted me into their lives like a father. I'm hoping Philip Larkin got it wrong.

The one casualty in my relationships that still weighs heavily on me is with Freya. I'm forever hopeful that we will see each other again soon before it's too late.

The sun is impossibly high here, the warm breezes coming in from the African continent in gentle waves. We're standing on Europa Point, my new wife and I. Spain to one side of us, Africa the other. We could be flying and in my heart I am. I've just married Karina. They say that love is all, and if that's true, then Karina is everything. One of my few regrets is that I didn't meet her earlier in life. After our plans for a wedding in the UK were scuppered by Covid, we made the impulsive decision to fly out to Gibraltar and marry here. I'm glad we did. It was perfect.

Marillion are in a good (some might say fantastic) place right now. We know who we are, and we know our place in the world. How many bands get to say that? As I write this, we have completed work on *An Hour Before It's Dark*, our twentieth album. It feels remarkable even writing that down. While the next two years of our lives are already mapped out, you will be pleased to hear that we have no desire to stop any time soon.

If, over the last 100,000 words or so, I've offended or upset you, forgot to single you out, or, much worse, failed to entertain you, then, hand on heart, I'm sorry. But not even 100,000 words could afford me the space for all the memories that have come echoing down the years as I sat to write this. And remember, it's just one man's story, one life, and, as a great woman once almost said, life is either a great adventure or nothing at all.

Here's to the next great adventure.

ACKNOWLEDGEMENTS

Patti Smith might have managed two memoirs, but let's face it, I'm probably only going to get one chance at this, so please indulge me. If you haven't made the meandering thank you list below and are mystified as to why, then you've either done me a terrible injustice in the past and I've silently held on to it for years, or it's simply an oversight on my part. It's probably the latter, so please forgive me and I promise to buy you a drink the next time we meet.

What's the saying? 'It takes a village…' and like most artistic endeavours, this book wasn't created in a vacuum. Enormous thanks then to Philip Wilding, who managed to make me funnier and more intelligent on the page and whose writing prowess even rubbed off on some of my own efforts along the way. And to Nick Shilton at Kingmaker Publishing, who initially suggested that I might have a story to tell, one which he would be happy to help to bring to life if I could just find the words. Nick, thank you.

Thanks also to Anne-Marie Forker for her marvellous photographs and to Professor Geoff Parks for his eagle proofreading eyes. Thank you to the keepers of the Marillion Archives, Mark McCormac, Claude Attard, Andre Kreutzmann and Keith Wickenden, for fact checking, live boots and photos. Thanks to Claus Nygaard for his archive and to Phil Simon for the title.

I'll always be grateful to my mum and dad, who always encouraged and believed in this dreamer, no matter how absurd some of those dreams.

All my family and friends, too numerous to mention (but let me try): Maia, Juliet, Max, Theo, Jude, Delilah, Tallulah, Kai, Sarah, Freya, Pedro, Arthur, Alex, Liz, Phil, Garrett, Sundar, Barry, Leslie, Greg, Mike, Liz, Conal, Caitlin, Jake, Scarlett, Aline, Thiago, Penha, Elesier, Phil, Adele, Colin, Susan, Clint, Deborah, Denis, Guy, Ginger, Storm, Marcelo, Flávia, Márcia, Nigel, Chris, Ollie, Henry, John, Woody, Erik, Ian, Paul, David, Lise, Tim, Fabian, Giorgio, Krix and Tally.

My heartfelt thanks to Ian, h, Pete and Steve, my four constant friends and companions, who have put up with me for two thirds of my life. They'll tell you it feels longer.

Thanks to the long suffering Lucy Jordache for keeping the good ship Marillion set on a steady course.

Thank you to Mike, Rich, Stephanie, Mark, Phil, Yenz, Nick, Tommy, Marcus, Pete, Nial and Stumpy for keeping the wheels on and rolling for all these years.

It goes without saying, but I'll say it anyway, that without our fans and supporters there would be no Marillion.

Thank you to everybody in the music industry who has helped further my career, by design or by chance.

And to you dear reader for getting this far. I hope you enjoyed the journey.

Last and certainly not least, Karina for showing me how to live in a world of possibilities. Thank you.

Photography Acknowledgements

The author would like to thank the following sincerely for their kind permission to use their photographs in this book as follows:

- » Anne-Marie Forker for (1) front cover; (2) inside back cover; (3) "Not just vapour trails…" and (4) "Blue Steel IV" photographs (www.forkerfotos.com).

- » Martin Collins for "Chemical Alice".

- » Paul Shorter for (1) "Giving it my best Rick Wakeman…"; (2) "Get the flock out!"; (3) "The ever adaptable Pete Trewavas"; (4) "Test one, two…"; (5) "Steve Rothery, still persisting with the sackcloth"; (6) "The smell of the greasepaint"; and (7) "My legendary jumpsuit" (www.picfair.com/users/GigBoots1980).

- » Justin Thomas for (1) "The eyes have it!"; (2) "With Andy Ward in 1983"; (3) "Fish, you've got something on your face."; and (4) "You hum it, I'll play it.".

- » Diz Minnitt for (1) "At the same Marquee show, my shirt …" and (2) "Steve takes flight at the Marquee".

- » Andy Phillips for "Market Square Heroes. The kings of Aylesbury in 1982."

- » Simon Hanhart for "The world is completely *Fugazi*…"

- » Marion Schult for "Why so serious?" (www.marionschult.com)

- » Clive Aspinall for (1) "For some reason I seem startled"; and (2) "Fish meeting his public".

- » Paul Lewis for (1) "What do you mean, 'Turn it off and turn it on again'?" and (2) "Like we'd stepped out of the pages of Italian *Vogue*".

- » Steve Rothery for (1) "Not quite a band of brothers" and (2) "Many happy returns."

» Márcia Caramati for "Love walked in."

» Pit Lad for "Every journey starts with a single step".

» Karina Tatagiba Kelly for (1) "Cruise to the Edge: reaching Key West", (2) "At Rock am Ring"; (3) "I finally got to duet with the great Arthur Rubinstein in Łódź"; (4) "And then there were three"; and (5) "Freewheeling at Port Zélande in 2017".

The author and publisher have been unable to trace the photographers of (1) "Man Of Steel"; (2) "Moving up to Marquee headliners"; (3) "Blue Steel II"; (4) "Utopia" and (5) "The sign of the cross".

All other photographs are copyright of the author.